SHIP IT
HOLLA
BALLAS!

How a Bunch of 19-Year-Old College Dropouts
Used the Internet to Become Poker's
LOUDEST, CRAZIEST, and RICHEST Crew

Jonathan Grotenstein
and Storms Reback

ST. MARTIN'S PRESS 🙟 NEW YORK

For Kristen and Nissa, and Jack, Sam, and Zephyr

ship it \\'ship 'it

1. In poker, an exclamation made after winning a big pot.
2. The affirmation of a suggested act of extreme awesomeness.

Authors' Note

This is a true story, though some names
and details have been changed.

For reasons that had little to do with taxes, April 15, 2011, was not a good day to be an online poker player in the United States of America—a group that, at the time, numbered somewhere between 2.5 million and 15 million people. Those who tried to log on to any of the biggest virtual cardrooms that Friday morning were greeted by official government seals and an ominous message: "This domain name has been seized by the Federal Bureau of Investigation."

While smoke had been in the air for a while, the shutdown had come without warning. Americans were suddenly unable to access the money in their online accounts, which in some cases meant several million dollars. More than 12,000 players rushed to Two Plus Two, a Web site that's home to the world's largest and most respected poker forum, looking for answers. The unexpected spike in traffic crashed the site's servers, further rattling the poker community.

Slowly information began to emerge. The Department of Justice had shut down the dot-com Internet addresses of the four largest sites in the world—PokerStars, Full Tilt Poker, Absolute Poker, and Ultimate Bet—alleging violations of the Illegal Gambling Business Act of

1955 and the Unlawful Internet Gambling Enforcement Act (UIGEA) of 2006. At least $500 million was frozen in seventy-five bank accounts across fourteen countries. Eleven people, poker site executives and the payment processors who brokered the transactions between the sites and players, were arrested and charged with bank fraud, money laundering, and illegal gambling.

With the exception of a few small rogue sites, "Black Friday" meant the end of online poker in the United States.

For the previous eight years—ever since an amateur named Chris Moneymaker upset the pros and won the World Series of Poker (WSOP) in 2003—America had been gripped by a poker craze. Televised tournaments filled the airwaves. The World Series had grown by a multiple of ten, one year awarding its winner $12 million—the largest payout ever given to an individual winner of a sporting event.

On Black Friday it became apparent just how much this craze owed to the multibillion-dollar online poker industry. The two biggest virtual cardrooms—PokerStars and Full Tilt Poker—had been spending $200 million each year in the United States on marketing and were the primary advertisers on poker-centric television shows like *Poker After Dark*, *The Big Game*, and *Million Dollar Challenge*. All three shows were quickly canceled. Sports giant ESPN immediately removed all of PokerStars' advertising from its Web site, ending a relationship that had been generating $22 million a year. ESPN also scratched plans to broadcast the 2011 North American Poker Tour, a series of big money tournaments that PokerStars had created the year before. Even the future of the World Series, the game's oldest and most prestigious tournament, grew murky: Moneymaker's victory may have lit the fire, but the explosion was fueled by the tens of thousands of entrants who qualified through online satellite tournaments and a singularly successful TV relationship with ESPN, which was strongly considering getting out of the poker business altogether.

The end of online poker also allowed for some perspective. The phenomenon that had kept millions of players enthralled for more than a decade could now be viewed as a historical event.

In many ways, online poker resembled a gold rush or investment bubble: Fortunes were made, sometimes literally overnight, and lost just as quickly. In other ways, it was a new twist on an old game, like day trading—a technological breakthrough that changed the preexisting paradigm, allowing its early adopters to pursue some form of the American dream while sitting in front of a computer in their bathrobes.

But what made the online poker craze truly unique was the extent to which it was powered by kids. You have to be twenty-one to gamble legally in the United States, but the online cardrooms—most of which were based overseas—allowed eighteen-year-olds to try their luck. At the peak of the boom, one out of every five college students was playing poker on the Internet. A significant number of even younger teens were able to bluff their way in as well.

The results were occasionally disastrous. An estimated one-quarter of the college players exhibited the kind of clinical symptoms that define problem gamblers. Many of them dropped out of school to play professionally, only to descend into financial ruin. Some even resorted to stealing money—typically from other players but in one notable case from a bank—to help fund their poker habits.

But poker is a zero-sum game—if there are losers, there are going to be winners—and college-age kids were in many ways the ones best positioned to take advantage of the opportunity. This was, after all, the first generation to have grown up with computer mice in their hands, making them ideally suited to the rapid-fire pace of online play. They were comfortable with the idea of spending hours playing a game on a screen and had copious free time to develop skills and strategies. Not surprisingly, some of them were wildly successful, creating a new economic caste of seventeen- and eighteen-year-olds suddenly bestowed with immediate riches.

Like many winners of the Mega Millions, these kids were ill-equipped to handle their success. They were earning too much to relate to their age-peers, and taking on too much risk to win the approval of their parents and teachers. Many of them were social misfits to begin with, the kind of teenagers you'd expect to latch on to the idea of spending most of their waking hours playing a computer game. In other eras they might have lived strange lives in relative isolation. But thanks to the Internet's evolution into the most powerful social networking tool in history, these kids were able to find one other. Through text messages and e-mails, discussion forums, and online chat, they formed powerful relationships that ultimately flourished into a full-on subculture with its own language, fashion, and customs.

In many cases their immersion into instant wealth coincided with living on their own for the first time, leaving a serious void in the whole authority figure department. These kids had the money and freedom to pursue a fantasy cobbled together from rap videos and late-night Cinemax. They developed expensive tastes and partied like rock stars around the world, dropping massive sums on bottle service, strip clubs, party drugs, fast cars, and the replacement cost of whatever property got destroyed along the way. The discovery of like-minds with similarly disposable income helped to reinforce and amplify the bad behavior.

But the connections weren't always negative. Some formed loose tribes that shared advice, support, and money. In the absence of adult supervision, they helped one another navigate the oftentimes treacherous waters of postadolescence and, eventually, mature into actual adults themselves.

The Ship It Holla Ballas were one of these communities, a loosely affiliated group of seventeen- to twenty-two-year-olds who chose their name to incite a reaction. You were either in on the joke or you weren't. The Ballas were young, rich, brash, arrogant, and, thanks to the pervasive media culture that raised them, remarkably self-aware. They knew the Internet wasn't just a tool for making money, but a place to create a reputation for themselves, defining and celebrating a new lifestyle that just a few years earlier never could have existed. They used it as a platform to wage war against the social idiosyncrasies that had previously defined them, the parents and teachers who doubted them, and a poker establishment that refused to take them seriously.

This is their story.

1

During this rigorous time in my life, several thoughts went through my mind: That chick is so hot. This bud is so sticky. This class is so lame. I want a beer. We should go surfing.

—Irieguy

FORT IRWIN, CALIFORNIA (September 2001)

Irieguy has seen plenty of gambles in his life. It's never taken much to convince him to bet all the money in his wallet on a football game or on the number of push-ups he can do in a day.

But this is the first wager that could conceivably be described as life or death, and he'd certainly prefer something better than fifty-fifty odds.

Maybe "life or death" is exaggerating the case. Then again, maybe not. Heads, he spends the next year and a half administering pap smears among the yuccas and Joshua trees of the California high desert. Tails, he's going to war. And Irieguy isn't exactly what you'd call "soldier material."

In fact, he's very nearly the embodiment of peace and love, a textbook California kid from Orange County who's about as laid-back as they come. Much of his don't-worry-be-happy personality can be traced to his father, SkipperBob, who earned his nickname during the seventies, when he bought the Newport Harbor Yacht Club and ran the place like a singles bar.

For college, Irieguy trades one hot spot of mellow for another, leaving the O.C. for Malibu. He spends four years at Pepperdine trying to perfect his Jeff Spicoli imitation. Waking and baking nearly every single day. Surfing, ideally when the tides coincide with the university's mandatory religion class. Drinking beer. Chasing girls. Drinking more beer.

Somehow Irieguy still manages to get into medical school at Nova Southeastern University in Florida, trading palm trees, an idyllic view of the Pacific Ocean, and reasonable proximity to L.A.'s glamour for palm trees, an idyllic view of the Atlantic Ocean, and reasonable proximity to Miami's glitz.

The original plan is to become a plastic surgeon, until a rotation in Obstetrics and Gynecology unexpectedly rocks his world. During the most exciting twenty-four hours of his life, he assists in two live births, an emergency C-section that saves a baby's life, and a successful cancer surgery. There's no combination of drugs and alcohol that can top the buzz he gets from introducing new lives into the world. He is literally delivering happiness. Forget face-lifts and tummy tucks. Irieguy has found his true calling.

There aren't any idyllic ocean views or palm trees in Detroit, where he does his residency. During the long, cold winters, he vows to set up his practice someplace warm and fun and full of beautiful women—he hopes to return to California or Florida, or maybe give Arizona or Las Vegas a try. There's just one hitch: the three-year commitment he owes Uncle Sam.

Between medical school and his residency, Irieguy has to attend

Officer Training School with the rest of the freshly minted doctors, lawyers, and chaplains who have volunteered for the military in exchange for tuition money. A two-star general strides briskly to the podium to deliver the orientation briefing.

It's called "Break Things, Kill People."

"I think I made a big mistake," Irieguy whispers to the doctor sitting next to him.

After finishing his residency, he gets assigned to Fort Irwin, a sleepy military base in the Mojave Desert about a half hour outside of Barstow, California. SkipperBob drives him to his post. "The good news," he tells his son, "is that we're probably living in the most peaceful and prosperous time in human history."

It's an era of peace and prosperity that will last for exactly two more days.

Irieguy is on a treadmill in the base's gym, gazing blankly at the TV across the room. More night owl than morning person, he's having trouble processing the image on the screen—a torrent of black smoke pouring into the sky from what appears to be a gaping hole in one of the World Trade Center towers. Several minutes later, he watches a Boeing 767 jetliner crash into the other tower.

Irieguy's first thought is, *Holy shit.*

Then he looks down at his clothes. Yup, that's an Air Force star on his T-shirt. His eyes drift across the room full of soldiers, faces hardening to a grim sense of purpose, and he gets struck by a second thought.

This is one hell of a time to be starting a career in the military.

There are two OB-GYNs stationed at Fort Irwin, Irieguy and Dr. Miguel Brizuela. They become fast friends, commiserating daily during the buildup to war; both got into this racket to save lives, not to

Break Things and Kill People. Then the inevitable orders roll in: one of them is going to be deployed to Iraq.

"Hey, Miguel," says Irieguy. "This might sound a little crazy, but . . . want to flip a coin for it?"

Which is how Miguel Brizuela winds up in Mosul with the 21st Combat Support Hospital North, stitching up soldiers, while Irieguy spends the next year and a half in the Mojave Desert, killing time.

2

There are only two signals emitted from the poker universe:

1. The universe will unfold as it should;

2. If you play the right way, and your opponents do not, you will win. Everything else is noise, and to make too much of anything that doesn't expressly involve the two above facts is to pave the road to failure.

—Irieguy

DETROIT, MICHIGAN (January 1998)

During one of the longest and coldest winters of his Detroit residency, three years before his stay in the desert, Irieguy gets a call from SkipperBob. "Hey, you can get on the World Wide Web, right?"

"No one calls it that anymore, Dad, but, yes, I've got Internet access. Why?"

"You won't believe this, but there's this place called Planet Poker where you can play cards for real money. Against real people, anywhere in the world."

Irieguy thinks this is pretty much the coolest thing he's ever heard.

He learned how to play poker from SkipperBob, who, after losing his shirt in the sailing business, spent a year working as a "prop" at L.A.'s Bicycle Club, employed by the casino to keep the action flowing at the poker tables. While at Pepperdine, Irieguy brought the skills his father taught him to nearby Hollywood Park, winning enough to keep his refrigerator stocked with beer. Now, thanks to online poker, he and SkipperBob can play at the same table, chatting with each other the entire time, even though they're separated by two thousand miles.

This discovery becomes particularly useful at Fort Irwin. During the long periods of extreme boredom that follow the occasional childbirth, Irieguy wonders if maybe he wasn't the coin flip's real loser. Online poker turns out to be a great way to break up the monotony. The site where he first plays, Paradise Poker, doesn't offer his game of choice—tournament no-limit Texas Hold'em, the same form of poker used to decide the world championship at the World Series of Poker—but they do have a rough approximation, something called a "Sit N Go."

The premise is simple: for an $11 entry fee—$10 toward the prize pool, $1 to the house—you get a seat at the table. As soon as nine players buy seats, the tournament begins.

Sit, and go.

You start with a fixed number of chips, and when they're gone, so are you. The "blinds," or forced bets required to play, increase every few minutes, compelling you to risk more and more of your chips, a neat bit of design that keeps the tournament from lasting more than an hour or so. The winner earns around $55, second place about half that, while coming in third gets you slightly better than a refund on the entry fee.

Irieguy quickly falls in love with Sit N Gos, because:

(a) the fixed buy-in prevents him from losing more than $11 at a time;

(b) they're only an hour long, so he can squeeze them into the cracks of his unpredictable schedule; and

(c) he seems to have a knack for winning them.

In fact, he's finishing in the money with such regularity that he starts to suspect there might be a science to it.

Irieguy has always loved numbers. During medical school he worked part time as a research assistant in a biomedical lab, where he spent hundreds of hours poring over statistics. It was the kind of work that most people would find insanely boring, but Irieguy knows that numbers, when looked at the right way, can tell you a story. Shed new light on the past. Predict the future. Explain everything in between.

Irieguy discovers that analyzing his Sit N Go results tickles the same part of his brain. He catches himself thinking about them even when he's away from the table. *Can I really keep winning this consistently, or am I just getting lucky? How often can I expect to win? Is it possible to predict how much money I can make?*

To the uninitiated, poker may seem like any other form of gambling. You've got to get lucky at the right time. The players who call themselves "pros" are basically shrewd masters of human psychology, able to outguess their opponents, spot their unconscious "tells," and pick the right time to make a daring bluff.

But Irieguy knows that there's more to it than observation and instincts. Poker is a game of probabilities. Some hands win more often than others. There are times when it's worth calling a bet in the hopes that your hand will improve, and times when it's not. By understanding these probabilities, you're able to make decisions that are mathematically correct. Great bluffs and brilliant reads—and, of course, the luck of the draw—might be a part of the game, but the real winners are the players who consistently make more profitable decisions than their opponents.

This is especially true for online poker—your opponent may scratch his left ear every time he bluffs, but you're not going to see it over the Internet. The best edge you can bring to the table is a deeper understanding of the game's mathematical foundation.

And the more Irieguy studies the mathematics that underlie Sit N Gos, the more he starts to believe that he's discovered the kind of can't-miss proposition that gamblers dream of: an investment with a steady rate of return.

3

Winning at gambling isn't about discovering some earth-shattering secret. It's about finding a whole bunch of small edges. We've uncovered all the edges.

—David Sklansky, quoted in *Cigar Aficionado*

COMMERCE, CALIFORNIA (February 2005)

In 1984, Mason Malmuth visited the Bicycle Casino—"the Bike" to locals—in search of advice. He'd been living in Los Angeles for the past two years, working as a probability theory expert for the defense contractor Northrop, but his dream job was 265 miles east in Las Vegas. Ever since stopping there during a business trip years earlier, he wanted to become a professional gambler.

A quixotic notion perhaps, but one pursued with utmost pragmatism. Malmuth had a master's degree in mathematics from Virginia Tech. He spent a year working for the U.S. Census. For him, everything boiled down to numbers. And according to the numbers, the only beatable games were blackjack and poker. Blackjack was illegal in Los Angeles, but the city had a thriving poker scene. With that in mind he began searching for someone who could teach him how to win.

Plenty were willing to try, but Malmuth needed someone who could explain the game in a way that would make sense to him, using math and logic, not intuition and hunches. He met his perfect match at the Bike, right down to their double-bridged, metal-framed nerd eyeglasses.

The son of a Columbia University professor of mathematics, David Sklansky scored a perfect 800 on the math portion of the SAT, ensuring his acceptance at the University of Pennsylvania. He went on to attend the Wharton School of Business but dropped out after a year to move to Las Vegas and become a professional poker player. He wasn't a particularly gifted player in terms of instincts, bravado, or creativity, but was able to succeed by mastering the game's probabilities, using mathematical reasoning to gain an edge over his opponents. Getting awarded a gold bracelet for winning a WSOP tournament is the most sought-after achievement in all of poker. Most poker players spend their entire careers hoping to win one. By the time he met Mason Malmuth, Sklansky had already won three.

Both men were enamored of their own intelligence and dismissive of most social graces. They got along famously. Sklansky agreed to teach Malmuth everything he knew about poker in exchange for 10 percent of his winnings. For the next four years, while Sklansky lectured him on the intricacies of the game, Malmuth compiled a thick dossier full of meticulous notes with the same diligence he'd used to earn his masters.

Malmuth had timed his jump from the corporate to the gambling world almost perfectly. The California casinos were in the midst of a small boom, thanks to a change in state law that allowed them to spread Texas Hold'em. New players were flocking to the game. Most of them didn't know what they were doing. How could they? Poker reference books were nearly nonexistent. The ones that did exist weren't very good.

Which gave Sklansky an idea: what if they took all the notes Malmuth had assembled and used them to write a book about Hold'em?

And so *Hold'em Poker for Advanced Players* was born. Self-published in 1988, it remains one of the most powerful books ever written about the game, a well-thumbed bible for anyone looking to understand and exploit the small edges that define one's results. It was so well received that the duo released a similarly detailed book on Seven-Card Stud just a year later. The demand for their work inspired Sklansky and Malmuth to form their own publishing company, which, in a nod to their commitment to mathematical reasoning, they named $2 + 2 = 4$. The imprint, affectionately known by its readers as "Two Plus Two," quickly became the gold standard for books about poker and gambling.

When the Internet began to emerge in the nineties, Sklansky and Malmuth were early adopters, creating twoplustwo.com. They didn't give away any of their secrets on the bare-bones, almost graphics-free site—the idea was to promote and sell their growing library of books—but they did encourage visitors to share knowledge with one another. A list of hyperlinks led to discussion forums like "Poker Theory" or "Books and Publications." Once in a while a conversation would intrigue Sklansky or Malmuth enough for them to weigh in with an opinion, which to their growing legion of fans sounded like the word of a mountaintop prophet. It didn't take long for Two Plus Two to become *the* place for serious players to compare strategies and seek guidance from one another and for lurking novices to learn from these exchanges.

Irieguy has been reading Two Plus Two books for years. The company hasn't produced anything about Sit N Gos yet, but on the Web site he discovers a message board called the "One-Table Forum," a small but dedicated community that's just as interested in these strange little online tournaments as he is.

There's FossilMan, a prolific poster who uses the forum to get feedback on the creative new maneuvers and strategies he loves to invent (and who will provide inspiration for them all when, putting the knowledge he gained from the forum to good use, he wins poker's world championship in 2004). A forum member named Aleo-Magus generously starts a thread called, "How to Win at $10+1 NLHE Partypoker sngs," which becomes a sort of dynamic, living bible to players hoping to master the one-table tournaments. Daliman, having spent much of his adult life figuring out how to beat the game of blackjack, offers theories about the optimal amounts to bet in certain situations. Bozeman develops the underpinnings of what comes to be known as the Independent Chip Model, or ICM, a complex set of mathematical calculations that can identify the most profitable moments to risk all of your remaining chips; Eastbay develops and distributes software that will actually do these calculations for you.

Every day, theories about Sit N Gos are raised and evaluated, amended or dismissed. There are lively debates and frequent arguments, but overall the tenor is marked by a spirit of discovery— everyone seems aware that, as a group, they're asking questions about a form of poker that very few people really understand. This us-vs.-them mentality helps to engender a deep sense of community.

It doesn't hurt that most of them are starting to make what feels like free money.

The popularity of online poker is exploding. By 2001—just three years after the first Internet cardroom, Planet Poker, deals its inaugural hand—the online poker industry generates annual revenues approaching $100 million. Sit N Gos are proving to be especially popular for the same reasons they're so appealing to Irieguy—a chance to experience tournament-style excitement, condensed into a brief period of time, that won't let you lose more than your entry fee. It's a perfect format for recreational players around the world who want to pursue their poker fantasies during lunch breaks or after the kids have gone to sleep.

The online poker sites quickly recognize and respond to the growing demand. They begin to offer Sit N Go tournaments with bigger entry fees—$22s, $33s, $55s, $109s, and even $215s—that, in many cases, allow players to gamble larger sums than they could in the more traditional cash games.

The pie may be getting bigger, but the strategies for winning Sit N Gos remain in the hands of a select few, mainly the regulars of Two Plus Two's One-Table Forum. Some of them are winning so consistently that they're able to contemplate quitting their day jobs.

Irieguy's not ready to ditch his stethoscope and speculum just yet, but he does make a concerted effort to stop lurking and actually join the conversation. As "Irieguy," a name chosen for his love of Rastafarian culture and philosophy, he quickly becomes one of the forum's most prolific contributors, averaging more than a post per day.

Many of his posts are wonky, number-crunching affairs, like "What's the highest ITM possible at each level?"—an effort to determine scientifically how often players can expect to finish "in the money" as they move up to higher stakes. He describes with academic clarity what statistics have to say about the types of winning and losing streaks that even the most skilled players should expect.

But it's his thoughtful posts about poker psychology that earn Irieguy an almost cult-like following within the forum. His self-proclaimed

"IrieZen philosophy" requires an almost masochistic indifference to the vagaries of luck inherent to the game. He encourages his fellow players to understand and accept poker's predictable unpredictability, helping them to avoid the irrational exuberance and crippling depression that can accompany the inevitable highs and lows.

He and the rest of the Two Plus Two regulars inevitably cross paths at the tables, but there's plenty of money to go around. Nobody puffs their chests; encounters are simply acknowledged with casual greetings. A seemingly innocuous "'Sup, bro?" might be the virtual equivalent of a Freemason's secret handshake, a tacit agreement not to butt heads until both players are safely in the money.

After finishing his military commitment, Irieguy settles in Las Vegas. Warm weather? Check. Beautiful women? Check. Medical practices aren't built overnight, however, so he finds himself with plenty of spare time for playing and posting. A social creature by nature, he wonders what kinds of "real" lives his fellow Two Plus Twoers are leading. Several of them live in Las Vegas, so he reaches out to a few.

He meets Daliman in a casino bar, discovering a guy in his mid-thirties with a wife and three kids who's making enough playing Sit N Gos (and winning the occasional karaoke contest) to quit a $36,000-a-year job selling tires. AleoMagus, McPherzen, and Lacky also turn out to be of similar age and temperament.

At the start of 2005, Irieguy puts word on the forum that he and SkipperBob are planning a trip to a tournament at L.A.'s Commerce Casino in February and asks if anyone wants to meet up. The most enthusiastic response comes from Raptor, who over the course of the last year has earned a lot of respect for his insightful strategic posts—many Two Plus Twoers credit a thread he starts about folding big hands near the end of a tournament as one of the greatest influences on their games. Raptor tells Irieguy he'd love to meet in L.A. and asks if he can share a hotel room with him and SkipperBob.

"What's this Raptor like?" SkipperBob asks as they approach the door to the room.

"Probably just like every other guy I've met on the forum," says Irieguy. "A college-educated professional in his thirties or forties with a degenerate streak."

SkipperBob grins. "Sounds like my kind of guy."

Which is why neither of them can say a word for a good thirty seconds after they open the door to find a teenager with a Beatles mop-top and a goofy grin sitting cross-legged on the bed between two laptops, stuffing his face with candy.

'Sup, bro.

MARCELLUS: Holla, Barnardo!

—*Hamlet*, Act I, Scene I

FORT WORTH, TEXAS (April 2004)

Raptor doesn't need a doctor to tell him his season's over.

Until now, his senior year at the Oakridge School in Arlington, Texas, has been a breeze. He's been getting As and Bs without cracking a book. He can't prove it, but his classes all seem to be dummied down to the lowest common denominator, ensuring that all the students go on to good colleges, so why bother? Besides, thanks to an academic scholarship, he already knows he's going to Texas Christian University, where he hopes to walk on to the baseball team.

If Texas high school football is a religion, baseball is the cool science class that everyone wants to take, the one with the young, fun teacher. Every kid in the state who can swing a bat dreams of playing for the Longhorns, Aggies, Red Raiders, or Horned Frogs before moving on to the Major Leagues.

Raptor's been playing baseball nearly every single day since the time he could first fit a glove onto his hand. He loves pitching more than anything else in the world—standing alone on the mound, engaged in a heads-up battle against the hitter, a contest that's every bit as psychological as it is physical.

He's sitting on a fastball, so I'll throw a changeup.

I'll bet I can get this guy to swing at a curveball in the dirt.

He's a pretty good hitter too, which is why, three games into the season, he's taking a routine lead off of first base. The pitcher makes a halfhearted attempt to pick him off. Raptor doesn't need his brain to tell his body how to respond, because his body has done it a thousand times before. He crosses one leg in front of the other and slides head-first back into the bag.

The shoulder is a ball-and-socket joint like the hip, only a lot shallower. The bones wouldn't stay together at all if it weren't for the labrum, a ring of cartilage that keeps the end of the humerus from slipping out of the shoulder socket.

His headfirst slide is only off by a fraction, but it's enough to tear Raptor's labrum in two. His right arm—his *pitching* arm—flaps around like a wet noodle. He's never experienced this kind of pain before, like someone repeatedly stabbing his shoulder with a knife. But that's not what causes the tears to pour from his eyes. It's the realization—confirmed by a quick glance at his coach, who can barely look at him—that his love affair with baseball has come to an abrupt end.

The doctor gives Raptor a choice: undergo surgery, followed by twelve to eighteen months of intense rehabilitation; or let it heal on its own, maybe recovering 75 percent of his original arm strength. For a high school senior, eighteen months might as well be eighteen years, so he chooses to forgo surgery and rehab his shoulder on his own. He thinks he can do anything as long as he puts his mind to it, and why should this be any different?

Three weeks later, Raptor is back in his high school baseball team's lineup, batting fifth and playing left field. He can swing the bat accurately enough to make contact, just not powerfully enough to hit home runs. He can track down just about anything hit to him in the field, but throwing the ball to the cutoff man requires an awkward sidearm motion that makes the severity of his injury apparent to all. He certainly won't be pitching for TCU next season. Or probably ever again for that matter. From here on out, he'll look at baseball with the same misty regard men normally reserve for women who have broken their hearts.

No other pursuit has ever worked its way into his being quite the way baseball has. He was on a swim team for ten years, but never felt entirely comfortable calling himself a swimmer. Same thing with singing, even after he joined his high school choir. Baseball has always been different, as connected to his identity as his name or the shrug he gives his teachers whenever they ask him to work a little harder. He spends the rest of his senior year doing whatever he can to keep himself from thinking about the game.

Parties.

A girlfriend.

Poker.

Lots and lots of poker.

$ $ $

The movie *Rounders* is released during Raptor's sophomore year in high school. Matt Damon plays Mike McDermott, a young gambler who dreams of one day winning the World Series of Poker. To get there he must first make his bones competing in New York's underground poker scene against a rogue's gallery of shady characters who narrate their high-stakes battles with the colorful and mysterious language unique to the game.

It's far too romantic a tableau for Raptor to resist, describing a world about as far as possible from the one he inhabits. He goes to private school. His parents belong to a country club. He is being groomed for a life of higher education, white-collar work, and, ultimately, leisure. He doesn't know any shady characters and he's never played a hand of poker, but he's so intrigued by the movie he sets aside any reservations. He and his friends begin playing for small stakes, $10 or $20 at most, throwing around chips and terms like "rags" and "the flop" just as they imagine the pros do.

At first, none of them know what the hell they're doing. But after a few weeks, it becomes obvious to Raptor that some of his friends are winning more consistently than others. Suspecting that there's skill involved, he does some research and orders a book by a guy named David Sklansky called *The Theory of Poker*. He devours it, and several more like it. Before long he's winning with such regularity that his friends can't afford to play with him anymore. Kind of a bummer, until someone reminds him that, just like in *Rounders*, Texas has a thriving underground poker scene.

Technically, the state says that playing poker for money is illegal within its borders, but sometimes tradition trumps law and this is one of those cases. Poker is as ingrained in Texas mythology as longhorns and six-shooters—hell, they don't decide the world championship playing *Mississippi* Hold'em. In the Lone Star State, backroom card games are every bit as ubiquitous as barbecue joints and taco shacks.

One such cardroom, the Poker Box, is just a short drive from Raptor's house, and from what he's heard its proprietors will let him play without having to show an ID. He knows that his parents won't approve and he doesn't like lying to them, so he tells them a half-truth—he'll be sleeping over at his friend Donald's house and he'll see them in the morning.

In the game Raptor's used to playing with his friends, you have to try really hard to lose $20, so the $3/$6 limit Hold'em game he joins at the Poker Box, with its $40 and $50 pots, feels like dizzying stakes for the sixteen-year-old. He's already prepared his concession speech.

If I run good, great, and if I don't, well, I got to play with some really good players at a real live poker club. What a cool experience.

Raptor makes plenty of rookie mistakes, but sometimes you make the wrong moves at the right time, and tonight is one of those nights. He's up about $200 when one of the regulars suggests they switch to pot-limit, a game with significantly higher stakes.

Raptor understands what's going on—these guys know he's getting lucky and are looking to accelerate the return of the money that, in their eyes, he's merely borrowed from them. "Nah," he says. "I'm happy with what we're playing."

"But we insist," they say.

Fine. I'll play with my profits. When I lose that, I'll quit.

Wary of getting beaten up or robbed, Raptor brought Donald and their friend Rei to the club with him. None of them can quite believe what happens next. In just two hours, Raptor wins more than $1,300, more money than any of them has seen outside of television.

Raptor has always prided himself on his self-control. Unlike most of his peers, he really doesn't enjoy the feeling of being drunk. Mind-altering drugs? No thanks. He doesn't even allow himself to get very excited about winning a baseball game, fearing that too much celebrating might somehow curse his ability to throw strikes. But this night at the poker tables feels different somehow, something worth cheering about.

On the drive back to Donald's house, Raptor pulls his winnings out of his pocket. "Man, can you believe this wad of cash!" he tells his friends. "I think I just might have figured this game out."

It only takes him six weeks to give it all back.

$ $ $

Good-looking jocks like Raptor tend to sail through high school, which makes his occasional bouts of emo angst all the more disconcerting for his parents.

"What are you interested in besides baseball?" they ask him.

"Nothing."

"Well, what *kinds* of things do you like?"

Raptor grimaces as if in actual physical pain. "I dunno. Everything's boring."

Poker might be changing his outlook on life. He's always been a jock first and a student second, but he loves the intellectual challenge the game poses. It inspires him in a way that history or calculus never has. He thinks about hands long after they're over, trying to figure out how he could have played them better.

One night, he bets heavily on a full house—one of the most powerful hands you can have—only to lose to a bigger full house. *Was there any way I could have gotten away from that hand?* he wonders. *Does anyone ever fold a full house?*

He can't find an answer in any of the strategy books he's been reading. And he knows that none of his friends are going to be much help—he's already thinking about the game in ways they wouldn't understand.

If this were a question about baseball, he'd ask a coach or a team-mate, but there aren't (yet) any coaches or teammates in poker. He's about to give up when he remembers the Web site mentioned on the back of Sklansky's book: twoplustwo.com.

Before he can post a question on the site, he has to register an account. He chooses the username "Raptor," the same one he used years earlier for his first AOL Instant Messenger (AIM) account, because, damn, dinosaurs were cool. He goes on to describe the hand that's been bothering him on one of the forums, fully expecting to get flamed for bothering everybody with such a n00b question.

But the responses turn out to be almost universally positive—thoughtful, encouraging, and, for Raptor, even a little therapeutic. He starts posting every time he has a question or concern, typically sign-ing off with "Holla!" because that's how Eminem would do it, and Eminem is even cooler than dinosaurs.

As he reads through all the other posts, he makes a surprising dis-covery: Very few of them are about live poker; nearly all of them de-scribe hands played on the Internet. Apparently the online cardrooms allow you to access blow-by-blow accounts of every hand you've ever played, and it's a simple task to cut and paste a "hand history" directly onto the Two Plus Two forum, where it can be communally dissected and analyzed by the poker hive-mind.

It's also easy to open an online account—all you need is a credit card—but Raptor is still a little anxious. *How do I know I won't get cheated? What if I lose all my money the first day? If I win, am I going to get paid?*

Life is funny. Had that headfirst slide into first base gone a fraction of an inch in either direction, he'd almost certainly be preparing to play baseball at TCU in the fall. Without baseball, he feels like just another high school senior playing out the string until graduation.

Screw it. What have I got to lose?

5

This is beyond fairy tale. It's inconceivable.

—ESPN commentator Norman Chad, describing
Chris Moneymaker's 2003 WSOP victory

OKEMOS, MICHIGAN (November 2003)

For the first fourteen years of his life, Good2cu has enjoyed being part of a perfect nuclear family. A loving, caring mom. A hard-working, good-natured dad. A younger sister who annoys him far less than he probably deserves. All living under the same roof in a comfortable house in Okemos, a quiet, upper-middle-class suburb of Lansing, Michigan. Sure, there are moments of tension, but all families experience tough times now and then.

His freshman year of high school, Good2cu's nuclear family gets hit by a nuclear bomb: Mom and Dad are getting a divorce. The only world Good2cu has ever known is being ripped apart. There's denial, anger, fear, and sadness. He can't remember ever crying as hard as he is now, with so much force he can hardly breathe.

But as the tears dry, he begins to see the angles.

His mother is only moving a few blocks away, but in terms of hands-on, parental supervision, she might as well be going to Mars. Nobody's going to be riding his ass about taking out the garbage or cleaning his room or playing too much Xbox. This divorce thing might not be such a bad deal after all.

For many teenagers, cynicism is as unavoidable as acne, and the end of his parents' supposedly lifelong commitment doesn't do anything to dissuade Good2cu from the notion that most of what he was told as a kid was a bunch of bullshit. He doesn't see much use in trying to make straight As, playing organized sports, or running for class president. He'd rather spend his time hanging out with his buddies, watching television, playing video games, and, once he gets his driver's license, making unsupervised forays into East Lansing, the nearby college town, to see hard-rocking bands like Taking Back Sunday, Brand New, and Green Day.

Good2cu and his dad occasionally find themselves battling over the remote control, but there's one TV show they always agree on. Every Tuesday night, in the fall of 2003, they meet on the couch, armed with popcorn and sodas, to watch new episodes of the World Series of Poker on ESPN.

They're not the only ones. All across the country viewers are getting caught up in the drama, thanks to the timely convergence of a couple of key factors.

The WSOP's Main Event has always been exciting in principle—a once-a-year gathering of the world's greatest poker players, each wagering $10,000 for the chance to call himself, as the colorful "Amarillo Slim" Preston once labeled the honorific, the *world champeen*. Not into titles? There's plenty to love about winning a cardboard box full of neatly wrapped bundles of hundred-dollar bills. Last year's first prize reached a record $2 million.

But despite the lively characters and lottery-like payouts, the event has never translated well to television.

Poker—especially no-limit poker, which allows players to risk all of their money at any point during a hand—can be an incredibly anxious business, a pressure cooker where even the right decision might be your last. The WSOP's Main Event requires players to make those decisions and abide by their consequences, again and again, twelve to fourteen hours a day, for almost a week. Winning requires the courage of a cliff diver and the stamina to survive multiple heart attacks.

Unfortunately, almost all of this tension takes place inside the players' heads. Poker couldn't be exciting on TV for the same reason that brilliant books are usually unfilmable—the tools for translation simply did not exist. Stone-faced men behaving inscrutably is no recipe for ratings success. The years the networks attempted to cover the WSOP, it was relegated to the same time slots as strongman competitions or celebrity basketball games, a sports oddity to fill the airwaves for insomniacs; many years, they didn't even bother to try.

But a couple of things are different in 2003. The first is a technological breakthrough, or at least a vast improvement: the "hole camera," a lipstick-sized camera that allows the television audience to see the players' hidden (or "hole") cards. The brainchild of Holocaust survivor Henry Orenstein, the hole camera has revolutionized televised poker, changing it from a sleep aid to something you can't *stop* watching. TV viewers are transformed from clueless conjecturers into omniscient know-it-alls, a horror-movie audience that can see the killer long before the intended victim. The 2003 WSOP isn't the first poker program to make use of the technology, but its impact is far greater, thanks to ESPN's relentless airing of the event.

But while the hole cameras make the game far more fun to watch, this year's cast of characters is what leads Good2cu and his dad to keep coming back for more, particularly a twenty-seven-year-old accountant from Tennessee with an unlikely name: Chris Money-maker.

The WSOP has always been a stage for professional angle-shooters with weathered faces and cool nicknames like "Puggy" and "Tree-top." On occasion, an amateur has crashed the party, like the 1979 winner Hal Fowler, a Hollywood marketing guy who managed to beat the pros at their own game with a combination of blind luck and mystical calm, which may or may not have been chemically produced by frequent visits to the small pharmacy he reportedly carried in his briefcase. But Fowler is the exception, not the rule. The pros have a name for the non-pros who dare to take them on: "dead money."

Chris Moneymaker is dead money. A goateed Everyman who looks like he'd be more comfortable sitting in the back of a fishing boat with a rod in one hand and a can of beer in the other, he's only in the event because he won a $39 "supersatellite" tournament in an online card-room. In a room full of ego-heavy cardsharps, Moneymaker constantly presents the picture of a guy who is humbled, even awed, by his proximity to the professionals. He keeps a low profile and struggles visibly with nervousness, which he attempts to hide beneath a baseball cap and reflective Oakley sunglasses.

Yet somehow he manages to survive the five-day grind against a record 838 opponents. When the tournament gets whittled down to its final two players, Moneymaker seems as surprised as everyone else to find himself sitting heads-up against Sammy Farha, a slick live wire with a predator's eyes and an unlit cigarette dangling from his mouth, some not-particularly-creative casting director's idea of a professional gambler. Per tradition, the first-place money—this year, $2.5 million—gets delivered by armed guards and dumped on the table, a mountain of cash to remind everyone exactly what's at stake.

Moneymaker does his best imitation of a stone, but it's far from flawless. Across the table, Farha casually drums his jeweled fingers on the table, probing his opponent with amiable chatter, the corners of his mouth upturned like a cat in no hurry to finish toying with a canary—sooner or later, dinner is going to be served.

On a pivotal hand near the finish, captured from every angle by ESPN's all-knowing cameras, Moneymaker bluffs with all of his remaining chips. Farha can smell deception and spends several minutes considering his response. Just enough time for the prickly feeling in his gut to give way to the more logical argument suggested by his ego: *There is no fucking way an amateur would dare bluff me in this spot.*

Farha throws away the winning hand and, along with it, any remaining momentum. A few minutes later, Moneymaker makes a legitimate hand and separates Farha from the rest of his chips.

The fish has eaten the shark.

A Category 5 hurricane might have less impact. The irresistible combination of his massive overnight success and his too-perfect name turns Chris Moneymaker into an instant folk hero. He gets barraged with requests for photo shoots and sponsorship deals. He makes an appearance on *The Late Show with David Letterman*. His story blazes a comet's trail from the Midwest to Macau, igniting the imagination of every accountant, doctor, lawyer, teacher, or other nine-to-five wage slave who's ever fantasized about an escape from the daily grind. Casual home games turn serious; online poker accounts spring up like weeds. Stories about great flops, scary turns, and brutal beats on the river slip into watercooler conversation. Poker tournaments grow as exponentially as the game's popularity: three years from now, Moneymaker's $2.5-million haul will represent seventh-place money in the World Series' Main Event—the winner will take home $12 million.

But frustrated salarymen aren't the only ones to catch the fever. Their kids have been watching too.

How could Good2cu not be entranced by the way the players riffle their chips with unconscious precision, the soul-reading stares, the seemingly idle chitchat that is anything but? Not to mention that cardboard box full of money. When ESPN's coverage finally concludes with Moneymaker hugging his father and raising bricks of cash high into the air, Good2cu's mind gets seared by one lasting impression.

Professional poker players are so fucking cool, and I want to be just like them.

When he was a little kid, you'd ask him what he wanted to grow up to be. He wanted to be a professional video game player.

—Good2cu's father

OKEMOS, MICHIGAN (April 2004)

Like any kid born in the 1980s, Good2cu has never known a world without video games.

He started when he was tall enough to reach his dad's computer, playing educational games like The Oregon Trail and DinoPark Tycoon, setting himself up for the discovery of SimCity. From there he moved on to real-time strategy games like Command and Conquer, StarCraft, and Warcraft I, II, and III, where success or failure was determined by resource management, rapid decision making, multitasking, and a fast finger on the mouse.

Good2cu loves entering these worlds, having to learn new rules on the fly and devise strategies that will (hopefully) lead to success. He gets an Xbox in high school and becomes so good at Halo he enters local competitions. A couple of times he actually comes home with prize money. While other kids his age harbor dreams of playing in the NBA or starring in a Hollywood movie, he fantasizes about following in the footsteps of Fatal1ty, the professional video gamer who is not much older than he is but who is already a full-on celebrity, thanks to his victories in the Cyberathlete Professional League and an appearance on MTV's *True Life*.

Good2cu's desire to become a pro gamer, when added to his thick glasses and conversational awkwardness, means he's never going to date the head cheerleader. Or, during his first sixteen years of life, anyone else. Talking to women feels like a video game whose rules he can't figure out. He wishes he could find the instruction manual.

But he's not exactly a nerd either. The I-don't-give-a-fuck attitude he's projected ever since his parents broke up plays well with the similarly jaded, which in high school leaves a lot of doors open. It helps that he likes to have a good time and laughs easily, an explosion of mirth that sometimes sounds like monkeys mating, other times like donkeys fighting. He's got a handful of really close friends, and they do just about everything together.

After Moneymaker wins the World Series of Poker, that means playing lots and lots of poker. This isn't exactly unique to Good2cu's clique. According to a study conducted by the University of Pennsylvania's Annenberg Public Policy Center, the number of fourteen- to twenty-two-year-old males playing cards for money has risen 84 percent between 2003 and 2004, with the greatest increase coming from those in high school and college. Dan Romer, director of the Adolescent Risk Communication Institute, calls the study "worrisome," adding that "these latest results suggest that the fad among teens is real and raise concerns that more young people will experience gambling problems as they age."

The poker craze isn't spreading as much as erupting: in every town, at every school, kids are dealing cards. Of the 1,600 students in Good2cu's high school, at least a hundred play on a regular basis.

Squint your eyes around lunchtime, and you might mistake the cafeteria for a Las Vegas cardroom, as there's nearly always action—a multicultural congregation of jocks, geeks, preps, and goths dealing no-limit Hold'em for quarters. After school, someone hosts a tournament nearly every day.

Good2cu wins about as often as he loses, $10 or $20 at a time, subsidizing the hobby with a part-time job as a janitor at the local YMCA. The job isn't his idea, but one foisted upon him by his parents, who, before he escapes their twin nests, want to make sure he learns proper Midwestern values, the underlying foundation of which is, "An honest day's work for an honest day's pay." Somehow scrubbing toilets for $7 an hour is supposed to make him a better person.

The lesson his parents are trying to impart either resonates profoundly or is entirely unnecessary—it might not always manifest itself in his academic life, but Good2cu possesses a stubborn work ethic. He attacks the game of poker as if it were a problem that needs to be solved, suspecting that, like video games, there must be some strategy to winning.

A trip to the bookstore confirms it. Reading every book on the subject he can get his hands on, Good2cu verifies what he was beginning to suspect: Most of the kids he battles in the lunch room are playing too many hands, bluffing too often, and focusing too much on their own cards instead of considering what their opponents might have. He puts his newly acquired knowledge to good use at his friend Jason's home game. After Good2cu leaves with all the money on the table four consecutive times, Jason asks him not to come back.

The same dynamic is playing itself out in home games all across the country. As the money gets redistributed from the weak players to the stronger ones, the smaller games start to dry up. The winning players gravitate toward one another, eager to use their bigger bank-rolls to compete in games with higher stakes.

Good2cu knows he's going to have to get a lot better if he's going to succeed against players with greater skills and bigger bankrolls. He's just not sure how. He's read nearly every poker strategy book in print, and, besides, there aren't very many books that focus on no-limit Hold'em, the game everyone likes to play.

His quest for knowledge leads him to the Two Plus Two forums. He's way too intimidated to join the conversation, but happily soaks up all the knowledge others are providing. The quality of his educa-tion can be measured by all the $5, $10, and $20 bills he keeps stuffing into his sock drawer. The socks are starting to complain.

His growing wealth allows him certain luxuries, like buying a high-quality fake ID on the Internet. The ID means Good2cu can buy beer, leading to several welcome discoveries. The idea of talking to a pretty girl is far less intimidating when he's got a beer in his hand, and the notion becomes even more palatable when he's got several of them in his belly. Alcohol doesn't just make him braver, but also wittier, more articulate, and more charming—at least that's how he feels under the influence.

Partying also levels the social hierarchy. The arrival of alcohol and drugs on the scene reshuffles the deck, so to speak, giving Good2cu a new way to prove his value to the pack and further increasing his confidence.

Suddenly he's getting invited to parties and, whenever his dad goes out of town, throwing ragers of his own. One of them gets out of hand. The police arrive. Good2cu gets arrested, charged with allow-ing minors to consume alcohol on the premises.

Choice A: Tell Dad, beg for forgiveness, and hope to see the keys to the car sometime before college.

Choice B: Hire the best criminal defense attorney in Okemos.

What would Sammy Farha do?

When the lawyer's bill arrives, Good2cu pays it with money he won in a home game just a couple of nights before.

7

Solved game: a game whose outcome can be correctly predicted from any position when each side plays optimally.

FORT WORTH, TEXAS (Summer 2004)

With his freshman year at TCU just a few weeks away, Raptor spends what's left of his summer mucking around Two Plus Two. It's become his default place to waste time on the Internet, a virtual home away from home (or, more precisely, a virtual home *inside* his home). When he's not posting questions about his play—an exercise in instant gratification, thanks to the mind-cloud of serious poker junkies—Raptor explores the site's nooks and crannies. He finds discussions on everything from hard-core poker theory to gossip about which famous pros are going broke. He loves that the site's founders, David Sklansky and Mason Malmuth—legends in the poker world, having written and published nearly every important strategy book at the time—are active participants on the site, weighing in on the topics that interest them. But it's the One-Table Forum, where a small community of players talk about Sit N Go tournaments as if they're a "solved game," that becomes the rabbit hole from which he can't escape.

The most obvious example of a solved game is tic-tac-toe—any two reasonably intelligent players, as long as neither makes a mistake, will always battle to a draw. A less obvious example would be Connect Four, where the player who goes first is always guaranteed to win as long as she plays a perfect strategy. (Pretty sneaky, sis!)

But poker? Poker seems like the opposite of a solved game. You're playing against unpredictable opponents, who don't always make rational decisions, and relying on cards, which were pretty much invented as a physical representation of the universe's crazy spirit of randomness.

Sifting through hundreds of threads started by guys like AleoMagus, Daliman, and Irieguy, Raptor learns that Sit N Gos haven't been "solved" in the sense that you can predict the winner of any particular game, but that this community of players, after years of theorizing and debate, have cobbled together an optimal strategy for success—a way of playing these interesting little tournaments that pretty much guarantees that you'll finish in the money more often than not.

The ideas that make up the strategy are wide-ranging and complex, but they more or less boil down to a single, unifying concept, a philosophy the Two Plus Twoers call "pushbotting."

At the start of a Sit N Go, you have a lot of chips relative to the size of the blinds. You can afford to play a lot of hands and to call a lot of bets once you're battling for a pot. Which is exactly what most people do. But as the blinds increase, your position reverses. You no longer have a lot of chips relative to the size of the betting. The decisions you make are riskier, forcing you to gamble with a larger percentage of your chip stack. Most people start to tighten up during the latter part of the tournament, playing fewer hands in order to preserve their chips as long as possible.

Most people are idiots. The best way to win a Sit N Go is to do the exact opposite. The smaller blinds at the beginning mean smaller pots that, in the larger context of the tournament, don't mean very much—it's not worth getting involved unless you've got a hand that's a lock to win. When the bigger blinds at the end of the Sit N Go force you to risk a larger percentage of your chips, you're very often "pot committed"—there's so much money at stake that it's worth taking a chance with a wider range of hands, even when your opponent is statistically favored to win.

Pushbotting is an effort to mechanize this strategy to the point where it no longer requires conscious thought: stay out of trouble in the beginning of the tournament, raise like a madman with all kinds of junk at the end.

The difficulty is in the details: knowing which hands to play at the beginning, which hands to play at the end, and the ability to recognize the "inflection point" where the beginning suddenly turns into the end, the moment when it's time to change gears.

But Raptor discovers most of that mystery has been eliminated as well. The members of the One-Table Forum have created a bunch of charts that let you know which hands to play when, and they've created something called an ICM calculator that helps you determine, with mathematical precision, the optimal time to stop playing conservatively and start playing hyperaggressively.

With the details more or less settled, most of the active debate in the forum centers around figuring out exactly how much money you can expect to make by playing this way. Success is measured not in wins or losses, but in "ROI"—return on investment, the size of your profit relative to the amount of money you've invested to earn it. The

Sit N Go specialists brag about ROI like it's penis size—probably exaggerated, unlikely to be verified—tossing around numbers like 10 or 20 percent. Some claim to have stretches where they're making as much as fifty cents on every dollar they risk.

Raptor can't believe what he's stumbled into. Poker's not gambling for these guys—it's investing. But it's the next discovery that really blows his mind.

You can play more than one table at a time.

It's a trick that would be nearly impossible in a live casino setting—how could you keep up with the action while racing among four separate tables? But online, you can move like a speed chess Grandmaster, clicking into a game, analyzing the board, making a play, then moving onto the next. And the beauty of pushbotting is that it's almost robotic—most of the strategic decisions don't require much active thought.

The regulars on the One-Table Forum have been experimenting with "multitabling" for years. *I'm earning a 10 percent ROI at one table. . . . What happens if I play two at the same time? Or four? Or eight?*

Most of them have come to the same conclusion: It's hard to increase the number of tables without suffering a drop in their ROI. There's no way to turn poker into a completely robotic activity—there are occasionally critical decisions that require concentration and thought—and spreading your attention over multiple games reduces the amount of focus you're able to give to any one in particular.

But Raptor wonders if the problem isn't more physical than mental. It's not easy to squeeze four tables onto a single screen—the age of giant flat-screen monitors has yet to arrive; most players are still using crate-sized CRT monitors with fifteen-inch screens. Clicking frantically from game to game, quickly trying to assess exactly what's going on and what you should do, creates a lot of heightened stress, and it's hard to play good poker while you're stressed.

Raptor alleviates this issue by plugging two different monitors into the same computer. With the games spread across a wider area, he finds that he's able to handle as many as eight tables at once without too much discomfort.

He puts this innovation to good use during the summer after graduating from high school, mastering Sit N Go strategy while playing eight to ten hours a day. By the time he moves into his new dorm room at TCU, he's often winning $300 to $400 a day. Good money for most adults.

For an eighteen-year-old entering college, it feels like winning the lottery.

I'm really glad I got all that, well, *most* of the degenerate gambling stuff out of my system before it was money that would actually impact my life in some way.

—**Raptor**

FORT WORTH, TEXAS (Fall 2004)

For Raptor, getting As and Bs in high school wasn't much harder than collecting Halloween candy. Not so in college, where just three days in, his professors are actually making demands of him. Read this book. Study for the test. Show up to class.

The demands are not playing nice with his *other* schedule. During the summer, Raptor had time to play at least eight hours of online poker nearly every day. He spent so many nights at the Poker Box that the owner invited him to take a 25-percent stake in the club. (An offer that Raptor happily accepted.) There's no way he can continue to make $300 a day if he has to read books and study for tests.

Three days into his first semester of college, and Raptor's already asking himself, *What's the point?*

When he can't come up with a good answer, he calls his parents, the happy loving couple who adopted him when he was two months old. Raptor won't ascribe too much meaning to his adoption, but countless academic studies have already done the work for him, citing social confusion and depression among the possible long-term effects. Raptor does in fact feel a vague mysterious void in his life, as if everything doesn't quite add up and he's the only one who feels that way, but he tries not to let the feelings control him. In his mind the man and woman who raised him are his real parents. He loves them with all his heart and what they say truly matters to him.

Now he's got to explain to Mom—an associate dean at TCU's School of Nursing—and Dad—a Naval Academy graduate who's been piloting American Airlines passenger jets for twenty years—that he's planning to drop out of college.

To play poker.

"I'm really not happy doing the whole school thing" is the opening he chooses.

"Is this about baseball, honey?" his mom asks. "I know how upset you are about that."

Raptor still can't rotate his shoulder with anything resembling full mobility, and it seems to hurt a little more every time he walks past the baseball stadium on campus. But these days he's so focused on poker he barely notices.

"Sort of. Well, not really. I told you guys I've been playing a little bit of poker online, right? I've also been playing at this club in town and doing pretty well."

" . . . "

"So I was thinking. Maybe I'll take the semester off and see where this whole poker thing takes me."

"We should probably talk about this a little more," says Mom, after taking a moment to consider her response. "But if that's really how you feel, you should do whatever makes you happy. If you're miserable at school, then obviously that's not the place for you. But . . . poker?"

"Yeah, I know how it sounds. And I'll admit that I have no idea where this whole online poker thing is going, whether it'll even be around next year or not. But right now I'm making insane amounts of money and I just don't feel like I'm ready for college."

Dad, who's been listening in from the phone upstairs, chimes in. "Do you really think three days is enough time to decide whether or not you're going to pursue a degree?"

"I'm just talking about taking the semester off. I can always go back in the Spring. I just need a little time to sort through some things. I'm eighteen, so this is probably a good time for me to be figuring this stuff out, right?"

"You've got to do what you've to do, son. Just . . . be careful. Don't go getting in over your head. And please keep us updated and let us know how everything's going. Don't be afraid to call us and ask if you need help with anything . . ."

"Thanks, Dad."

". . . as long as it's not money you're looking for or a place to live. You're on your own now, son."

Well, thinks Raptor as he hangs up the phone, *that went better than expected.*

Next up: the TCU administrative office. He tells the counselor he meets with that he wants to take a leave of absence for psychological reasons. Not a problem—plenty of kids get too depressed to finish their first semester of college. But in truth, he's anything but sad. He can't wait to start his new life as a professional gambler.

He moves into a run-down off-campus apartment with Deuce-2High, one of his best friends from high school who's now enrolled at TCU. Raptor's share of the rent is only $400 a month, so it's easy to set aside enough money to cover the year.

He uses another chunk of his bankroll to purchase a computer system that will turn him into a cult hero on Two Plus Two: the Quad Monitor Set-Up. Like a proud father Raptor posts pictures of it on the forum—four monitors, stacked two by two, connected to a computer with multiple graphics cards. He's now able to see sixteen online poker tables at once, although he quickly discovers through trial and error that his results suffer if he plays more than twelve games at the same time.

Free of any obligations outside of poker, Raptor multitables Sit N Gos all day, every day, rapidly rising up the ranks until he's regularly playing the $109s and $215s. Deuce2High is so impressed that he sells Raptor his radar detector for $250—with a few clicks, Raptor transfers the money into Deuce2High's new poker account, seed money for grinding the $11 Sit N Gos. He will soon be winning with enough consistency to join Raptor as a college dropout.

The online cardrooms have been quick to realize that these sorts of referrals are an easy way to keep growing their business, so many have established Amway-style affiliate programs to reward players who are willing to evangelize. Raptor steers his friends to a site called Empire Poker in exchange for a percentage of the "rake."

Most casino games are insanely profitable because they're rigged in favor of the house. Not so with poker, where the house is relegated to spectator as the players battle among themselves. The casinos—including the online poker rooms—compensate themselves by taking a small cut out of every pot: the rake. It's usually just a couple of dollars, so the players hardly feel the pinch, but they're being pinched nonetheless. If the house is dealing a hundred hands an hour and taking $2 out of every pot, it's like having an invisible player at the table who's guaranteed to win $200 every hour. It's not enough for a poker player to outdo his opponents; if he's going to turn a profit, he's got to beat this invisible player too.

As long as his friends keep playing, Raptor gets a portion of their rake in the form of a check from the card room at the end of each month. It's almost like having a steady paycheck, which frees him up psychologically to play his best poker. He's able to quickly build his bankroll up to $25,000, which to an eighteen-year-old feels like a grand fortune.

But after a few weeks, Raptor worries that something is missing from his life. A quick glance at his daily routine, which rarely sees him stray farther from his computer than the bathroom to take a leak or the front door to pick up delivery food, reminds him that his world lacks any kind of social life or sense of community. For the first time in his life he's not part of a team. He'd planned to join a fraternity, but that option's no longer available to him. He has a lot of friends at TCU and goes to plenty of college parties, but he usually feels like an outsider, disconnected from the rhythms of campus life, coping with a radically different set of concerns than the students who surround him.

It occurs to him that, as a professional gambler, the Two Plus Two site would probably be a good place to seek camaraderie. He begins to post more often, and when Irieguy throws out the idea of sharing a room at the Commerce Casino for an upcoming tournament, Raptor jumps at the chance to fly to Los Angeles.

$ $ $

Raptor is every bit as surprised by Irieguy and SkipperBob as they are by him. Irieguy is *way* older than he'd expected, like, in his thirties or something, and SkipperBob clearly gets into movies for half-price.

The awkwardness slowly dissipates as they launch into an esoteric poker discussion, then disappears altogether once TheUsher, a Two Plus Twoer from nearby Santa Monica who named himself after a villainous character from HBO's *Carnivale*, arrives on the scene.

Raptor and TheUsher have traded messages on AIM, but they've never actually met in person before. Raptor's relieved to discover that TheUsher's only twenty years old—a contemporary who speaks the same language and gets the same cultural references. The two hit it off, strutting around the Commerce Casino as if they own the place, getting so caught up in the moment that they put their names on the waiting list for a $100/$200 limit Hold'em game. It's by far the biggest game Raptor has ever considered playing, but he has $12,000 in his pocket and he's feeling plenty confident, especially after seeing how awful—"terribad" in his vernacular—many of the players are.

While waiting to get in the game, they drift into the adjoining room, where a group of Asian gamblers are whooping it up. Whatever strange card game they're playing is clearly the most entertaining activity in the world.

"What the heck is that?" Raptor asks.

"Pai Gow," TheUsher replies. "You know you can play as the bank here?"

"So what?"

"So, the bank has like a two percent edge."

"Wait a minute. You can gamble here *plus EV*?"

"EV" stands for expected value, gamblerspeak for the amount of money that any given decision will win or lose over the long run. When you talk about the house having an edge, what you're really saying is that casino games like craps or slot machines force players to make decisions with negative expected value—you may enjoy some short-term success, but keep betting a dollar and, once the law of averages has a chance to work its magic, you'll only be getting back ninety-eight cents.

Savvy gamblers live for opportunities that carry positive expected value. Blackjack card-counters aren't psychic; they don't have any way of knowing exactly which cards are going to come out of the shoe. What they can do, by keeping close track of all the cards that have been played, is identify moments where the odds have shifted subtly in their favor, creating "plus-EV" situations. Seizing these opportunities, they suddenly increase the size of their bets, hoping to take advantage of the winds that are, however briefly, blowing their way. Winning poker relies on a similar ethic: nearly every move that a knowledgeable player makes at the table is governed by the hopes that he's making a plus-EV decision.

Raptor, having committed himself to the life of a savvy gambler, can't believe that this casino is going to give him an opportunity to gamble plus EV.

Or rather, he *totally* believes it. He sidles up to the table and pulls out his bankroll, quickly bringing himself up to speed on the rules of the game as it progresses.

Less than an hour later, a floorman calls his name for the poker game, but Raptor isn't around to hear it. He's back in his hotel room with TheUsher, feeling terribad, trying to figure out how much grinding at the poker tables it's going to take to win back the $12,000 he just lost at Pai Gow.

9

Once I came upon Two Plus Two, I saw all these people who were playing poker on the Internet for a living. In the Midwest you're told you have to finish high school, go to college, get a corporate job or whatever. It gave me confidence that there were actually people living outside of that system making a living playing poker. That it was more than a crazy idea.

—**Good2cu**

OKEMOS, MICHIGAN (Fall 2004)

In addition to allowing him to buy beer for half of underage Okemos, Good2cu's fake ID turns out to have another benefit: access to Soaring Eagle, an Indian casino an hour's drive north on Highway 127.

Here he finds the kind of poker he sees on TV. Real felt tables. Professional dealers. Interesting characters. The hypnotic clickety-clack of hundreds of players simultaneously riffling their chips. In this seductive environment Good2cu's desire to become a professional video gamer comes to an end, supplanted by the fantasy that's been prickling his imagination for the past year. He wants to be a professional gambler, a well-heeled scoundrel living by his ingenuity and wits, a "balla" in the parlance of the rap world. Good2cu understands that he's not a natural fit, that to be a true balla he's going to have to overcome his social awkwardness and find a girl who's actually interested in him, but there's no reason he can't embark on the gambling part right now.

His first few sessions at Soaring Eagle teach him that his dream job comes weighted with certain harsh realities. The wait-list to get into a $6/$12 or $10/$20 limit Hold'em game often exceeds an hour, plenty of time for a bored gambler to lose all his money playing black-jack. The poker games themselves aren't quite boom-or-bust—"boom" is much too strong of a word to describe his piddling success. Good2cu tends to string together a few decent wins, only to wipe them out in a single bad session, sending him all the way back to square one. Or, rather, to the YMCA, to scrub a few more toilets, and to Two Plus Two, to search for ways to clean up his game.

While lurking on the site, Good2cu picks up some valuable infor-mation. The conventional wisdom among poker players is that, in the long run, solid play can reasonably be expected to net around one "big blind"—the betting unit that dictates the size of a game—every hour he plays. In other words, even if Good2cu plays flawlessly, the kinds of games they're spreading at Soaring Eagle probably won't earn him more than $10 or $20 an hour. It's certainly better than the $7 an hour he's making at the Y, but not exactly a path to riches.

Internet poker presents an interesting challenge to this long-maintained belief, offering an accelerated version of the game. Live poker is riddled with all sorts of tedious conventions that prevent swifter play. Human dealers have to collect and shuffle the cards. Bets have to be counted out and confirmed. Players ask other players for chip counts, dealers to change the decks when they're running bad, and floormen to resolve arguments over even the most trivial of slights.

According to Two Plus Twoers, the Internet has redefined or elim-inated many of these hurdles. Where in a live game you can expect to be dealt maybe twenty hands an hour, in an Internet game you might see a hundred or more. Online players have discovered that they've been driving the car in first gear. With the emergency brake on.

Taking the logic one step further, it stands to reason that a player who can make $10 an hour in a game where twenty hands are dealt can make $50 an hour in a game where he's dealt five times as many hands.

And if you can handle playing four or eight or twelve of these tables at the same time . . .

Reading this inspires seventeen-year-old Good2cu to take the leap and make a deposit online. He chooses PokerStars, the site where Chris Moneymaker started his miraculous run to the world championship. He doesn't have a credit card, so he uses Western Union to wire some of the money he's won playing home games to his new online account. When prompted for his date of birth, he enters the same one that's on his fake ID—if this is going to present a problem when he goes to cash out his winnings, well, he'll worry about that when the time comes.

Turns out he doesn't have to worry—in his first few days on the site, Good2cu learns another important lesson about Internet poker: you can lose your money a lot faster too.

He returns to Two Plus Two to learn a few more tricks. One is bankroll management, the discipline to choose games you can actually afford to play without fear of losing all your money in one sitting. Another is a form of bargain shopping specific to online poker—the competition among virtual card rooms is so fierce that most offer special deals to attract players, like cash bonuses for new deposits and "rakeback," which rewards loyal players by refunding a portion of their rake. After comparing sites for the best deal, Good2cu makes another deposit, vowing to stick to a lower-stakes game he knows he can afford.

He also has a goal to keep him focused. Spring Break is only three months away and some of his friends are going to Mexico, a trip that promises epic drunkenness and, possibly, drunken hookups with drunken girls. His parents are willing to pay for college, but they're not interested in subsidizing this particular aspect of their son's education.

To go, Good2cu needs to make $2,000, and with margaritas and bikinis serving as a carrot, he manages to do just that. He flies to Playa del Carmen, drinks a thousand Coronas and half as many tequila shots, and comes awfully close, on one or two occasions, to hooking up with girls who are every bit as drunk as he.

Upon his return to Michigan, Good2cu can't wait to get back to the tables to begin funding his next adventure. He parks himself in front of the computer in his dad's home office, a development that does not go unnoticed by Dad, who from time to time likes to pop his head in to see what his son is up to. Sometimes Dad even likes to take a seat beside him and watch him play.

Uh-oh.

Despite the fact that one of the world's most celebrated poker players, 1989 WSOP champion Phil Hellmuth, hails from Madison, Wisconsin, most folks in the Midwest still equate poker with gambling, and gambling with sin. Good2cu's father is hardly a puritan, but he doesn't take regular junkets to Las Vegas either. All he knows about poker is what he's seen on television, and, despite his son's admiration for them, he wouldn't trust Sammy Farha or Chris Moneymaker to give him proper change.

Good2cu doesn't want his dad to know he's playing with, and therefore risking, actual American dollars, but the $.50/$1 limit Hold'em game he's settled into is clearly identified with boldface letters in the top-left corner of the window as being a **Real Money Game.**

Which is how he discovers Sit N Gos. After buying into one of these single-table tournaments, there's no further mention of real money being involved until the payouts are issued at the end. The bets and raises are made with tournament chips, which have no cash value, and the top-left corner offers a far more innocent-looking heading: **Tournament Table.**

"Just messing around," Good2cu tells his father.

During his frequent visits to the One-Table Forum he discovers that there are even better reasons to cast his lot with Sit N Gos. He reads nearly every post written by guys like Daliman and Irieguy, who insist that these online tournaments are cash cows that can be steadily milked. Raptor, a regular contributor who ends each of his posts with his signature catchphrase "holla!", claims he's consistently making a 30 percent ROI.

Good2cu's journey begins with an epic heater, a textbook episode of beginner's luck. He quickly jumps from the $22s and $33s to the $55s and $109s, playing as many as eight tables at once. During one stretch he plays 449 Sit N Gos and achieves an ROI of 208 percent, a number that's twice as big as it has to be to be called a statistical anomaly.

This windfall allows him to start living in a way he couldn't have imagined just three months before. He pays $3,000 for a top-of-the-line laptop. He buys an expensive necklace for the girl he's starting to call his girlfriend. While his peers drink Natty Ice (a catchall term for shitty beer) and Popov vodka and smoke Mexican dirt weed, Good2cu treats himself to more exotic Coronas, Hpnotiq (a trendy blue liqueur popular in the New York club scene), and sticky kind bud.

His parents can't help noticing the influx of disposable income their son is enjoying, and share with him the predictable concerns about his new hobby. Good2cu mollifies them by promising to set aside enough money so that he—not they—will be paying for his first semester of college. It's an angle that will cost him roughly $5,000, but it allows him to go on playing poker.

It turns out to be the correct play. By the time Good2cu makes the three-mile trip down Grand River Avenue to the freshman dorms at Michigan State, he's pushed his bankroll all the way up to $43,000.

10

Wake up whenever I wake up, take a piss, brush my teeth, sit down at my computer and immediately fire up as many Sit N Gos as possible. Order some food, run to door when it rings. Keep firing up Sit N Gos. Post on Two Plus Two and AIM with friends, talk about hand histories throughout the day while playing nonstop. When my eyes hurt, go lie down and watch a movie or a TV series. Fall asleep. Sleep until I wake up. Repeat.

—**Raptor**

FORT WORTH, TEXAS (Fall 2005)

With the one-year anniversary of his decision to become a professional gambler fast approaching, Raptor is ready to take stock.

At times, it's been a grand adventure. This summer, he made his first trip to Las Vegas for the World Series of Poker. Barely nineteen, he wasn't old enough to enter any of the tournaments, but that didn't prevent him from playing cash games in any casinos that didn't bother checking his ID. Nor did it stop him from experimenting with blackjack, specifically the Martingale Betting System, a creation of the eighteenth-century French mathematician Paul Pierre Lévy that suggests you double the size of your bet every time you lose a hand. It's more or less foolproof if you have an infinitely large bankroll.

Raptor—whose resources were not infinitely large—chased a $1,000 loss with a $2,000 wager, bet $4,000 hoping to win back the $2,000, then threw down his last $7,200 in an effort to recoup all his losses, successfully wiping out his $14,200 bankroll in under three minutes.

It made for a great story on Two Plus Two—Daliman, a skilled blackjack card counter, got a lot of comic mileage out of retelling it— and Raptor doesn't have a problem laughing at himself. But he also felt sick to his stomach, unable to distance himself from the idea that the money he lost could have been converted into, say, a brand-new car.

Over the course of the past year, he's also become one of the most frequent posters on his favorite Two Plus Two message board, which, during an overhaul of the site, got renamed the "Single-Table Tournament Forum" (STTF). He likes to propose informal competitions— for example, "Who can play five hundred $109 Sit N Gos in a week while achieving an 8 percent ROI?"—that will motivate him to put in even more hours at the tables. They come to be known as Raptor Challenges, and inspire many of the regulars on the forum to play longer, higher, and better than they ever have before.

But looking back on the year, he's also ready to admit that the glamorous life of a gambling man hasn't turned out to be quite as glamorous as he'd imagined. He spends most of his days and nights staring at a computer screen, clicking a mouse, making decisions that, 99 percent of the time, don't require an iota of conscious thought. The only humans he interacts with are poker players, and that's mostly through online forums and instant messages. He's definitely not meeting any girls. Depression has become a very viable diagnosis.

Hoping to fill the growing void inside him, Raptor reenrolls for the fall semester at TCU. He cashes out all the money he has in his online accounts except for $450, enough to fool around at some low-limit games should he feel the itch, but vows to take the entire first semester off from poker.

For a last hurrah he returns to Vegas over Labor Day weekend to play in a "heads-up" (one-on-one) poker tournament hosted by Irieguy. Many of the regular posters on the Single-Table Tournament Forum fly in from all over the country to play what they dub the inaugural STTF-HU Championship. Raptor manages to finish in second place and, for the first time, leaves Las Vegas with more money than he brought with him.

Back in Fort Worth, he does his best impersonation of a normal college student. He pledges a fraternity. He begins dating again and lands a serious girlfriend. His off-campus apartment becomes a popular place to party into the wee hours of the morning. A little too popular—after the eighth noise complaint, the property management company evicts him. Luckily his friend TravestyFund has a spare bedroom to rent, but the change of scenery doesn't do anything to curb the partying. One morning Raptor wakes up and realizes he hasn't been to class in two weeks. His grades are so poor he's not going to get initiated into the fraternity. And there's no way the school is going to let him take another leave of absence. If he flunks out this time, it will almost certainly be for good. He needs a plan.

Or an escape. His eyes drift to the Quad Monitor Set-Up in the corner of the room. He brushes dust from the screens and fires up the computer. In one of his accounts he finds the $450 he's been saving for a rainy day.

The smart move would be to stick to low-stakes—he hasn't played in a while, and he could easily lose all his money in one sitting. Hell, the smart move would be turning off the computer and going to the library to study.

Instead, he spreads his entire poker bankroll across four $109 Sit N Go tables.

All right, time to run good. Either I win or I'm done.

In the parlance of the game, he "runs good," winning three of the tournaments and finishing second in the fourth. He doesn't bother standing up, using his winnings to enter eight more Sit N Gos. Then twelve. When he feels like his bankroll will allow it, he moves up from the $109s to the $215s.

Thirty-six hours later, he's too bleary-eyed to see the cards on the screen. It takes all his remaining energy just to power down his computer, but before he does he takes one last look at his bottom line, just to reassure himself that what he thinks just happened really did happen.

Thirty-six hours of poker, and he's transformed the last $450 in his online accounts into a $20,000 bankroll.

Well, I guess I'm a poker player again.

11

The Single-Table Tournament Forum on Two Plus Two was a small community. There were probably less than a hundred people who played those games for a living, so everyone kind of knew each other. I started talking to Raptor on AOL. He and I were playing a lot of the same games against the same opponents, and we would talk strategy. He was probably making more money playing those games than anybody else, so everybody knew who he was.

—Good2cu

EAST LANSING, MICHIGAN (Fall 2005)

Almost everyone Good2cu knows in Okemos is going to the University of Michigan or Michigan State. His girlfriend is going to Michigan, where applicants are required to write a bunch of essays. Michigan State does not require essays, a comparative lack of rigor that is rumored to result in better-looking girls and wilder parties.

Well, it wasn't like they were going to get married.

The classes at Michigan State aren't very tough. Good2cu is able to maintain nearly an A average in all of them with plenty of hours left in the day to play online poker and get drunk nearly every night. He's in the middle of a session, multitabling $15/$30 limit Hold'em, when there's a knock on his dorm room door.

"Come in!"

Two police officers accept his invitation. They've come to arrest him for throwing rocks through a window last night while he was stumbling home, drunk off his ass.

But it's the cops who get arrested by the sight of the side-by-side flat-screen monitors on his desk. Good2cu has four tables open on each screen, and at each table he has at least $1,000 in play.

"Is that Texas Hold'em?" asks one of the officers.

"Yeah," Good2cu replies. "Do you play?"

"A little," the cop answers sheepishly. "But not at those stakes."

"Do you mind if I keep playing until my big blinds come around?"

The cops each pull up a chair. "No problem. Go right ahead."

The police officers eventually get around to charging him with Willful and Malicious Destruction of Property. Luckily, Good2cu already has Okemos's best criminal defense attorney on speed dial. He gives the man $2,000 to make the charges disappear, while setting two new goals for himself: (1) stay out of trouble; (2) win back the two grand as quickly as possible.

$ $ $

During the many hours Good2cu spends playing poker on his computer, he also finds time to surf the Web, check his e-mail, and talk on AIM. One of his favorite people to chat with is Raptor. The kid is clearly a skilled player as well as something of a celebrity on Two Plus Two.

What does it mean to be a celebrity on Two Plus Two? It means that an older STTF regular might write a tongue-in-cheek post about you, like the one entitled, "Why I Hate Raptor," a top ten list that's simultaneously envious of your youth and success while making fun of said youth and success. The kid's enthusiasm for the world "holla" is particularly irritating to many of the site's elders, but for the young players like Good2cu, it's a generational touchstone, an edgy greeting like " 'Sup, bro" that distinguishes them from the old farts.

Good2cu often runs into Raptor at the online tables and the two build an Internet friendship, mostly through instant messages. Soon they're sharing details about their personal lives. Good2cu learns that Raptor, who's only four months older than him, has dropped out of college—twice!—to play poker full time. From time to time he recommends that Good2cu do the same, a suggestion Good2cu laughs off.

But it's harder to ignore Raptor's advice that he attend something called the STTF-HUC II, a tournament that Irieguy, one of the message board's elder statesmen, plans to host in Las Vegas in February. Raptor promises Good2cu that there will be girls, booze, and the chance to win some decent money.

Good2cu has never been to Vegas, and he's intrigued by the idea of meeting some of the Two Plus Two guys face-to-face, so he introduces himself to Irieguy via instant message and asks about the tournament.

"We still have a couple spots open," Irieguy replies. "You interested?"

"It's $200, right?"

Irieguy has structured the tournament with two different prize tiers created by two different entry fees, $200 and $500. There are still a few $200 seats available, but he doesn't know Good2cu and is looking to build a bigger prize pool.

"Sorry, just sold the last $200 seat," Irieguy bluffs. "If you want to play, ship me $500 online, plus another $170 for food, beverages, and incidentals."

"Incidentals?"

"Let's just say that if you like drinking alcohol and/or naked women, you won't be disappointed."

Good2cu's run of beginner's luck has come to an end; he's still winning more than he loses, but at a much slower rate. After paying for his first semester at Michigan State—a tab that includes lots of marijuana, even more alcohol, and Okemos's most expensive criminal attorney—his $43,000 bankroll has been substantially reduced. The tournament buy-in, the "incidentals," plus hotel, food, and airfare, represent a significant portion of his net worth.

"$670, huh?" he writes back. "I don't know. I'm not that big of a balla."

A balla? Irieguy chuckles inwardly. *What is it with these kids?*

"Well, think it over," he responds.

That's not a problem—Good2cu can't think about anything else. It's not even December, and the ground's already covered with dirty slush. He has to bundle up like an Eskimo just to go to the gym or the food court. Most of the girls on campus have started wearing thick sweaters and ski hats everywhere they go, which, if you ask him, is a crime against humanity. And it's going to be this way for another five long months.

Fuck it. This is a once-in-a-lifetime opportunity. I'm going to Vegas.

Using one of his online poker accounts, he ships Irieguy the money.

12

This kid was asking me if he could buy in for $200 instead of $500 and says he's no balla, but on his first night in Vegas he's running the party at the Rhino.

—Irieguy

LAS VEGAS, NEVADA (February 2006)

There are many reasons why people love Las Vegas. Around-the-clock action. The smell of easy money. Beautiful women. Handsome men. Gourmet restaurants. Spectacular shows. The high-octane oxygen that, it's rumored, flows through every casino's ventilation system and negates the need for sleep.

But the most compelling reason—the one that the city, circa 2006, is just coming to embrace—is wish fulfillment. Las Vegas is (once again) in the process of reinventing itself, tossing away an unsuccessful branding effort at becoming a destination for the whole family, and wants its visitors to feel comfortable doing the same. Accountants can undo their top two (or three) buttons and turn into high-rolling VIPs. Schoolteachers unleash the leopard-print mini they never get to wear back home. Typically faithful husbands and wives, prowling for a spark of the naughty, well . . . , as Sin City's new ad campaign goes: "What happens here, stays here."

Back in East Lansing, Good2cu already feels like he's living a double life. By day, he's your typical college student, spending more time partying and less time on classwork than he should, growing in fits and spurts out of his social awkwardness. But when he's logged into an online card room, routinely winning hundreds, sometimes thousands, of dollars in a single night . . . he's motherfucking Superman.

He's never been to Vegas before, but he's heard enough to know he can leave his glasses at home—all he needs to pack is his red cape.

The descent into McCarran Airport feels like the beginning of a great movie. Through the plane's window, Technicolor lights erupt out of the stark desert. The glowing casinos, currently trending toward international sophistication, smorgasbord-style—Paris, New York, Venice, Rome, and Monte Carlo all share the same stretch of road—promise the kind of adventure that simply can't be found in the Midwest.

His plane is two hours late, so Good2cu jogs through the airport, hoping Slim Pickens isn't too upset. He's never met Slim in person, but knows enough about him from the Two Plus Two message boards—like, for example, he isn't a poker pro, but a grad student studying nuclear engineering—to know that he probably isn't too happy about having to wait at Arrivals for some guy he's only talked to on AIM.

Slim turns out to be a surprisingly laid-back guy for an aspiring nuclear engineer, but he's got work to do, so Good2cu's on his own. Raptor's not answering his phone, but Good2cu has no trouble figuring out how to kill a little time in a city full of casinos. He asks Slim to drop him off at the Wynn Las Vegas, which is supposed to have one of the best poker rooms in town.

Good2cu has already logged considerable hours at Soaring Eagle and made occasional border crossings to play cards at the Caesars Windsor in Canada, but the Wynn is in an entirely different class. Not even a year old, it's the casino of the moment, a nearly $3-billion play-ground with a man-made waterfall cascading off a man-made moun-tain into a man-made lake that inspired its owner, Las Vegas's biggest real-estate mogul, to name it after himself. Everything is decorated in plush velvet and almost all of it is red, the color considered luckiest by the high-rolling Asian gamblers the casino hopes to attract.

Good2cu struts into the poker room like he owns the place, figur-ing that if he acts as if he belongs, he won't get carded. He's right. A floorman ushers him to a table spreading $15/$30 limit Hold'em, a game where the average pot usually exceeds $100. Good2cu casually presses a red $5 chip into the floorman's hand like he's been doing it all his life.

He's not quite sure what to expect from the game, but quickly fig-ures it out. Most of the guys at his table aren't tourists, but local "nits" who refuse to put a chip into the pot unless they believe it's going to come right back to them. He might be able to bluff them out of a few small pots, but he knows they won't risk significant money without a hand that's heavily favored to win.

Great. I came to Vegas to fold every single hand.

But the cards fall his way, and he manages to win a few decent-sized pots. With his confidence on the rise, his ears perk up when the floorman announces an open seat at the $80/$160 game, where the pots routinely approach $1,000. It's a quantum leap above the game he's currently sitting in. In fact, he's never played anywhere close to that high before. And he's doing just fine where he is . . . but he didn't come to Vegas to win a couple hundred bucks in a low-stakes game. He's here to leap tall buildings.

How much harder can it be to win in that game than the one I'm in right now? It's still just poker, right?

Good2cu moves to the bigger game, and, just a couple of hours later, rises from the table carrying two racks full of chips, $4,000 richer.

Up, up, and away, bitches!

But his confidence dims when he gets to the cashier's cage, where he learns that for tax purposes, they're going to need to see an ID. Good2cu's fake has seen better days—it fell apart after his mom threw his pants in the washing machine, and when he put it back together he accidentally glued the back on upside down. If the ID fails, he'll not only lose the money, but may possibly face charges of tax fraud. He's debating the risk-reward when he spots a spaghetti-thin guy, not much older than he is, sitting at a low-stakes table. On a hunch, Good2cu approaches him.

"You aren't by any chance here for Irieguy's tournament, are you?"

"Sure am. I'm TheNoodleman."

"Good2cu."

"You too."

"I mean, that's my name on Two Plus Two. Good2cu."

"Never heard of you."

"Yeah, I mostly just lurk, but I'm here to play the heads-up thing. And right now I have a bit of a problem."

"Yeah, what's that?"

"I'm only nineteen." Good2cu's grinning so hard it makes his face look crooked. "And I need to cash out these chips."

TheNoodleman, who makes $10 an hour working for a local-access television station back in Indiana, stares, slack-jawed, at the racks Good2cu's holding in his hands. This goofy kid's got more chips than everybody at TheNoodleman's table put together.

Who is this kid, he wonders, *and if he plays this big, why the hell haven't I heard of him before?*

$ $ $

"Who?" asks the voice on the other end of the line.

Good2cu repeats his Two Plus Two user name into his phone before tossing out his given name for good measure.

"Never heard of you," replies Daliman. "Plus I'm drunk, I'm playing blackjack for five hundred dollars a hand, and I don't give a fuck." He hangs up before Good2cu has a chance to respond.

After TheNoodleman helped him cash out his chips, Good2cu traded the commotion at the Wynn for the quiet of Slim Pickens's house, where he took a disco nap on the couch. When he woke, he politely declined Slim's invitation to join him at the Orleans for a low-stakes game, where the pots would rarely top $20 or $30. He tried calling Raptor, but got his voice mail once again. The only other number Good2cu has belongs to Daliman.

After Daliman abruptly terminates the call, Good2cu tries him again. "Raptor's not with you, is he?"

"Here, talk to Irieguy."

There are muffled noises as the phone gets handed from one person to the next. Good2cu can hear the unmistakable sound of a slots payout in the background: *ding ding ding!*

A few seconds later, Irieguy gets on the line. "We're at TI donking off money in the pits. We're heading over to a craps tables next. You can't miss us."

Treasure Island was originally envisioned as a cornerstone of Las Vegas's family-friendly motif, a Disneyesque theme park where choreographed battles between pirate ships played out in an artificial lagoon seven times a day. Three years ago, when the city decided to abandon the kids, Treasure Island became TI, a swashbuckling fantasy for adults hosted by buxom cocktail waitresses stuffed into low-cut halter tops.

Good2cu exits his cab in front of the casino and dials Daliman for the third time. "I'm here. Where are you guys?"

"I'm still drunk, and I still don't give a fuck. Call someone else."

Click.

Fortunately, the few bits of intel Good2cu has at his disposal—young, drunk, playing craps—are enough to lead him straight to the group. He approaches them with equal parts excitement and nervousness—it feels like he's on a blind date—and introduces himself. The fact that everyone's already drunk helps break the ice. Soon he's able to attach names to faces: Raptor, Irieguy, Daliman, Apathy, Bonafone, Deuce2High. When the dice get passed his way, Good2cu puts aside his inhibitions over negative-EV gambling and rolls the bones down the table.

As it turns out, getting drunk and donking on craps is a hell of a lot of fun. For a while, anyway. When the allure of betting on dice starts to fade, they decide to move the party to the world-famous Spearmint Rhino.

$ $ $

Of all the occasions Irieguy's been to the Rhino (and let's just say there have been a few) this is the first time he's ever had to sweat getting in. Not for himself obviously—he's much closer to forty than twenty-one—but for the entourage of underage kids trailing him. Bonafone, a seventeen-year-old from Colorado, looks too young to be left at home without a babysitter. Good2cu appears a little older, but thanks to his shaggy bowl cut, Coke bottle glasses, and the rolling suitcase he's for some reason lugging behind him, he also looks like someone that even a good-natured Vegas bouncer would relish barring from the club.

But after a coordinated effort by the older guys, redistributing their IDs to the younger members of the crew, everyone—except for Bonafone and Deuce2High; there's only so much looking the other way that a bouncer can do—gets in. Irieguy suggests Good2cu check his bag at the door, which he manages to do despite all the distractions.

And by "distractions," we mean tits. The Rhino is swimming in them. Good2cu wonders if it's possible to see so many perfect breasts in such a short period of time as to become completely immune to their charms. He hurries through the math: in the last two minutes, he's probably increased his lifetime intake of live, naked, female bosom by a multiple of ten. Twice that, if you count each breast separately.

They come in nearly every color, shape, and size, as do the women they're attached to, a fickle raja's fantasy harem. White and black. Hispanic and Asian. Cute and slutty. Mysterious and girl-next-door. As varied as the women who work here are, there's one area where they hardly differ at all. After another quick calculation, Good2cu estimates that he's looking at more than a half-million dollars in top-shelf plastic surgery.

Raptor, feeling like an old hand on his third trip to Vegas, notes the awed expression on Good2cu's face. "What do you think?"

"I think I need a drink."

"How about a dance? My treat." Raptor pulls a gangster roll out of his pocket, peels off a couple of twenties, and waves them in the air. A few seconds later, one of the hottest women Good2cu has ever seen materializes out of the darkness.

In Good2cu's eyes it's just about the smoothest move he's ever seen. He didn't think Raptor would be able to measure up to the image he projects online, and he was right—the guy's way cooler in real life. He's got an easy smile and a self-assuredness about him that belies his youth. It doesn't hurt that he stands several inches over six feet and sports the kind of unblemished face and chiseled features that girls can't ignore. He looks like the type of guy Good2cu would have mocked or avoided in high school, the student body president or the captain of the football team, but he has to admit that right about now it feels good to be hanging out with the cool crowd. And that's before the dancer starts grinding her perfect ass into his lap.

A round of drinks appears. Then another. In between lap dances, the Two Plus Twoers down shots and brag to one another about their prowess.

Their online poker prowess.

"So you've been eight-tabling the $215s, huh?"

"Yeah, I used to do that, but lately I've been twelve-tabling the Step 5s."

The strippers in their company pretend to be impressed, the same way their sisters in New York and Los Angeles humor hedge fund traders and movie producers. Money sounds the same in every language. One of the dancers leans in close and whispers into Good2cu's ear. "How about a private dance in the back, you sexy stud?"

If a beautiful, half-naked woman had asked him the same question back in Michigan, Good2cu probably would have erupted into that nervous donkey laugh of his. But here in Vegas he can be anyone he wants to be, and right now, he's a guy carrying several thousand dollars in cash, stuffed into the front pocket of his jeans like the proverbial banana.

"How much are you going to pay me?" he replies.

It's an old routine she's heard countless times before, but she still smiles sweetly. "You know that's not how it works, honey."

A few of the Two Plus Twoers have already ventured into the "Champagne Room" in the back of the club, where wild, private dances are chipping away at their bankrolls like the world's most expensive taxi ride.

"Maybe later," says Good2cu.

"I hope so," she replies before resuming her rounds.

The aroma of her perfume is still lingering in the air when a balding guy in a jacket and loosened tie—the universal workday's-finally-over look—grabs Good2cu by the shirt.

"Hey, kid. . . . You want to make a quick hundred?" Good2cu's drunk, but it's obvious from the way this man is swaying that he's even drunker. As the man lets go of Good2cu's shirt, he rests one hand on the wall to steady himself. "You won't have to do anything weird, I promise."

Good2cu might have thousands of dollars of cash in his pocket, but thanks to the Rhino's $22 cover charge, $10 cocktails, and $20 lap dances, it's disappearing fast. At heart he's still just a kid from Okemos, where $100 feels like an enormous sum. He's also drunk enough not to think too deeply about what might happen next.

"Well, okay, I guess. . . ."

He follows his new patron into one of the VIP rooms where the man's friend is enjoying the company of a stripper on a small couch. Two other strippers occupy an adjacent love seat.

"What's up?" Good2cu asks a little suspiciously.

"The ladies want somebody to dance for them," explains the drunken businessman, waving a bill in the air. "I'll pay you a hundred bucks a song."

Good2cu isn't a great dancer. With lessons and practice, he might get to below average. But over the last semester he's been hitting the weights five days a week, part of a calculated strategy to improve his lot with the opposite sex. Now it's time to get rewarded for all the hours he's spent at the gym. He takes off his shirt, approaching the two strippers on the love seat like they're wild animals who might attack if provoked.

Instead they reach out and caress him, running their hands over his six-pack.

"Feel his ass!" one of them yells while doing just that.

Typically, the person getting a lap dance is not allowed to touch the person giving it, but Good2cu's not about to complain. He tries to imagine what the dancers would do, were the situation reversed. He leans in so close to them his nipples nearly make contact with their faces. He straddles their legs and assumes the cowgirl—*cowboy?*—position, then turns around and grinds his ass into their crotches, giving them a little reverse cowboy for good measure. When the song comes to end, his patron hands him a $100 bill, pulls another from his wallet, and waves it in the air: one more?

Hell fucking yeah.

Any inhibitions Good2cu brought with him into the room have disappeared. One of the strippers slips a $20 bill into the elastic waistband of his boxers. The other buys him drinks. Not just any drinks, but bottles of Cristal. The stuff Jay-Z drinks.

After several songs, Good2cu takes a breather, sliding into the love seat between the two topless women. The drunk businessman has seen enough. "All right, party's over," he tells Good2cu. "Time for you to jet. Just tip the girls first."

"Me tip them?" Good2cu replies with mock astonishment. "I dance better than they do. They should be tipping me."

The ladies giggle and nod their heads in agreement. The man is less amused. He pays Good2cu what he's owed and escorts him out of the VIP room.

A few minutes later, one of the strippers catches up with Good2cu. "You should have tipped us," she says. "If you had, that guy was going to give you like a thousand dollars or something."

Good2cu just grins.

Whatever.

Yesterday, he was a college student worrying about midterms and suffering through a typically frigid Michigan winter. Today, he's a high-rolling poker god who just got paid to dance for strippers.

Look, up in the sky! It's a bird, it's a plane . . .

13

Why would I want to run bad? That's not how you win.

—Good2cu

LAS VEGAS, NEVADA (February 2006)

Good2cu isn't sure why he bothered sleeping. The two or three hours he managed to sneak in only make the loss of those he missed that much more painful. He has no idea what time it was when he passed out on Slim Pickens's couch. All he knows is that the sun was shining.

It's only 9:00 A.M., but the tournament is scheduled to start in an hour. Fortunately, he's still drunk enough from the night before to ward off the hangover he knows is coming. After his lap dancing debut at the Spearmint Rhino, Good2cu split off from the group to check out TAO, the swanky nightclub inside the Venetian, with his new buddy Apathy.

Apathy is from Canada, but Michigan is so close to the border it might as well be one of its territories, and he and Good2cu quickly discovered that they share many of the same values, namely the three P's: playing poker, partying, and, *cough*, pursuing the ladies. Both of them are also under twenty-one, so they were a little hesitant to face the bouncer guarding the entrance to the club, choosing to duck into a nearby bar instead.

Apathy picked his screen name to express his worldview, but "carefree" would have been a better choice. He doesn't get too worked up about the things that drive other players crazy: bad beats, cold decks, grandstanding opponents. And while he strives to play poker like an emotionless automaton, away from the tables he fairly pulsates with positive energy. He's an effervescent raconteur with enough rascally charm to make most of the people who meet him immediately want to become his friend, rip off his clothes, or both.

Within minutes of sitting down at the bar, Apathy starts chatting up the two girls sitting next to them. They're also underage, but they decide that the four of them together might stand a better chance of getting into TAO. Apathy's cherubic face makes him look a good three years younger than his actual age of twenty, but he has no trouble convincing the doorman that he's thirty-four, just like it says on his fake Canadian driver's license. The girls are hot enough to avoid getting carded at all. Which leaves Good2cu and his New York driver's license with the upside-down back.

"This shit is fake," the bouncer says, sounding pretty sure of himself. He hasn't even seen the other side of the license.

"No, it's not."

"Um, yeah, it is." The bouncer lowers his voice. "I *make* fake IDs for a living."

There's something inherently corrupt in a world where age-verifying bouncers make fake IDs on the side. *But hey,* thinks Good2cu, *we don't always get to choose the world we live in, do we?* He removes the $10,000 roll from his front pocket and peels off two bills. "Here's $200, bro. We all good?"

A quick look into the bouncer's eyes, and Good2cu realizes he's made a rookie mistake. Not his attempt to bribe a bouncer—that's standard. And $200 would definitely have been enough. Probably too much. No, the error was flashing his entire bankroll.

The bouncer's eyes narrow greedily as he takes in the sight of all that cash. "Make it a thousand," he says. "Then we'll be good, *bro*."

"No fucking way am I giving you a thousand dollars just to get into a nightclub."

"Then you won't be needing this anymore."

The bouncer moves to pocket the fake ID, but before he can Good2cu rips it out of his hand and takes off running, stumbling over the velvet rope and sprinting down the up escalator. A backward glance reveals two security guards barking commands into walkie-talkies. Good2cu ducks into the Venetian's casino, hoping to blend in with the tourists, and doesn't turn around until he's out the front door and safely ensconced in a cab.

$ $ $

By the light of day, Good2cu's able to better appreciate the Venetian. Its cavernous lobby is an extravagant homage to the churches and palazzi of Italy, a Baroque era's greatest hits collection—frescoes on the ceiling, gold and marble everywhere else. There's even a canal with real gondolas, and the hotel's art exhibit includes works by Picasso, van Gogh, and Matisse.

Praying that the hotel's security staff has turned over since the night shift, he doesn't linger long in the lobby. Besides, the tournament's about to start. He hurries toward the elevators, rides to the third floor, and approaches the hospitality suite Irieguy has rented for the occasion. The sight of a linebacker-sized security guard makes Good2cu stop in his tracks.

"Name?" asks the guard.

As the first tendrils of his hangover creep around the sides of his skull, Good2cu croaks out the name his parents slapped him with at birth.

The guard scans the clipboard he's holding and shakes his head. "Not on the list."

"How about 'Good2cu'?"

The guard smiles and checks off the name on the list. "I love this gig. I don't know what's going on in there, but you guys got some really great names. IHateKeithSmart. SkipperBob. TheNoodleman. Is this some sort of fraternity thing?"

Good2cu forces a smile. "Something like that."

The atmosphere inside the suite pulls him out of his stupor. Like a packed concert hall moments before the headliner takes the stage, the room is buzzing with expectant energy. There are a few older guys milling around, but they are far outnumbered by kids his age. Despite their youth, most of them project showy confidence and sport gaudy watches—a skilled thief could easily pull several hundred thousand dollars worth of timepieces from this room.

Nearly twenty tables are scattered throughout, each decorated with two identical stacks of chips and a deck of cards, solid evidence that a poker tournament is about to get under way. But most poker tournaments don't have open bars and a stripper pole. The pole is currently being used by a topless woman who clearly spends a lot of time working on her flexibility. The bar is being put to good use by almost everyone else. More topless women circulate throughout the room.

Some are serving drinks; some are serving in other ways. Good2cu spots a very happy-looking Bonafone sitting beneath a half-naked woman, compensation for not being allowed into the Rhino the night before.

Wow.

Good2cu's on his way to the bar when he gets intercepted by Irie-guy, who is accompanied by one of the few women in the room wearing a shirt, albeit one that's several sizes too small and reads: I ♥ TO MAKE BOYS CRY. Not to be outdone, Irieguy's wearing a T-shirt that announces, I'M HERE FOR THE LAP DANCE.

"Ready to play some poker?" asks Irieguy.

"All I need are some chips and a chair," says Good2cu gamely. "And maybe some aspirin and a Bloody Mary."

"That's the spirit. The pairings for the first-round matches are over there." Irieguy points to a large poster on the wall. "As for the rules, you can cuss or swear or say whatever the fuck you want. You can even expose your cards while you're still in a hand if it floats your boat. The only big no-no is behaving rudely toward the lap artists. If you do that, I'll kick your ass out, or worse, make you listen to Dali-man's bad beat stories. Dinner will be catered. And I hope you like alcohol, or you're going to be severely disappointed by the beverage selection."

A Bloody Mary helps part the fog, but there's still a lot to take in. Beyond the thirty-two Two Plus Twoers actually playing in the tournament, there are twenty to thirty other people in the room, each of whom has paid $170 for the right to hang out, eat catered food, drink massive quantities of alcohol, and enjoy a few lap dances.

The tournament promises to be entertaining as well, as there's a fair amount of money at stake. Those who paid the $200 entry fee can win as much as $3,650, while the players who put in $500, like Good2cu did, are vying for the top prize of $6,400. Each match features two players squaring off against each other, with the winner moving on and the loser getting shunted into the consolation bracket. Some of the matches will be over in four or five hands; others will go on for two or three hours.

A second Bloody Mary restores Good2cu's swagger and loosens his tongue. He loudly announces that he'll bet anyone $200 that he's going to win his first match. Given that the room is split pretty much evenly between the Two Plus Twoers who have never heard of him before and those who witnessed his drunken exploits the night before, a line quickly forms. By the time the first cards hit the felt, Good2cu has wagered over $2,000 on himself.

A few minutes later, the players who bet against him are lining up once again, this time to pay him his money.

14

"They were eighteen or nineteen and they had it all. They had the world by the balls, so they had a little bit of attitude because they'd had way more success than any person should have at that age. I remember thinking, *These kids have way too much money for their own good right now. But they've all earned it. They've all gotten it by being this good at this game.* But it definitely seemed like . . . you just worry."

—**TheNoodleman**

LAS VEGAS, NEVADA (February 2006)

Irieguy can't believe it. All he asked of these guys was that they follow one simple rule—don't mess with the lap artists!—and here they've gone and broken it. *Twice!*

ZeroPointMachine is tripping on acid or mushrooms, possibly both, which Irieguy wouldn't consider a problem if the creepy old guy weren't relentlessly urging all the strippers to do the same. Irieguy doesn't waste much time contemplating the proper response—he boots ZeroPointMachine out of the suite.

But he's not so sure what to do about durrrr. One of the lap artists claims the kid flicked water in her face, then gave her some attitude when she complained about it.

Irieguy's never met durrrr before, but knows him by reputation.

Only nineteen years old, durrrr regularly competes in the biggest games you can play online. Some are calling him a poker prodigy. Others joke that he's not entirely human.

Irieguy just wants to know what to make of the stripper's story, so he seeks out Raptor, who knows durrrr better than anyone else in the room. Raptor and durrrr struck up a virtual friendship via AIM last fall. In January they met at a tournament in the Bahamas, where they hung out together nearly every single minute and went from being virtual friends to actual ones.

Raptor explains to Irieguy that the woman probably mistook durrrr's aloofness for condescension, an explanation that gains merit when Irieguy introduces himself to the lanky kid with the probing eyes, owlish eyebrows, and Spock-like ears. Durrrr takes in the lecture from Irieguy as if he doesn't quite comprehend the words coming from his mouth. The effect is unsettling, almost otherworldly.

When Irieguy finishes, durrrr chuckles nervously, explaining that he wasn't aware that he'd splashed anyone with water and that if he did he was sorry. The kid seems sincere, so Irieguy lets him stick around.

Getting kicked out of the room wouldn't have affected durrrr's plans all that much, as he's not even playing in the tournament. Despite paying the $170 entertainment fee, he's been spending most of his time in the suite he rented next door, quietly engaged in an online battle for stakes that make Irieguy's entry fee look like pocket change.

Nearly every day for the past several weeks, durrrr has been playing against Spirit Rock, one of the most successful online poker players in the world, noted for breaking a few well-known pros who dared to venture into the online realm. They've been playing heads-up for tens of thousands of dollars each sitting.

Because you're playing every hand against the same opponent, heads-up poker is a lot like an expensive game of Rock, Paper, Scissors. *Is he raising here because he's bluffing, because he wants me to* think *he's bluffing, or because he's bluffing and knows that I'll think he's pretending to bluff?* These long psychological clashes tend to leave the winner just as drained as the loser.

Which is why durrrr didn't bother to enter Irieguy's tournament. He also skipped the Calcutta-style auction at the start of the day, but plenty of other players took part, wagering on the tournament's participants, a monetary incentive that, coupled with the open bar and copious female nudity, has encouraged most of them to stick around long after they get knocked out. Some watch the matches that are still in progress. Others have heated discussions about strategy, or bet hundreds of dollars on arm wrestling, or on who can draw the highest card from a deck.

Almost everybody is drinking as if exhausting the contents of the bar were a moral imperative. Several joints have been passed around, adding their fragrance to the room. Some of the younger guys have taken hits of Ecstasy and, if their blissed-out smiles are any indication, are enjoying their lap dances on a cosmic level.

Throughout it all, Good2cu remains in character, the one he's adopted for his Vegas adventure. He's double-fisting drinks from the bar and needling his opponents the way he's seen players on television do. Every time he wins a big pot he shouts, "Ship it!" and his growing legion of supporters reply, in a call-and-response pattern that will continue deep into the night, with a perfectly timed, "Holla!" The roll Good2cu's on carries him all the way to the finals, where he squares off against Yugo, a longtime Two Plus Twoer with an uncanny resemblance to former NBA All-Star Peja Stojakovic.

Yugo is more of a recreational player than a pro, and for the first time all day, Good2cu is actually favored to win the match, but the cards don't fall his way. Irieguy awards Yugo a gold medal for winning the tournament. As a $200 entrant, however, he's only eligible to win the smaller portion of the prize pool.

Good2cu is the day's real winner. Between the prize money and all his side bets, he's earned more than $8,000. It's the biggest score of his life, and it works on his confidence like a flattering remark from a beautiful woman. Chatting up strippers is one thing; separating thousands of dollars from a group of players whose games he admires shoots him into an entirely different zip code. He wraps all the hundreds and fifties Irieguy hands him into a roll, stuffs the cash burrito into his pocket, and grabs an enormous bottle of Grey Goose vodka from the bar. Trailed by a ragtag processional of drunken, stoned, and tripping teenagers, Good2cu marches out of the suite and through the frescoed lobby, swigging from the bottle with every step.

Irieguy knows he needs to get a hold of this situation quickly before it spirals out of control, so he steers the kids toward a fleet of limousines parked in front of the casino and tells the drivers to take them to Déjà Vu, an eighteen-and-over "gentleman's club." Despite the exotic name, Déjà Vu doesn't have the same class of dancers as the Rhino and they don't serve alcohol either, but everyone's been drinking for twelve straight hours, so who cares?

Added bonus: full nudity.

Last night, Good2cu was a strip club newbie, but tonight he feels like a veteran. In between shouts of "I am the world champion!" he buys lap dances for all his new best friends and bottle after bottle of nonalcoholic champagne, and tips extravagantly in response to even the most mundane acts of service. His neatly wrapped bankroll quickly turns into a disheveled head of Ben Franklin lettuce, stray leaves occasionally fluttering to the ground while he negotiates prices with the saucer-eyed strippers who trace each bill's descent.

In the midst of all this fun Good2cu gets struck by a serious thought. Two days ago, he was a fairly typical college student, studying for midterms and hating life because of all the reading he still had to do. Between hitting the books and grinding online he's hardly spoken to a member of the opposite sex in weeks. He's made some good friends at Michigan State, but none of them can do more than nod dumbly when he wants to talk poker.

The last two days have offered him a glimpse of a far more glamorous life. He's been living like a balla, buying rounds of fancy cocktails and lap dances from gorgeous women and paying for it all with money he's won off of poker players with legitimate skills. He's made a bunch of new friends who, despite knowing him less than forty-eight hours, already seem to understand him better than anyone else in the world. And, to top it all off, he's $12,000 richer, or at least he was at the beginning of the night.

Drunk and surrounded by naked women who won't leave you alone because your pockets are overflowing with cash probably isn't the best time to make an important decision about your academic career, but Good2cu doesn't care.

To hell with midterms. I'm not ready to go home yet.

15

Going to classes just didn't seem like the right thing to do on a lot
of days.

—**Apathy**

LAS VEGAS, NEVADA (February 2006)

Apathy's not ready to go home either.

The twenty-year-old Canadian is supposed to be in his second year of college at the University of Western Ontario, but, distracted by poker, hasn't sat through a lecture since the fall. Ever since he won $75 in a freeroll tournament his freshman year of college, Apathy's bankroll has been on a rapid ascent. Once poker made him a hundred-thousandaire, he began to focus all of his attention on the things he loves—food, travel, nightlife, women—and ditch the things he didn't, namely studying. He never officially quit school; that would have required way too much motivation. One day, last fall, he simply stopped going to class.

When Good2cu announces his desire to stay in Vegas for a few more days, Apathy suggests they rent a room together at TI. They spend the next four days playing poker and sampling the city's nightlife, or at least the portions accessible without a decent fake ID.

The budding bromance proves highly educational for both. While similarities drew them together, it's their differences that cement the bond. Each sees in the other a quality he lacks. Apathy emanates the sort of charisma and natural ease with women that Good2cu craves, and Good2cu has an honest-to-god work ethic, whether it's keeping meticulous records so he can analyze his results at the poker tables, adhering to a gym schedule, or practicing pickup lines in the hopes of improving his lot with the ladies.

They spend most of their days at the Bellagio, which has been *the* place to play poker in Las Vegas ever since it opened its doors in 1998. Tourists flock to the low-stakes tables in a never-ending stream, while high-stakes pros and the high-rolling businessmen who come to challenge them sequester themselves in Bobby's Room, home to the biggest cash games in the world. Good2cu and Apathy occasionally peer into that special section of the card room, dreaming of a day when they might play there themselves. For now, they're content to take money off the tourists, with Good2cu concentrating on the cash games and Apathy winning several thousand dollars in a tournament.

They've just emerged from the Bellagio's card room and are walking back to their hotel when Good2cu realizes that the most exciting week of his life is about to come to an end. In four hours he'll be getting on a plane that will carry him back to the frozen tundra of Michigan, where he'll go back to being just another college kid.

"Fuck it." Good2cu points at the Forum Shops at Caesar's Palace. "I've got $8,000 in my pocket, and I want to spend it all before I leave town. Let's go shopping."

From its marble floors to its Corinthian pillars, the Forum Shops are designed to evoke a spirit of Roman decadence. Good2cu and Apathy ride down a three-story spiral escalator into an underground cavern where the blue skies and puffy white clouds painted on the ceiling combine with climate control to simulate the most perfect day in the history of the Empire. In the subterranean depths they find 160 of the world's most exclusive brand-name stores, from Armani to Zegna. The Forum Shops gross more per square foot than any shopping center in America, including Rodeo Drive. And there are more than 600,000 square feet.

It's just a glorified shopping mall, but the contrived opulence still provides an amusing contrast to Good2cu's provincialism. He can't tell you the difference between a Cabernet and a Chardonnay, although that didn't stop him from ordering a bottle of each at dinner last night. He owns a sport coat, but it was purchased at a thrift store and is made out of velour. He likes to wear baseball caps with the brim turned sideways, as if protecting one ear from the elements, and nearly all of his jeans have gaping holes in them, including the ones he's wearing now.

Adding to his disheveled appearance, he hasn't slept more than four hours any night this week. Amid all the high-end shops, he looks like a street urchin. He feels like Julia Roberts in *Pretty Woman* as he glides from store to store on a spree that would make any shopaholic jealous. His bags are full of expensive designer clothes—part of his plan to woo the ladies—and a painting that promises to look completely out of place in his dorm room.

"But what I really need," he tells Apathy, "is a Rolex."

While it sounds like a spur-of-the-moment decision, he's actually been thinking about it ever since he observed all the extravagant wristwear at Irieguy's tournament. A cultural anthropologist studying young online poker players might identify a sort of fun house version of Maslow's hierarchy of needs. The first big acquisition is a brand-new, top-of-the-line computer, a prudent attempt to shore up their business infrastructure. The purchase of a blatantly expensive watch often comes next, letting everyone know just how successful that business is.

Good2cu walks into Tourneau and loudly declares his desire to buy a Rolex. When that fails to get the desired response, he pulls out a wad of cash and starts waving it in the air. Apathy laughs so hard his stomach hurts and he can't catch his breath.

A saleswoman practically runs to assist them. "Perhaps you'd like to consider a Patek Phillippe?" she says. "They keep better time than Rolexes do."

Patek Phillippe makes the more expensive watch. Technically superior. Understated. Elegant. The Rolex is large. Attention-grabbing. Ostentatious.

No-brainer.

"I'll take the Rolex," he says. "I guess I'll just have to live with losing a second every half-million years instead of a million."

"You're cute." She removes the Rolex from the glass case. "And how will you be paying for this? Credit card?"

"Credit card?" He plunks what remains of his bankroll down on the counter and starts laughing like a donkey. "Ship it!"

$ $ $

The next morning, Good2cu wakes up in his dorm room. He looks around at the drably painted cinder-block walls and the piles of books sitting on his desk.

He's definitely not in Vegas anymore.

But the Rolex on his wrist is proof that it wasn't all just a dream.

For nearly a week, he lived his vision of a rock star's life. He won a tournament against some of the best Sit N Go players in the world. Doesn't that mean he's one of the best Sit N Go players in the world?

That's what he keeps telling himself as, instead of going to class, he logs onto Party Poker, where he plays confidently and well. Over the next four days, he wins $35,000, by far the best run of poker he's ever had.

Good2cu's roommate takes it all in with detached bemusement. Somehow in Vegas the kid who earned a 3.9 GPA his first semester got replaced by a poker-playing extraterrestrial who never goes to class or opens a book. The roommate doesn't want to sound like a public service announcement, but after ten days he just can't take it anymore. He has to say *something*.

"Hey, man, is this poker thing becoming, like, a problem?"

16

Never before have the means to lose so much been so available to so many at such a young age.

—Mattathias Schwartz, "The Hold-'Em Holdup,"
The New York Times, June 11, 2006

In 1988, during a typically cold and brief summer in Oulu, Finland, a programmer working for the local university's Department of Information Processing Science grew frustrated with the department's Bulletin Board System. A rudimentary antecedent of the World Wide Web, the BBS allowed users to connect to the university's computer server using their modems and, at least in theory, chat with one another in real time. In reality, as observed by the programmer Jarrko Oikarien—or "WiZ" to his programming buddies—the BBS relied on software that suffered from "a bad habit of not working properly." WiZ took advantage of a lull in his schedule to try to create a better way to communicate online.

Two years later, journalists in Iraq used WiZ's creation—Internet Relay Chat—to circumvent a media blackout and continue reporting during Operation Desert Storm. IRC quickly became the standard protocol for real-time text communication, the precursor to today's instant messages.

In the early 1990s, Todd Mummert and Greg Reynolds, developers at Carnegie Mellon University's School of Computer Science, created a script that allowed IRC users to play poker against one another. Despite a complete lack of graphics, their "IRCBot" was a huge hit among poker-loving computer geeks, even if it failed to attract a mainstream following.

If IRCBot was Project Mercury, Planet Poker was the Apollo Program. The site, launched in 1998 by Randy Blumer, a former Marine Systems Engineer in the Canadian Navy, was the first Internet card room to offer real-money games—the same place that introduced Irieguy and SkipperBob to online poker. Overshadowing its novelty were frequent crashes and the discovery that the random number generator they had licensed to deal the cards wasn't so random after all, but Planet Poker gave the world a taste of what could be.

By 2005, online poker had grown into a $2.4 billion industry. Scores of competitors had entered the business, and the fight to attract and retain clients turned increasingly aggressive. Their number one target: college students, a clientele blessed with easy access to the Internet, their first credit cards, plenty of unstructured time, and a national gambling law that barred them from setting foot inside a brick-and-mortar casino.

Take Absolute Poker, which in an effort to lure college students to its site began enlisting campus representatives to recruit players into free tournaments, rewarding winners with real-money deposits into newly opened online accounts the way a drug dealer hands out the first taste for free. Absolute also bought promotions during halftime of N.C.A.A. basketball games to advertise their "Win Your Tuition" campaign, a series of tournaments promising a free semester of college to the champion. The event attracted more than eight thousand students from more than three hundred schools.

Setting aside any argument about the chicken and the egg, hundreds of thousands of college kids were playing online poker as if it were the fifth class on their schedule. Or the only class. According to a report published by the Annenberg Public Policy Center, 20 percent of all college students played online poker at least once a month in 2005. A study from the University of Connecticut's Health Center claimed that one out of every four college-age players fit the clinical definition of a pathological gambler.

Stories of kids failing out of school and amassing substantial debts were becoming commonplace. Gamblers Anonymous meetings experienced an unexpected shift in demographics.

A few of the most desperate even resorted to crime: Two months before Irieguy hosted his heads-up tournament at the Venetian in Las Vegas, Greg Hogan, the president of his class at Lehigh University, walked into a Wachovia Bank in Bethlehem, Pennsylvania, handed the teller a note claiming he had a gun, and made off with nearly $3,000 in cash. It was enough to get the nineteen-year-old son of a Baptist minister sentenced to twenty-two months in prison.

But not enough to pay off the $5,000 debt he'd accrued playing online poker.

17

Ship It Holla Ballas is original and patented henceforth.

—Apathy

TORONTO, CANADA (March 2006)

Good2cu is already stuck a grand when his Internet connection craps out.

He can handle losing a thousand dollars in a day. He's done it before. The first time he felt sick to his stomach for two days. The second time was pretty goddamn aggravating, but at least it didn't make him want to puke. Soon the number 1,000 becomes a video game score, a regular part of his daily routine. Right now he's working on his tolerance for five-figure swings—after running his bankroll up to nearly $100,000 in the weeks following his trip to Vegas, he's lost $30,000.

Just a number on a screen, he assures himself.

The $2,000 he's about to lose, on the other hand, is driving him batshit crazy. The money is spread across eight Sit N Gos. By the time his Internet connection is restored, the tournaments are likely to be over. He can live with getting outdrawn, or even outplayed, but losing money to technical glitches feels like the worst kind of bad luck.

Good2cu is ready to eat the loss when he realizes he might not have to. He calls Apathy and explains the situation.

"Epic fail," says Apathy. "Maybe you should remember to pay your cable bill. Or have you gone busto since Vegas?"

"I actually went on a sick heater as soon as I got back," Good2cu replies. "This week, not so much. Where are you anyway? You logged in yet?"

"Toronto. Chilling here for a few days. Recovering from Monte Carlo."

"How was Monte Carlo?"

"I'll tell you all about it later." Apathy uses Good2cu's user name and password to sign into the poker site. "You've got seventy grand in your account? Nice. You *have* been running well."

"Don't fuck it up."

Logged in as Good2cu, Apathy finishes all eight of his friend's Sit N Gos for him. Not only does he save Good2cu from taking a $2,000 loss, he actually makes $400 for him, news he's happy to report.

"I owe you big time," says Good2cu. "How about I ship you half the profit?"

"Why don't you just buy me some drinks? How about this weekend? Inyaface and I are going out with some friends. You should come on up."

"Holla!"

$ $ $

Good2cu has been to Canada a few times, both to play poker and to exploit the lower drinking age, but never to Toronto and never with Apathy as a guide.

They start off at the bar where Apathy worked the previous summer, making just over minimum wage busing trays of food up three flights of stairs, shooting the shit with the old barflies during the moments of calm. A charming summer job, at least until he enjoyed a string of large cashes in online tournaments.

After Apathy quit, his friend Inyaface was rewarded for staying onboard with a promotion to bartender. Inyaface still works there part time while attending the University of Toronto, even though he really doesn't have to—he often earns more in a single night playing online poker than he does tending bar for an entire month.

The screen name reflects a Canadian sense of irony—in real life, Inyaface is anything but. He's a mild-mannered twenty-year-old college kid with a round, pleasant face and a self-deprecating sense of humor. He likes that the name makes him sound like an asshole. Players tend to give more action to people they think are assholes.

He's an excellent hockey player too, not the aggressive type who delivers ferocious body checks into the boards, but a goalie, protecting the net for his college team. If every group of friends has a Responsible Guy, someone who can sober up when the cops are knocking at the door or whose parents trust him with the car, Inyaface is that guy. Which helps explain how he's managed to keep his job at the bar, despite five mornings a week of hockey practice, a full course load at school, and poker almost every night.

In other words, he's the opposite of Apathy, who, despite their many differences, has been one of his best friends since the seventh grade. Like connecting jigsaw puzzle pieces, they complement each other perfectly.

Convincing Inyaface that it's a little lame to hang out at the same bar you work at, Apathy steers him, their friend Nick, and Good2cu to King Street, where they bounce from one club to the next before landing at the C Lounge, an upscale nightclub with plush couches and VIP cabanas. Apathy orders a round of Jägermeister shots. Good2cu buys a $200 bottle of Ketel One.

"Damn," says Nick. "You guys are such *ballas*. Like you've got money to burn."

"Literally," says Inyaface, smirking at Apathy. "Tell them about Monte Carlo."

The legal gambling age in the United States is twenty-one and Canada doesn't host very many major tournaments, but in Europe you only have to be eighteen to gamble and there are plenty of big events to choose from. Apathy and Inyaface just got back from playing in the European Poker Tour's end-of-the-season championship, the Grand Final in Monte Carlo. They'd flown there hoping to make a big splash, which they did, even if it wasn't in quite the way they'd imagined.

Apathy's cheeks turn red. "What can I say? I got wasted and acted like a donkey. Inyaface and I were debating whether you could light a cigar with a euro note, like whether it would actually burn."

"Turns out the hundred burns the cleanest," adds Inyaface.

"I was on tilt after getting knocked out of the tournament," Apathy explains.

"Seriously?" says Good2cu. "You? Tilting?"

Apathy shrugs. "Happens to the best of us. I'd gotten deep in the main event when some joker sucked out on me and sent me to the rail. Back in our hotel room I got *completely* hammered and allegedly did some stupid stuff."

"'Allegedly' my ass," says Inyaface. "I've got photos of you lighting the C-note. You going to tell them about the furniture?"

From the way his eyes are crinkled and his mouth's upturned it's hard to tell if Apathy's smiling or cringing. "We were staying in this sick hotel. Sixth floor with a balcony overlooking the Mediterranean. We'd just finished eating room service, and there was this little dock below and, you know, it looked like a good target. So I tried to hit it with a plate."

"How'd that go?" Good2cu asks.

"Missed by a mile. But the second one was a lot closer. When we ran out of plates, I switched to glasses."

"Then a coffeepot," says Inyaface. "Then the furniture. End table. Lamps. The armchair. Good thing the mattress wouldn't fit through the door."

"Hitting that dock," Apathy admits, "was a lot harder than I thought it would be."

"Oh, snap," says Nick. "How much trouble did you get in?"

"The hotel charged me an extra thirty-five hundred euros to cover the damages."

"Ouch."

"I know. I probably should have fought it. There's no way that armchair was worth five hundred euros."

Good2cu's donkey laugh can be heard in every corner of the club. "That sounds so rock star. Man, I wish I could have been there to see it."

"It was pretty hilarious. But I felt like a complete asshole afterward. I donated twenty percent of my bankroll to charity the second I got home. Figured I could use the karma points."

"Hey," says Good2cu. "You guys planning on going to the World Series this summer?"

"Sure, why not?" Apathy replies. "We should rent the pimpest suite the Rio's got for the whole six weeks."

"If we're going to be there that long," says Inyaface, "we should rent a house."

"I don't know," Apathy says. "That sounds like a lot of motivation."

"I'll do it," says Inyaface, voicing the familiar lament of the Responsible Guy.

"Ship it!"

"Holla!"

Nick smiles at them drunkenly. "You guys are such ballas," he slurs. "'Ship this ridiculously expensive bottle of vodka over here! Holla! Ship these fine-looking ladies over there! Holla!' You know what you guys are? You're Ship It Holla Ballas!"

"Oh, man, that's it!" says Good2cu.

"That's what?" Apathy asks.

"The name of our crew!"

"The Ship It Holla Ballas?" Inyaface laughs. "That might be the dumbest name I've ever heard."

"No way," says Apathy. "It's perfect. ESPN is going to fucking love us!"

In the beginning if one of us found ten dollars on the street, it would've gone into the bankroll. It was like a commune or something. But I don't know why I didn't see that Dutch is basically a con artist. Maybe I was smoking too much weed.

—**Gank to** *Rolling Stone*

For as long as there has been poker, there have been poker "crews." In the 1800s, when the game as we know it today first appeared on steamboats traveling up and down the Mississippi River, cardsharps worked in teams to cheat unsuspecting high rollers out of their money, dealing useful cards to each other from the bottom of the deck and using signals to relay the strength of their hands.

By the middle of the twentieth century, such rampant cheating had for the most part been eradicated, but there were still legitimate reasons for players to work together as a team. In 1957, three young Texas road gamblers, Doyle "Texas Dolly" Brunson, Thomas "Amarillo Slim" Preston, and Brian "Sailor" Roberts, decided to pool their bankrolls and start traveling together. "Any one of us could pinch-hit for the other when he was tired or just not feelin' right," Amarillo Slim later recalled.

The partnership was intended to prevent any of them from ever going broke, but the most important resource they shared turned out to be something other than money: they supported one another emotionally and intellectually as well. "After a long session, none of us could hardly sleep from being so wound up," Slim said. "And we would just stay awake for hours talking about the hands we played that night, the players in the game, and all different sorts of strategies. Imagine what it would have been like if Paul 'Bear' Bryant, Vince Lombardi, and George 'Papa Bear' Halas traveled together for ten years and did nothing but talk football. Or if Warren Buffet, Peter Lynch, and George Soros went around the world picking stocks together and exchanging investment ideas. Let's just say there was a lot of knowledge changing hands."

Later, the concept of a crew would undergo another evolution, offering its members something that Dolly, Slim, and Sailor never could have imagined:

Media exposure.

$ $ $

One of the stories overshadowed by Chris Moneymaker's 2003 victory at the World Series of Poker was the twelfth-place finish by a twenty-three-year-old prodigy named Russ "Dutch" Boyd.

"Prodigy" is a word that gets thrown around loosely, but how else do you describe a kid from Missouri, raised by a single mom bouncing between welfare and minimum wage, who starts taking college classes at the age of eleven and is accepted to law school three years later?

After earning a Juris Doctor from the University of Missouri, eighteen-year-old Dutch chose to follow the same path as Matt Damon's character in *Rounders*, shelving the idea of practicing law in favor of playing poker for a living. Settling in Silicon Valley with his brother Robert, a computer whiz who helped build one of the world's first high-speed Internet backbones, Dutch spent his nights selling men's underwear at Macy's so he could spend his days playing poker in the rundown card rooms that dot the San Francisco Peninsula.

Dutch loved the idea of online poker and was an early adopter, but hated its execution. The most popular site at the time, Planet Poker, didn't offer tournaments or any cash games other than Hold'em or draw, and the frequent software crashes in the middle of hands were infuriating and occasionally expensive.

Sitting in a hot tub at 3:00 A.M., twenty-year-old Dutch and nineteen-year-old Robert decided they could do better. They borrowed $80,000 of seed money from friends and family, and Robert, who had always wanted to create video games, began writing one.

The result was an online card room named PokerSpot. In September 2000, PokerSpot became the first Internet casino to host multitable tournaments, and by December it had grown into the third-biggest online poker room in the world. Dutch and his brother were making $160,000 a month and making bold predictions about their future prospects.

Until Dutch became the most hated man in poker.

He claimed it wasn't PokerSpot's fault, blaming the company that processed the card room's credit card transactions. Wherever the fault lay, PokerSpot suddenly found itself short on funds, lacking the cash reserves to pay its players. Instead of coming clean with his customers, Dutch opted to stick to the classic "the check's in the mail" strategy, figuring that if he bought some time, his company could generate enough new deposits to cover its debts.

But these were wild and woolly days. Online poker operated

without any regulations or oversight. When PokerSpot went belly-up, the players who were owed money had little recourse other than venting their anger on Internet message boards. (To date, many of those customers are still waiting on their refunds.)

Just when it seemed things couldn't get any crazier for Dutch, they did. Or, rather, *he* did. On New Year's Eve, he suffered the first in a series of psychotic breaks. The mild ones involved public nudity. A more intense episode led to his confinement in a concrete cell at an Antiguan mental institution.

No one wants to get diagnosed with bipolar disorder, but Dutch saw a silver lining. The affliction didn't necessarily erode his poker skills; in fact, many of his greatest insights into the game occurred in the midst of his manic episodes.

In May 2003, Dutch rode one of these streaks deep into the WSOP Main Event. Sporting John Lennon glasses and a mischievous grin, he played brilliantly through the first three days of the tournament and was among the chip leaders late on the fourth day when he tried to run an ill-timed bluff past Chris Moneymaker. A few hands later, Sammy Farha took the last of his chips, eliminating Dutch just three places short of the final table. With ESPN's cameras following his exit from the room, he used the moment to make a bold announcement: He'd formed a poker crew, and they were going to "take over the poker world."

Their ambition extended to the name they adopted: "The Crew." Other than their youth—most were in their early twenties—its members were an eclectic bunch. Besides Dutch and his brother Robert, The Crew included a model and full-time pothead named Brett "Gank" Jungblut and a street-savvy pool hustler named Joe

Bartholdi, Jr. A few months later, they were joined by Scott Fischman, an ex-poker dealer whose rheumatoid arthritis forced him to move to the other side of the table.

Using the $80,000 he won at the World Series, Dutch rented a five-bedroom house in Culver City, California, and turned it into their headquarters. They pooled their bankrolls, shared strategies, ate and slept only when necessary, and played online poker nearly every other minute of the day.

At the 2004 World Series, The Crew backed up all the brash talk. Gank won a gold bracelet; Fischman earned two; and Dutch, three weeks removed from his most recent psychotic break, came tantalizingly close to winning one of his own, finishing second to the legendary T. J. Cloutier in a Razz event. Over the course of that summer's thirty-three events, The Crew won nearly $1 million.

Cocky kids who trained online, promised to beat the pros, then did just that? The media ate it up. Newspapers ran lengthy features. ESPN's cameras followed them throughout the World Series. An article in *Rolling Stone* made them look like the Rolling Stones.

By the time the article hit the stands, infighting had driven The Crew to disband, but their impressive performance that summer helped establish them in the poker world. Fischman parlayed his two WSOP victories into a regular column for *Card Player* magazine, a book about how to master Internet poker, and a sponsorship deal from Full Tilt Poker. Dutch and Gank would go on to earn sponsorship deals of their own.

Ah, the sponsorship deal. In the eyes of online poker players who aspired to turn their hobby into a job, this was how you got made. Such endorsements were tangible proof of your skill at the game. While few deals were structured the same way, all offered the opportunity to boost one's bottom line. Online sites often paid their sponsored players' tournament entry fees and refunded their rake in cash games. Some sites even paid their players regular salaries, the best-known players making more than $1 million a year just for playing on the site.

These deals turned the game of poker on its head, offering a new template for success. For most of his career Doyle Brunson had tried to keep his profession a secret to avoid moral judgment from friends and family. The Crew came along and proved that fame could be just as valuable a commodity as money itself. Texas Dolly is famously old-school in his ways, but even he was persuaded, lending his name to an online poker site called Doyle's Room.

Thanks to The Crew, the kids who grew up watching poker on television had been handed a road map showing them a new route to poker stardom.

Play online.

Form a crew.

Talk a big game.

Take over the poker world.

Q: What exactly does "Ship It Holla" mean?

A: When you win a big pot in poker and you want to be funny—or maybe a little bit of a dick—you yell, "Ship it," as in telling the dealer to "ship," or push, the pot to you. Then, in celebration, it is correct to yell "holla." "Ship it" can also be used in a variety of other ways—when you are sending someone money online you are "shipping them money," or when you are ordering food you can tell the fast food employees to "ship the food." "Holla" is also the customary greeting between young degenerate gamblers.

—**Good2cu**

EAST LANSING, MICHIGAN (April 2006)

After a late-night session of online poker played at Inyaface's house in Toronto, Good2cu drunk dials all the young Two Plus Twoers he bonded with in Vegas to informally invite them to join the "Ship It Holla Ballas."

The reactions are mixed. Raptor thinks it's ridiculously silly. Others don't think it's silly enough. "You know what would be funny?" suggests Jman, a twenty-one-year-old Jason Biggs look-alike and amateur stand-up comedian who just dropped out of the University of Wisconsin to play more poker. "If we give ourselves a really gay name, so that the ESPN announcers have to say it every time one of us makes a final table at the World Series. How about 'Pushbotting Panthers'?"

"I'm hanging up now," says Good2cu.

But all of them do agree on one thing: renting a house in Vegas for the summer is an excellent idea.

Good2cu is especially excited. Upon his return to East Lansing, he starts counting down the days until he will be reunited with his new best friends. The two halves of his double life no longer feel equal— he's starting to think of himself as more of a Ship It Holla Balla than a Michigan State Spartan.

Despite the growing divide between him and academic life, Good2cu is becoming something of a celebrity on campus. Every-one's talking about the professional poker player living in the fresh-man dorms, and Good2cu, for the first time in his life, is becoming a person that other people want to know. He's achieved the kind of rock-star status normally reserved for members of the university's football and basketball teams. Every time he goes out, he gets bom-barded with questions.

"So how much money have you made?"

"What's the most you've ever lost in a night?"

"Have you ever played against Phil Hellmuth?"

Good2cu tries to stay modest about his success, as long as he isn't piss-drunk or trying to impress a girl. Then stories about booking five-figure wins and drinking bottles of Cristal start to roll off his tongue. His fellow students—and even a few teachers—look at him the same way people observed successful day traders nearly a decade before, with awe and envy of a life led above the daily grind.

There's only one question that bothers him: "When do you find time to study?"

The answer is he doesn't, although it's not from a lack of effort. There simply aren't enough hours in the day. The rigorous daily routine he follows leaves him with little time to do anything else. Each morning, he plays four hours of poker, then chugs a Red Bull and heads to the gym. After downing another Red Bull, he returns to his computer and plays for another four to eight hours. Following this strict regimen is helping him earn him between $150 and $200 an hour.

His robust earning power comes with an unexpected downside. Every time Good2cu thinks about doing something other than play poker, he has to consider the opportunity cost, a concept he first encountered in Econ last semester when he was still going to classes.

Should I spend the next two hours playing poker or watching a movie? Play poker, and my expected return is $300, money I can't earn if I watch a movie. Watching a movie will effectively cost me $300. It'd better be a damn good film!

The same thinking carries over to his studies. Even though he's stopped attending his computer class, his professor offers to pass Good2cu as long as he completes the final project. Good2cu weighs the estimated sixty hours of work it will take to pass the class against the $12,000 he could make if he were playing poker.

Needless to say, the computer project doesn't get done.

One day his routine gets disrupted by a surprise visitor. Returning to his dorm from the gym, Good2cu finds his father standing outside his door.

"Uh, hi, Dad. What are you doing here?"

"We need to talk."

He knows what his dad wants to talk about. It's not a conversation Good2cu wants to have right now. He has plans. He and a friend are about to drive to the Caesars Windsor in Canada to play in a live game. But this conversation is pretty much inevitable, so he might as well get it over with.

"I guess you got the letter."

Good2cu is referring to the official notification from MSU's administrative offices, sent yesterday to both him and his father via certified mail, informing him that he's no longer eligible to live in student housing on account of his "light course load." Good2cu didn't bother to open the letter—there was no way it could be good news—but got the message when he discovered his food card had been deactivated.

"Sounds like you've been missing some classes?"

"Yeah, I know. I just haven't had time lately. Poker has kind of become a full-time thing."

Dad sighs, wondering how much he's to blame. After all, hadn't he encouraged his son to join him on the couch to watch ESPN's coverage of the World Series of Poker? And didn't he let Good2cu use the computer in his home office to play online?

"I know you've been making some money at the game, but can't you stay in school and play poker in your free time?"

"Sure, if I only wanted to be a low-stakes grinder," Good2cu replies. "Someone who's happy to win a hundred dollars so they can buy their friends a round of cheap beer."

"That sounds pretty good to me."

"I think I can do so much better than that. I want to make enough money to buy a car or a house. I mean, I want to buy a plane."

"All the more reason why staying in college . . ."

It can be argued that, in 2006, the value of a college education has never been higher. A college diploma halves your chances of unemployment and doubles your lifetime earnings. On paper, it's certainly a wise investment.

But Good2cu can't help but think that he's looking at a once-in-a-lifetime opportunity to make boatloads of money, travel the world, party with beautiful women, and quite possibly avoid getting a real job forever. If there's a social stigma attached to quitting college, his peers on Two Plus Two don't seem too worried about it. Apathy, durrrr, Jman, Deuce2High, FieryJustice, Bonafone, and Raptor have all dropped out, and none of them seem to have any regrets.

But "all my friends are doing it" isn't going to fly with Dad. So Good2cu takes a different tack. "Look, the world is changing. Go to college, get a good job, suffer through sixty-hour workweeks—it doesn't work that way anymore. I can make more money in a day, sitting in my underwear in front of a computer, than most recent college graduates are going to make in a month."

"But it's gambling! What happens when your luck changes?"

"Let me show you something." Good2cu opens a file on his computer—a detailed spreadsheet chronicling his daily poker results—and points to a number at the bottom of the screen.

"You've made $70,000?"

"Yeah, *last month.*"

His father looks over the spreadsheet. It shows a profit, often four figures, nearly every single day. He can't help but admire Good2cu's organization. He's broken down every aspect of his play—how much he bought in for, how much he won, where he finished in tournaments, even how often he folded.

Good2cu senses his father's resistance slipping. "You're right," he admits. "It may not last forever. Online poker could disappear tomorrow for all I know. But right now, today, it's like when they first discovered gold in California. People from all over the country headed out there, hoping to get rich, but by the time most of them got there nearly all the gold was gone. I don't want to miss out on this, Dad. Just give me a year. If I haven't made over $200,000 by this time next year, I'll reenroll in school. I promise."

Good2cu's father turns to face his son. "It's your life. If this is how you want to live it, well, that's up to you. But I want you to do one thing for me. Your academic counselor, she had a lot of very good reasons why you should be staying in school. She really wants to talk to you. Can you at least listen to what she has to say?"

"No problem. I'll make an appointment to talk to her in the morning."

"I mean *now.*"

Father and son walk up the steps of the administration building, both feeling a little shell-shocked by the unexpected turn the day has taken. When they enter the academic counselor's office, they're told to have a seat by a stick figure of a woman who looks like she's been working at the university since the Roosevelt administration.

Dad doesn't waste any time putting his son on the spot. "I want you to tell her what you told me."

"I'm dropping out of school," says Good2cu, maybe a little too casually, "to play poker for a living."

The horrified expression on the old woman's face could have said it all, but she reinforces it with a litany of sympathy for Dad and disappointment for his son. "Oh, my God," she says. "I'm so sorry. I feel *so* bad for you. I can't tell you how many students have sat in that chair and told me the exact same thing. They start chasing this cockamamie dream of an easy life. Then they lose all of their money gambling, and they're left with . . . nothing. No degree, no money, no friends. I truly am sorry."

Good2cu can't hide his frustration. "Easy? Do you know how hard I work? And I'm not *gambling*. Poker is a skill game. My ROI—"

"Your what?"

"My ROI. You know, return on investment? It's over ten percent."

"What I see is a young man caught in the throes of a sickness he doesn't even understand. . . ."

Good2cu's thoughts start to drift. *This woman doesn't know what the hell she's talking about. The whole work-nine-to-five-and-retire-at-sixty-five mentality is a recipe for unhappiness. Why would you want to make yourself miserable doing something you hate if you could make a lot of money doing something you love? This woman is stuck in the Dark Ages, and I can't wait to prove her wrong. I wonder what the game is like at Caesar's. . . .*

". . . and I think you're making a terrible choice. But if you insist upon dropping out of school, I can't stop you. You just need to sign these release papers to make it official."

She digs through her files until she finds the proper form, then slides it across her desk, thrusting it at Good2cu like a challenge.

He signs with a flourish, pushes the form back to her, and smiles. His days as a Michigan State Spartan are officially over. He's a Ship It Holla Balla now, and he's ready to get real paid.

20

It's this expensive million-dollar house and there's no furniture any-where. Just laptops and video games and a big-screen TV. And I remember walking in and thinking it's as though the parents were kidnapped and all of the furniture was jacked and pawned for video game money. The kids took the parents hostage, sold all of their household goods, and bought big-screen TVs and computers with the money.

—Irieguy

DALLAS, TEXAS/LAS VEGAS, NEVADA (Spring 2006)

Raptor lucked out when, after his second sabbatical from college, he moved in with TravestyFund, who turns out to be a near-perfect roommate. He's four years older than Raptor, so he tends to offer a more mature perspective on things. He actually cleans up af-ter himself and while he likes to party, he doesn't equate getting wasted every night with coolness. These days Raptor is in a similar frame of mind. He just started dating a TCU coed named Haley and, as an admitted girlfriend guy, prefers spending quiet nights at home with her to getting trashed in bars.

During a rare foray into the Dallas bar scene, Raptor and Travesty-Fund run into DocHolatchya, an old friend of theirs from the Poker-Box. Doc's a former varsity soccer player at TCU who started playing poker professionally soon after graduating. He earned a reputation for solid and profitable play in the local card rooms before moving back to his hometown—Las Vegas—where he planned to become a high-stakes cash game player.

So far, the plan seems to be working. "Vegas is awesome," Doc tells Raptor during his visit to Texas. "I just bought a new house. You should come check it out. Shit, you can come live there if you want. I have like three spare bedrooms."

"Seriously?"

"Sure. I'll rent you a room for, I don't know, eight hundred a month?"

Raptor likes the idea. To break up the monotony of playing one Sit N Go after another, lately he's been spending more of his time playing cash games. He's been doing well enough to officially declare himself a hundred-thousandaire, but he still spends way too much time staring at a computer screen.

Living in Vegas would allow him to fully commit to the poker lifestyle and help him figure out if this is really what he wants to do with his life. The free education he'd get from "sweating" Doc and his friends—watching over their shoulders as they play—is an added bonus. He imagines the city's easy access to live games will encourage him to get out of the house more often so he won't feel like such a hermit all the time. The affordable rent seals the deal; it's cheap enough to allow him to keep his room at TravestyFund's, so he'll have a place to stay in Fort Worth whenever he returns to visit his family or Haley.

Doc's house is in Southern Highlands, an affluent neighborhood with picturesque views fifteen-minutes by car from the madness of the Strip. There's a swimming pool and a basketball court. The place is officially listed as a 3,500-square-foot single-family home, but feels even bigger because, besides the beds, the only furniture is a couch in the living room and a foosball table in the breakfast nook. The sparse décor forces one to consider the pink walls and lavender carpeting, a combination that makes Irieguy, when he stops by to welcome Raptor to Vegas, feel like he's stepped inside Willy Wonka's Chocolate Factory.

Raptor's quarters could easily be mistaken for a room in a flophouse, were it not for the enormous flat-screen TV mounted to the wall. The mattress on the floor holds a rat's nest of sheets and dirty clothes. Half-eaten boxes of Sour Patch Kids and Cinnamon Toast Crunch litter the carpet, making a simple traverse of the room feel like a journey through a minefield. He doesn't care. He spends most of his time in the computer room around the corner.

In contrast to the rest of the house, the computer room looks like a place where work actually gets done. The centerpiece is Raptor's now-famous Quad Monitor Set-Up, which he brought with him from Texas. In addition to its kickass graphics cards and four monitors, he's upgraded the system with state-of-the-art software that helps him keep track of his opponents—what kinds of hands they play and how they like to play them. A heads-up display on the screen gives him instant access to this information, allowing him to make more informed decisions. While he loves (and profits by) all the bells and whistles, he can't take credit for the technical wizardry—he flew his computer genius friend Rhino from Texas to Las Vegas to set up the rig. The $500 plane ticket was a small price to pay, especially when Raptor can make that much in just a couple of hours at the tables.

For the first few weeks of his new existence, Raptor is loving life. He's living in a million-dollar fraternity house, improving his game daily, getting what amounts to a graduate-level education in poker. But the dynamic gets shattered when Doc returns from a tournament in Tunica, Mississippi, with a girl on his arm.

"This is Chantel," he says. "We're engaged. She's moving in."

Raptor prides himself on his ability to get inside his opponents' heads and figure out what they're thinking, but he can't get a read on this pretty twenty-one-year-old brunette from Dallas. One minute, she's an archetypal Southern belle, all grace and manners and smiles; the next, she's every bit as coarse and temperamental as an escapee from a women's prison.

The first couple of months after Chantel moves in aren't so bad. She and Doc fill the air with romantic overtures and declarations of eternal love, nauseating but ultimately harmless. But soon they're getting into big fights over small issues. Chantel gets upset when other women post on Doc's MySpace page. When the lovebirds return from a Caribbean cruise—a Party Poker tournament that skirts age requirements by sticking to international waters—they're barely speaking to each other. When they do, there's a lot of screaming involved.

To avoid the drama, Raptor spends more and more time holed up in his room, enjoying low-key sessions on his laptop and scrolling through messages on Two Plus Two. One afternoon he spies an intriguing new thread started by Good2cu: "Where Should I Live?" The kid has either dropped out or flunked out of school and is looking for advice on where to go next. Many of the responses, especially from the older guys, are unkind, painting Good2cu as the poster child for everything that's wrong with online poker—*a few months of what is probably beginner's luck and these dopey kids think they're ready to go pro.*

But there's plenty of heartfelt advice as well, encouraging Good2cu to buy health insurance, open an IRA account, or travel the world.

There are also numerous offers of couches to crash on, from Pennsylvania to Paris. But as usual, it's a post by Irieguy that puts everything into perspective.

"Vegas is where you want to be if you are a cardplayer," he writes. "Failing to realize that is much worse than dropping out of school."

Raptor agrees and responds with his usual bravado. "Pack yer shit, jump around the world till u get bored, then 'settle' down in Vegas. Get a nice place, buy a nice car, meet some strippers you can hang out with on a non-pay-for-lap-dance basis, get them to introduce you to all their eighteen to twenty-three-year-old friends, party and club with them, play poker, visit friends whenever u want, laugh at all the people that tell you to go back to school because they are jealous and don't want you to have fun, and enjoy the fuck out of your life."

He concludes the rant with a concrete offer—there's an extra room in Doc's house he can probably squat in for a week or so. That, combined with another week or two on Irieguy's couch, and he'll have plenty of time to find a place of his own.

Thirty seconds later, Good2cu is on AIM telling Raptor he can be there in three days. Raptor loves the kid's enthusiasm, but knows he needs to run it by Doc first.

He plans to do so over dinner, a feeding at the nearby Olive Garden, but forgets amid all the cheap pasta and wine. After dinner, he and Doc pay a visit to another friend, WSOP2005, to check out his new home theater system and play a fun, drunken, poker session online. But immediately after logging in, Doc turns stone-cold sober.

His account, which had $9,000 in it the last time he checked, is now empty.

It's the same account Doc's been letting Chantel use to work on her online game. She did quite well for herself playing limit poker in the underground games back in Texas, and now she's hoping to start playing more online. Doc agreed to help her as long as she promised to stick to low-stakes Sit N Gos, but tonight she's apparently decided to take a shot at a high-stakes cash game.

The result? Not good.

Doc gets Chantel on the phone and starts venting his rage.

"He might want to reconsider those wedding plans," Raptor jokes.

WSOP2005 snickers.

"What?" asks Raptor.

"Dude, they've been married since January."

Back at Doc's house, the fight stretches deep into the night. Raptor plugs his ears and tries to get some sleep, but not before firing off a quick message to Good2cu:

"About that offer of an extra room here in Vegas. . . . Probably not such a good idea right about now."

21

If I'm going to be a degenerate college dropout, I have to culture myself somewhat.

—Good2cu

OKEMOS, MICHIGAN (April 2006)

Good2cu doesn't know why Raptor has suddenly rescinded the invitation to crash in his house in Vegas, but he takes it in stride.

Plan B: *As long as I keep winning online, I can go wherever the hell I want.*

He picks Italy because Kelsey, a girl he knows from high school, is studying abroad in Florence. The red-tiled houses, hillside vineyards, and craggy mountains of the Italian countryside leave a deep impression on him. The cities aren't bad either. The Venetian wowed him when he first set eyes on it two months ago; now he realizes the casino was just an homage. This—everything he sees before him—is the real deal, and he spends each day trying to take it all in. He visits art galleries and museums, historical sites and old ruins, but it's the churches that make the biggest impact on him. The part of him that remains innocent and impressionable can't get over the idea that these architectural masterpieces are more than five hundred years old, while the part of his brain he uses for poker sees the underlying scam—many of these "holy sites" are also tourist traps raking in huge amounts of money for the house, i.e. the Vatican.

From Florence he travels with Kelsey to Cinque Terre—five picturesque villages, nestled into a rugged section of coastline along the Italian Riviera, connected by walking trails offering some of the most breathtaking views in the world. Good2cu does a little hiking and a lot of drinking. On his last night in town he gets slapped in the face by a bartender and passes out in a youth hostel between two girls he barely knows.

Parting ways with Kelsey, he heads to Rome, where, freed from her budgetary constraints, he checks into a five-star hotel. He laughs every time someone on the staff asks him when his parents are arriving. In the hotel's restaurant he meets Ron, a fifty-year-old American, who invites him to sit at his table. He's from Las Vegas where he works as a pit boss, supervising the floormen at TI. Good2cu can't believe he's stumbled across a true Vegas character in Europe. They're deep into a serious discussion about gambling by the time the antipasti arrives.

Ron knows plenty, and shares some of his favorite theories. Using stop-losses and win limits to regulate your time at the tables. Employing the hit-and-run strategy to help build your bankroll.

What's funny, from Good2cu's point of view, is that Ron doesn't have any idea what the hell he's talking about. His theories are all mathematical losers, "fish logic" based on superstition instead of statistics. And Ron is a guy who, given his line of work, should know better.

Good2cu can't help but smile. *These are the kinds of mathematical and psychological flaws that are going to allow me to make a living playing a card game.*

Their differences don't prevent them from having a good time. They knock off two or three bottles of wine, smoke some of Ron's hash, and visit a local "strip club," which is actually a brothel. Tom disappears into a back room with one of the girls. Good2cu spends the rest of the night chatting up a Polish dancer until her boss yells at her for neglecting the paying customers.

For a nineteen-year-old kid from the Midwest, the trip to Italy is an Indiana Jones–style adventure. During a rare sliver of down time, Good2cu logs on to the Two Plus Two forum and posts a detailed trip report.

"This is how I roll," he brags.

$ $ $

He's home in Michigan less than three days when he gets a phone call from Apathy. "Road trip."

"Can't do it," Good2cu protests. "I spent like four grand in Italy. I've got to get back to grinding. I'm pretty partied out too."

"Who am I even talking to right now? Can you please put Good2cu back on the phone?"

"Seriously. I was living large in Italy. But now it's time to punch the clock."

"Dude, we're not going to Mars. They have wireless in the Bahamas."

"The Bahamas?"

"Yeah, you know, rum drinks, girls in bikinis. And, oh yeah, poker. Paradise Poker is sponsoring a five K on Paradise Island. What is there to even think about?"

"You only have to be eighteen to play there, right?"

"And only eighteen to drink. We'll stop off in Texas on the way to see Raptor, then maybe spend a night or two with DonButtons in Miami."

"When would this supposed trip take place?"

"I can be at your place in three hours." Apathy hears silence on the other end and knows that he's won. "Well?"

"Well, I guess I'd better tell my mom to start doing my laundry."

Most people don't understand. You have to lead this lifestyle to understand.

—Deuce2High

FORT WORTH, TEXAS (April 2006)

Detroit Metro Airport is one of the world's busiest international hubs, a heavy-flow spigot to Europe and Asia. Still, Good2cu and Apathy manage to stand out.

It's not the way they're dressed; there's nothing about their uniforms—hooded sweatshirts, jeans, and sneakers—to distinguish them from any other college-age kids. It's not the intense focus on their computers either; plenty of travelers are zoning out on their laptops, even if their eyes aren't darting across every inch of the screen, rarely bothering to look up.

No, it's the outbursts—

"Ship it!"

"Holla!"

—every time one of them wins a big pot, which seems like every few minutes.

Of course they missed their flight. After boozing all night with some of Good2cu's friends, oversleeping was inevitable. But they lucked out: There's another flight in two hours, and the airport has wireless. By the time they're called to board their plane to Dallas-Fort Worth, each of them is more than $1,000 richer.

Texas doesn't conform to their expectations—it's surprisingly lush and green and contains fewer cowboys and less big hair than they'd imagined. Neither does Raptor's place. If his posts on Two Plus Two are to be believed, he's been doing *extremely* well at the poker tables lately, so Good2cu and Apathy are a little surprised when the taxi delivering them from the airport comes to a stop outside a ramshackle house in a sketchy neighborhood full of fast-food restaurants and car dealerships. They're double-checking the address when Raptor opens the door and greets them with a smile.

"Welcome to Texas, y'all."

Belying its ghetto exterior, the inside of the house could be a Best Buy showroom. A Nintendo GameCube and an Xbox 360 sit on the floor next to a tall stack of games. A sixty-inch plasma TV hangs on the wall, plugged into a state-of-the-art, surround-sound system. Spread around the living room are about a dozen high-end laptops and giant flat-screen monitors, most of which are currently in use. Good2cu recognizes most of the faces from his trip to Vegas: durrrr, TheUsher, Deuce2High, Bonafone, and FieryJustice. They all briefly lift their heads to say hello, then immediately return their focus to the poker games on their computer screens.

"Hey, you guys ever meet my buddy TravestyFund?" Raptor asks Good2cu and Apathy. "This is his place. I rent a room from him."

"I thought you were living in Vegas," Good2cu says.

"I was. I am. I kinda go back and forth," Raptor explains. "Durrrr and I are actually thinking about buying a place together here in Fort

Worth. He doesn't really care where he lives, and my family and my girlfriend are here. Speaking of . . ."

A blond sorority girl emerges from one of the bedrooms, sporting the look favored by college-age females throughout the Lone Star State: cowboy boots, blue jeans, black camisole.

"So what's the plan for the evening?" asks Good2cu.

"We goin' to da club!" shouts Deuce2High.

"Not me," says Raptor. "Haley's dragging me to a country-western concert."

She rolls her eyes. *"Dragging* you?"

"Just kidding, babe."

"Shouldn't you be in the shower?"

Raptor smiles apologetically at Good2cu and Apathy. "I'll catch up with y'all later."

"You know your boyfriend's, like, famous on the Internet, right?" Good2cu says to Haley as soon as Raptor's left the room.

"That's what he keeps telling me."

"Is it weird dating a celebrity?"

"A celebrity? Yeah, right. The celebrities I read about in the magazines don't spend all their time sitting in front of a computer playing some dorky game."

$ $ $

Good2cu and Apathy pull out their laptops. It's easy to slip into the flow. Hours pass. Like the video games all of them grew up playing, online poker has a way of devouring massive quantities of time. No one really notices when Raptor and Haley leave. Or when they return, only to quickly turn around and leave again, this time for a party at Raptor's old frat house.

"Anyone want pizza?" asks Bonafone whose hunger can be traced, at least partly, to all the bong hits he's been taking in between hands.

"Get ten larges. I'll buy," says durrrr.

"For eight people?"

"Shit, you're right. Get twelve."

When Bonafone answers the door a half hour later, he can barely see the delivery guy's face behind the enormous stack of boxes he's carrying.

"Where are the Cokes?" Deuce2High asks.

Delivery Guy places the pizzas on a table. "You guys didn't order any."

Durrrr pulls a wad of bills out of his pocket and peels off $160 for the pizza. Then another $40 for the tip. "There's a 7-Eleven next door. I'll give you another twenty if you run get us some Cokes."

Delivery Guy breaks into a smile. "Sure. Need anything else?"

"Just for my bottom pair to hold up against my opponent's flush draw," mumbles durrrr, racing back to his laptop.

Delivery Guy can't believe how lucky he is to have stumbled across this pack of kids whose laziness is only exceeded by their total disregard for the value of money. What he doesn't understand is that the five minutes it would take durrrr to walk over to the 7-Eleven and back might cost him hundreds of dollars in expected value. When time is money, life becomes a pretty simple series of mathematical calculations.

One by one they pull themselves away from their screens. Poker, when played correctly, is a boring game occasionally interrupted by heart-stopping moments of anticipation. Online multitabling filters out a lot of the tedium, distilling the game to a rapid-fire frenzy of intense decisions and a steady barrage of gut-wrenching showdowns. After toiling for several hours in this state, everyone's nerves are jangled, bodies buzzing with adrenal residue. It's going to take a while for the energy in the room to return to something resembling normal. A bottle of Crown Royal gets passed around. So do a bong and several tabs of Ecstasy.

Recharged, they arrive at an enormous nightclub in Dallas like a pack of wolves, howling, play fighting, battling for space. The club has four dance floors, each with its own particular music and vibe. There's crunk rap for those looking to get down and hook up; techno for the voyagers rolling on E.

Good2cu chooses crunk. Soon he's chatting with a pair of girls wearing identical T-shirts that read TAKE ME TO AMSTERDAM. He offers to buy them drinks if they can guess what line of work connects him and his group of friends.

"Auto mechanics?"

"Oil workers?"

"Cowboys?"

When the club shuts down at 4:00 A.M., the crew moves to an after-hours lounge. Deuce2High runs around the room playing with glow-sticks. The rest of them plant themselves on a couch. Raptor joins them, having tucked his girlfriend into bed. The place is full of beautiful women, but these guys are content to hang out with one another.

They talk about poker.

They talk about girls.

They talk about life.

Before Irieguy's tournament, each of them had been living in relative isolation. Their passion for online poker confused and, in some cases, terrified their parents and teachers. As for their friends, how could they possibly understand? They lack the insight required to appreciate the moments of inspired ingenuity, or the empathy to truly grasp the bad beats and the psychological ups and downs. What it feels like to suffer four- and, occasionally, five-figure wins and losses. The decision, and its attendant difficulties, to drop out of college. But now that they've found one another, a company of like minds, it feels like a revelation.

"It still blows my mind that I'm able to do shit like this," says Bonafone. "Just hop on a plane and go to Texas. I mean, a year ago I was in high school. Now Deuce2High and I are talking about traveling to Thailand and hanging out for a while. Pretty fucking amazing."

"I hear you," says Apathy. "A year ago I was stressing about having to write papers and study for tests."

"Now you're a Ship It Holla Balla!" says Good2cu.

"Such an idiotic name," grumbles Raptor. He raises a glass of scotch that costs as much as a tank of gas. "But you guys are all right in my book."

Good2cu spots a trio of attractive women standing nearby and, hit by a flash of inspiration, hands his camera to durrrr.

"Follow me."

Good2cu positions himself in the middle of the women, wraps his arms around their shoulders, and tells them to smile. Durrrr dutifully snaps a picture. Two of the girls think it's the cheesiest move they've ever seen. The third smiles at him flirtatiously.

Life, like poker, is a numbers game.

"Sorry to scare away your friends," says Good2cu.

"That's okay," she replies, putting her hands on his chest and feeling his upper body. It turns out the Ballas aren't the only ones rolling on Ecstasy. "I saw you from across the room. I think you're the best-looking guy here."

"Thank you," he replies. "You look like a model."

"That's funny. I just did a shoot for *Playboy*."

"Yo, Good2cu!" Deuce2High calls from across the room. "We're going to bounce."

A drink in one hand, an honest-to-god *Playboy* model who clearly wants to have sex with him hanging on the other—Good2cu is living the dream.

But he's no ladies' man. At heart he's still a socially awkward nineteen-year-old who spends most of his time playing a computer game. There aren't many people in the world who understand him, and the few who do are on their way out the door.

"Nice meeting you," he stammers to the Playmate before sprinting across the room to catch up with his friends.

23

This is what I get for: (a) leaving my laptop on, and (b) sleeping longer than other poker players you're traveling with.

—Apathy

MIAMI, FLORIDA (May 2006)

DonButtons lives in a luxurious condominium on Brickell Key, a man-made island in the waters east of downtown Miami. The building has an underground garage, where DonButtons parks his Lamborghini and his Range Rover, and a doorman, who carries Good2cu and Apathy's bags into the apartment.

The condo's floors are made of imported white marble, and every window provides a view of the Atlantic Ocean. A sixty-inch plasma TV hangs on the wall, as do various pieces of art from a noted gallery in South Beach. This could be the pied-à-terre for a successful Wall Street trader undergoing a midlife crisis. Instead it's being rented by DonButtons, who won't turn twenty-one for a few more months.

The glamour is, in large part, superficial. The artwork comes included with the rent. The cars are leased. DonButtons does not have a million dollars in the bank. He probably doesn't even have $100,000. But by spending five hours each day playing ten tables of low-stakes no-limit Hold'em at the same time, he's able to earn several thousand dollars a month, and as a twenty-year-old bachelor in Miami, what the hell else is he going to spend it on?

A balla condo. Pimp rides. Expensive dinners with gorgeous women. Bottle service at the clubs. The affluence, real or otherwise, is an eye-opener. For Good2cu, home is a spare bedroom at Mom or Dad's house, and his ride is a Saturn with 150,000 miles of wear. Apathy's Pontiac Pursuit—the fancy Canadian name for the very modest Chevy Cobalt—is, well, a Chevy Cobalt, and he still lives with five other guys in an off-campus flophouse near the University of Western Ontario.

DonButtons clearly knows how to live.

On their first night in town, he takes his guests out for a fancy meal that they wash down with several $100 bottles of wine. Good2cu can't pronounce whatever they're drinking, but he sure does like the way it tastes. That, and the feeling that comes with drinking something that carries such an expensive price tag.

After dinner, DonButtons leads them to a club, where the promoter, a good friend of his, hooks them up with a prime table and a bottomless supply of free cranberry vodkas. Good2cu spends the early part of the night dancing on the bar alongside fifteen women. He'll finish it by spilling drinks on two of them, puking in a garbage can, and passing out on the sidewalk just outside the club.

The next night they hire a twenty-four-person stretch Hummer limousine and cram it full of champagne, Grey Goose, and DonButtons's friends—fashionable club kids, most of whom are too young to drink. One of them tells Good2cu she's worried that she won't be able to get into the club without a fake ID.

"I don't think that's going to be a problem," he assures her.

"Why, are you that big of a balla?" she asks. "Please tell me yes because it turns me on."

Another girl keeps stealing the hipster fedora he bought earlier in the day during a shopping spree to update his wardrobe. He asks her to give it back.

"But I want it," she insists. "What do I have to do for you to let me wear it?"

"Kiss me."

She does. Good2cu could get used to this.

The line to get into the club wraps all the way around the corner of the building, but DonButtons's club-promoter friend whispers into the bouncer's ear and the bouncer waves the two dozen drunk underage kids past the velvet rope. They dance all night, drink Dom Pérignon, and smoke a blunt that appears as if by magic. This time it's Apathy who consumes too much. As soon as they get back to the condo, he passes out in DonButtons's bed.

It doesn't matter how much Good2cu and Apathy spend on clothes, alcohol, or stylish transportation—they're still just a couple of kids a year or two removed from high school. Good2cu hands out Sharpies to the girls they brought home and encourages them to draw penises all over Apathy's body.

In a previous era Good2cu might have shaved off one of Apathy's eyebrows, but the Information Age allows for more devious pranks. Good2cu opens Apathy's laptop, logs on to Two Plus Two using Apathy's account, and contributes a post to the message board:

OT: Going Busto

This is kind of embrassing but I decided to post it for educational purposes.

Those of you who know me well know that I don't practice the best money mangement skills. I have spent the past year of my life traveling the world living like a huge balla. I always had to take limos to the club, and upon arrival order $300+ bottles of Don and Grey Goose. When I went to circuit events I'd get drunk and go donk off stacks in 50/100 Triple Draw and other stupid games. This combined with purchasing a new car, a Pontaic Pursit and a bad run at 50/100 Ohamo 8 better online has resulted in me going busto. I plan on returning to SNGs to grind out a new roll until I get a roll for cash games again.

There is also a very dark underground to poker that I don't think gets enough atteion on these forums or gets taken as joke. When I was in Vegas for the STFF:HUC2 I ended up spending $10,000 on hookers and strippers. This was a significant portion of my bankroll and defentaily not something I could afford. I also don't think it was that uncommon at the tournament as apperntly none of us can get laid. Furthermore, I also took some cocaine off Raptors ass that re-sulted me in becoming addicted to cocaine. Since going busto I have resorted to sucking cock to support my cocaine addiction.

By the time Apathy regains consciousness the following afternoon, the thread has inspired five pages of comments, running the gamut from sympathy to mockery to offers of financial support to help him get back on his feet. Some of the more astute posters are also able to correctly identify the architect of the practical joke—only Good2cu could mangle the English language so badly.

Revenge comes swiftly. As soon as Good2cu falls asleep the next night, Apathy commandeers his phone and sends what he thinks is the most hilarious message ever to half the names in the contact list. Good2cu awakens to dozens of new voice mails—Mom, Dad, his lawyer, the family doctor—all curious about his decision to announce his homosexuality via text message.

24

Moral of the story: don't risk your life for 5K then get pwned by Matusow.

—Good2cu

PARADISE ISLAND, BAHAMAS (May 2006)

It's been three years since Chris Moneymaker's victory at the World Series of Poker, but the poker economy, powered by recreational players with dreams of winning millions on TV, shows no signs of slowing down. Online poker rooms host around-the-clock satellites and supersatellites—inexpensive tournaments whose winners gain admission into tournaments with much bigger entry fees. The swell of new entrants inflates the prize pool, which in turn attracts even more attention from amateurs hoping to become the next Money-maker. They are participating in what economists call a "virtuous circle," a feedback loop that builds on its own positive momentum. By 2006, the circle has become so culturally entrenched as to have earned a nickname from the mainstream media: the "poker boom."

The World Series of Poker still rules in terms of prestige, but it only happens once a year. Upstarts such as the World Poker Tour and the European Poker Tour fill the void with a new business model: smaller, lesser-known tournaments get aggregated and packaged into television-friendly "seasons" culminating in championships. The virtuous circle spins a few more times. Where the WSOP Main Event used to be the only tournament with a $10,000 buy-in and a seven-figure prize for the winner, now there are dozens.

When the online card rooms aren't feeding players into live tournaments, they're creating tournaments of their own. In 2002, Party Poker hosted the inaugural Party Poker Million aboard a cruise ship on the Mexican Riviera. The event was a hit—one year later, the World Poker Tour added the Party Poker Million II to its first season's schedule. In its second season, the WPT added a tournament in Aruba sponsored by Ultimate Bet and a tournament aboard a Caribbean-bound cruise ship hosted by PokerStars.

The Caribbean theme isn't coincidental—by hosting their events on tropical islands or cruise ships, the online card rooms can skirt U.S. law and allow players as young as eighteen, their bread-and-butter clientele, to play in the kind of tournaments they grew up watching on TV. It's why Paradise Poker chooses the Atlantis, an enormous resort and water park on the Bahamas' Paradise Island, to host its first ever brick-and-mortar tournament: "The Conquest of Paradise Island."

The Conquest fails to secure any TV coverage or commitments from well-known pros—in the months leading up to the event, there's some speculation whether it will even take place. But the allure of lax gambling and drinking laws in a tropical setting is enough for the tournament to attract more than three hundred players, a large percentage of whom are under twenty-one.

Good2cu, Apathy, and DonButtons fly there from Miami. Raptor, durrrr, Deuce2High, Bonafone, TheUsher, and FieryJustice meet them at the resort. They're buzzed before the first round of boat drinks even hits their lips—for most of them, this is the biggest tournament they've ever entered.

Only durrrr can laugh off the $5,000 entry fee. While the rest of them are still devoting most of their attention to Sit N Gos, durrrr is regularly playing in the biggest cash games on the Internet. He probably shouldn't be—any old-school player would scoff at his horrendous bankroll management, which sees him routinely flirt with going broke—but what does he really have to lose? He's nineteen years old, has no wife or kids to support, is blessed with an active intelligence, and is fully capable of returning to college if the whole poker thing doesn't work out. Why wouldn't he take shots at the biggest games? When he loses—an inevitability for even the best poker players—he simply drops down to smaller stakes, rebuilds his bankroll, and waits for the chance to take another shot. But when he wins . . . No one's sure exactly how much money durrrr has, as it's an ever-changing number, but for several brief stretches lately he's been, at least according to the pixels on the screen, a millionaire.

The rest of the Ballas are doing their best to catch up to him. Most of them are now hundred-thousandaires. Good2cu has pushed his net worth close to $200,000. Raptor's earned enough money to buy himself a brand-new car—a sporty Subaru Impreza WRX—and is looking to buy a house with durrrr in Fort Worth.

The Ballas are brimming with confidence as they take their seats in the tournament room at the Atlantis, but, one by one, they get eliminated. Only FieryJustice makes it past the first day, hanging around just long enough to win back his entry fee.

Not the experience they'd hoped for, but hardly the end of the world—Paradise Island is aptly named. The sky is blue, the weather warm, the summer humidity a few weeks away. There are swimming pools and fruity drinks, plenty of craps and blackjack tables, and a murderer's row of waterslides, apparently designed by an imaginative child touched by madness: "the Abyss" begins with a fifty-foot vertical drop into total darkness; "the Leap of Faith" travels through a lagoon teeming with sharks.

But this week the most popular activity takes place in the hotel lobby. The wireless Internet in the rooms doesn't work for shit, forcing guests to gather in the only decent hot spot. No matter what time of day or night, at least fifty young online players are there, hunched over their laptops, madly clicking away.

Amped by one of these sessions, Good2cu, Apathy, durrrr, and FieryJustice decide to pay a nighttime visit to the Mayan Temple. A random mom overhears their plans and, in need of some adult time (and possibly a stern talking-to in regards to good parental judgment), asks if her sixteen-year-old daughter can tag along. "Take good care of her," Mom says before disappearing into a bar.

The girl, half-mortified, half-intrigued, and probably a little drunk herself, attaches herself to the group. So does sublime8700, a Two Plus Twoer enjoying a long weekend away from the University of Michigan.

The Mayan Temple turns out to be closed—an unsurprising development, given that it's past 2:00 A.M. What is surprising is that the lagoon full of sharks, with the minor exception of a waist-high railing, is wide-open and easily accessible.

"This would *never* fly in America," observes FieryJustice. "There'd be like seven security guards here to keep some idiot from jumping in."

They all stare into the water. Lights line the pool, clearly illuminating the sharks as they make their predatory rounds.

"Two thousand dollars," says durrrr.

"What are you talking about?" asks the sixteen-year-old girl.

"I'll give anyone here two thousand bucks if they swim down and touch the bottom."

"Hell no," says Good2cu. "It's like twenty feet deep. Oh yeah, and *it's filled with sharks.*"

"Fine. Three thousand."

"I might consider it," says FieryJustice, "for fifty K."

"Four thousand."

"No fucking way," says Apathy, "but I'll kick in five hundred bucks if anyone's actually thinking about it."

"Me too," adds FieryJustice.

"Are you guys serious?" asks the girl. "That's enough to buy a car."

"A crappy one." Durrrr laughs. "But, hey, if you do it, you can spend the money any way you want."

"If you're still alive," says Good2cu.

The girl appraises the tank. "You'll seriously give me five thousand dollars if I do it?"

"He's good for it," Apathy assures her.

Taking a deep breath, she takes off her shoes, strips down to her bikini, and steps out onto the ledge overlooking the pool.

A wave of terror and excitement passes through them: *Holy shit. She's actually going to do it.*

Several sharks draw near. The sight of them triggers an eruption of fear from some recessed area of her lizard-brain, and the girl, legs shaking, steps back from the edge. "No freaking way!"

For a moment, no one knows whether to be disappointed or relieved.

"Screw it," says sublime8700. "I'll do it for five K."

Sublime8700 started playing poker online a year ago. He's made enough money to be able to travel to the Bahamas, put himself up in a $300-a-night room, and enter a $5,000 tournament, but not enough to drop out of college and play the game for a living. For him, $5,000 isn't life-changing money, but it isn't chump change either.

Before he can change his mind, he whips off his shirt, climbs over the railing, and jumps into the water.

For a second, no one can believe he's actually done it.

Then panic sets in. Durrrr runs to a nearby tree, trying to rip off one of its branches.

"What are you doing?" Good2cu yells.

"Trying to find something to throw at the sharks!"

But sublime8700 is already pulling himself out of the water, no worse for wear, with a huge smile on his face.

"Ship it!"

Back in the lobby, durrrr transfers $5,000 into sublime8700's on-line poker account. Having swum with sharks and lived to tell about it, he's feeling about as good as a human being can without benefit of sex or drugs, and he doesn't want that sensation to go away. "I'm going to take a shot!" he announces to everyone within earshot.

Using the money he just won from durrrr, sublime8700 buys into a $25/$50 no-limit cash game, the biggest he's ever played. The adrenaline builds as he realizes he's sitting at the same table as Mike Matusow, a world-famous pro.

Seconds later, sublime8700 gets dealt an ace and a queen, a premium hand with only five players in the game. There is a raise and a call in front of him, but his instincts tell him that neither player is particularly strong. He figures that if he bets all of his chips, he'll scare the other two players into folding, allowing him to win a decent-sized pot without too much stress.

But sublime8700 forgets to take one thing into account: while a $5,000 bet might feel intimidating to him, it means virtually nothing to Matusow, who has won and lost millions of dollars in his career. "Smells like ace-queen," Matusow types in the chat box before calling with a measly pair of deuces.

The odds are more or less fifty-fifty, but the onus is on sublime8700 to improve. He needs to catch an ace or a queen to win the hand. Neither card arrives. Fifteen minutes after risking his life for $5,000, he's lost it all to Mike Matusow on a single hand of poker.

There are sharks, and then there are *sharks*.

25

As the United States completes its transition to an all-gambling economy, perhaps you're wondering what your place is likely to be in it. Depends. If the sentence "Another good scenario for a stack is a flush that's made on the river" means something to you, you have a shot at membership in the new socioeconomic elite. If not, you can plan on washing that elite's cars or watering its lawns.

—Neil Genzlinger, *The New York Times Book Review,*
January 8, 2006

EAST LANSING, MICHIGAN (May 2006)

Had Good2cu been born twenty years earlier, he might have felt the lure of Wall Street, where bright college graduates were discovering lucrative signing bonuses and expensive cocaine habits. Ten years later, it could have been the Internet and its promise of IPO-minted millions.

For Good2cu's generation, the poker boom is its California gold rush, offering everyone, regardless of background or education, the opportunity to strike it rich. But, as is rapidly becoming apparent, the poker boom isn't just an economic phenomenon—it's also producing celebrities.

Professional poker players have never had unions or guilds. Few barriers stand in the way of membership. There's an argument to be made that it's not even a real profession, at least as far as the IRS is concerned: poker winnings aren't taxed as earnings, as they are for a real job, but at the higher rate reserved for windfalls like the lottery. For most of the game's history, professional poker players have been equated with outlaws, living on the financial and social margins of society.

But for the last few years, you can't turn on a TV without stumbling across a poker tournament. The incessant coverage is breeding familiarity, and familiarity creates fans. We've entered the age of the poker superstar. No longer considered outlaws, they've been recast as brilliant math wizards, masters of human psychology, disciplined warriors with nerves of steel. Three decades ago, Doyle Brunson had to put up his own money to get his instructional book *Super/System* published; now the septuagenarian pro has to fend off autograph seekers and photo hounds at every turn, fleeing as fast as his walker will allow.

Other players embrace the spotlight with open arms. The most popular write books, create instructional videos, and hire themselves out as private coaches or motivational speakers. Annie Duke, who won a World Series of Poker bracelet in 2004, has moved from Portland, Oregon, to the Hollywood Hills, where she's producing a poker-themed game show, dating an actor, and dabbling in screenwriting. Her brother, Howard Lederer, has teamed up with a group of fellow poker celebrities to start an online card room—in under two years, Full Tilt Poker has become one of the biggest sites in the world, shrewdly marketing itself as the place where the game's superstars come to play.

Other pros take advantage of the lucrative sponsorship deals the online sites seem to be doling out like wartime promotions. Some of these deals promise a steady salary, offering lucky poker players something like legitimate financial security for the first time in their lives.

These are uncharted waters, but if you're not already a poker celebrity, the path to sponsorship typically begins with a victory in a major televised tournament. No one really believes that Chris Moneymaker is the best poker player in the world, or even among the top one hundred, but the marketing team at PokerStars—the site where he began his Cinderella-like journey in a $39 satellite—understands the value of reminding everyone exactly which company made this fairy tale possible. Moneymaker and 2005 WSOP champion Joe Hachem become the most prominent faces of Team PokerStars, a stable of sponsored pros who serve as human billboards decked out in company-logoed schwag.

The final tables of televised tournaments begin to look like NAS-CAR races. Plastered with ads, the sponsored players are impossible to miss, especially if you're an aspiring young pro looking for someone to pay your way into all the tournaments. To get there, all you've got to do is get famous, which so far has meant outplaying, outlasting, and outlucking a ballroom full of cutthroat angle-shooters to win a major tournament.

But the Internet offers a new path to fame, a viable alternative to the old monolithic media model. Successful online players might not be world-famous, but being "Internet famous" has got to count for something, right?

A Two Plus Twoer named ZeeJustin is one of the first to solve this puzzle. A year earlier, at age nineteen, he became the youngest player in history to make a televised final table, taking advantage of Europe's more kid-friendly gambling laws to finish fourth in an EPT tournament in Deauville, France. The accomplishment isn't enough to turn him into a poker superstar, but it does provide the impetus and the money to hire a Web site designer. ZeeJustin starts blogging about his experiences touring the world as a professional poker player, and when the site starts to generate traffic, he monetizes it, selling banner ads and driving visitors to online poker rooms.

This spring, ZeeJustin gains even more notoriety when it's discovered that he's been playing tournaments on PokerStars using more than one account. In what is mostly a self-regulated industry, "multi-accounting" is one of those gray areas that straddle the lines between legal and illegal, ethical and unethical. For years, it was a standard practice among online players. In fact, it's how many of the Ballas built up their initial bankrolls, opening accounts under different user names to take advantage of as many sign-up bonuses as they could. But ZeeJustin has been accused of using his multiple accounts to enter the same tournament more than once. PokerStars decides to make an example of the young pro, banning him from the site for three years.

The harsh punishment generates a lot of press. Good2cu is jealous—in his eyes, any publicity, even scandal, is good publicity. The proverbial lightbulb appears over his head: why not skip the TV part of the equation and try to become an Internet celebrity from the very beginning?

After returning from the Bahamas, he makes a road trip to London, Ontario, to visit Apathy. Against the backdrop of three kegs and the better part of a local sorority, Good2cu pitches him the idea for ShipItHollaBalla.com, a place for them to share their stories and inflate their reputations. Dancing for strippers and swimming with sharks is a lot more interesting than anything ZeeJustin is putting on his site.

Apathy, fending off the sorority girls long enough to hear the pitch, loves the idea. His constitution prevents him from doing any actual work, but he's willing to put up half the seed money.

Good2cu returns to East Lansing, where he's sharing an apartment with a friend from college, and sets the plan into motion. There's no need to reinvent the wheel: he hires the same Web designer who built ZeeJustin's site. The first couple of posts on ShipItHollaBalla.com are commercial enticements to visit certain online poker rooms, but Good-2cu's first travel report will set the tone for the site and help define the Ballas' identity:

"I've spent the past forty days of my life, traveling, meeting random Two Plus Twoers, partying like a rock star, and mercilessly hitting on girls," it begins. "God, do I regret dropping out of college. . . ."

26

FROM: good2cu@shipithollaballa.com
TO: XXXXXXXX@mtv.com
SUBJECT: MTV "True Life: I'm Moving to Vegas"

HOLLA.

I'm a 19-year-old college dropout/professional poker player/ straight balla. I dropped out of college at Michigan State University after taking a week long trip to Vegas that netted me over $8k.

(Too bad I spent $10k+ on booze, clothes, strippers and a Rolex.)

In the past year I've made over six figures playing poker online on PartyPoker.com and Pokerstars.com. I think I'll bring in $300k+ this tax year. Yeah, that's right. SHIPPPPPPPPPP IT, HOLLA.

I am a semi-well-known online pro in the Two Plus Two poker community (a forum for pro poker players). I recently finished in 2nd place in the Two Plus Two Single Table Tournament Forum Heads-Up Championship which netted me just under $6K.

Since dropping all of my classes at MSU, my days consist of sitting in front of the computer for ten hours a day playing eight tables of poker, so I can really move anywhere I want. I mean assuming I can get time off of "work." (My boss is a real badass . . . BWHAHAHA.)

After making a post in the Two Plus Two forums about it, I decided there is no better place for a cardplayer to live than in Las Vegas. In my opinion not realizing that I belong in Vegas must be a much bigger mistake then dropping out of school!

I have a mansion in Vegas lined up for June 28th to August 13th with three other professional poker players (all between the ages of 19–28), which will surely be a party mansion. Yeah, drunken rich kids with more money than they know what to do with. SHIPPPPPPP the ladies. In the meantime I'm thinking about packing up all my shit, flying down and living with a doctor (semi-professional poker player), or in a mansion with three other pros until I find my own place. I currently have a bankroll/life savings of $200,000.

Besides playing poker I am becoming a member of the PUA (pickup artist) community. I've read "The Game" and avidly read seduction forums on the Internet. Despite my amazingly sexy looks and classic charm, I've only had marginal success so far. My crowning achievement so far was getting paid in a strip club to dance for the strippers! YEAH, SHIPPPP IT HOLLA!! I suppose I'm still a nice guy at heart. Anyways, put me on MTV and the ladies will love me even more, I'll keep shit exciting, and SHIPPPPPPPPPPPPPPPPP THE MTV CAMERAS THIS WAY.

PEACE OUT. HOLLA.

Irieguy (and friends). *(Photo courtesy Craig Hartman)*

Good2cu (center, in white) on his way to the prom. *(Photo courtesy Andrew Robl)*

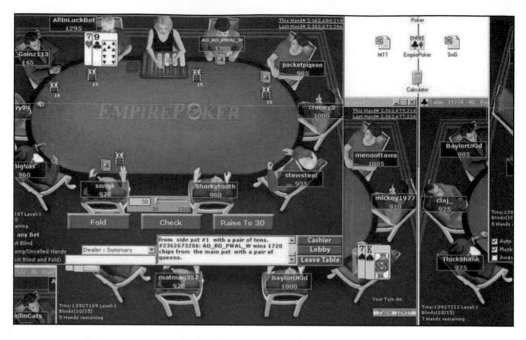

Early attempts at multitabling weren't easy . . . *(Photo courtesy Mario Silvestri)*

. . . until Raptor cracks the problem with his Quad Monitor Set-Up. *(Photo courtesy David Benefield)*

Game Level	Total Hands	Vol. Put $ In The Pot	Vol. Put $ In From SB	Folded SB To Steal	Folded BB To Steal	Att. To Steal Blinds	Won $ WSF %	Amount Won	BB/100 Hands	Went To SD %
NL $5,000	1,015	17.54	32.64	69.23	70.73	30.33	42.95	$22,239.53	21.91	19.46
NL $5000	3,826	21.28	22.38	83.24	76.64	34.30	44.07	$17,880.19	4.67	28.85
NL ($20) (1	64	46.88	65.63	0.00	0.00	0.00	45.83	($1,264.50)	(49.39)	37.50
NL $2000	23,771	25.56	25.98	84.72	75.07	36.10	43.62	$70,429.20	7.41	27.14
NL ($20) (6	113	32.74	20.83	77.78	61.54	53.13	50.00	$899.50	19.90	50.00
NL $2,000	7,480	23.82	25.47	85.77	74.46	33.09	45.12	$5,304.41	1.77	25.52
NL ($10)	161	24.22	27.78	100.00	87.50	37.29	46.67	($209.00)	(6.49)	20.00
NL ($10) (6	2,881	21.10	20.00	90.71	79.62	29.99	39.95	($8,043.35)	(13.96)	25.27
23 Levels	104,704	23.84	24.43	84.94	75.94	34.42	44.78	$158,557.86	4.44	25.38
Totals:	1,738 Session(s)						61,022	$158,557.90	104,704	4.
True Win Rate:	223.35 hrs.		MT Ratio:	4.55			13,401	$709.91	468.79	20.

Most of the Ballas kept meticulous records. *(Photo courtesy Andrew Robl)*

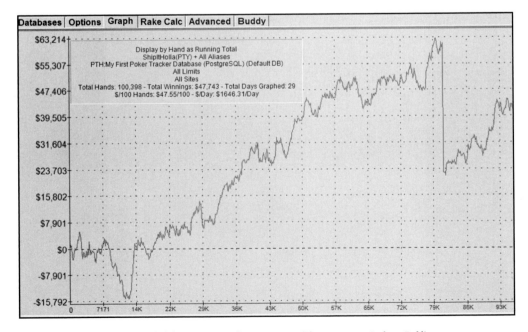

The ups and downs were often extreme. *(Photo courtesy Andrew Robl)*

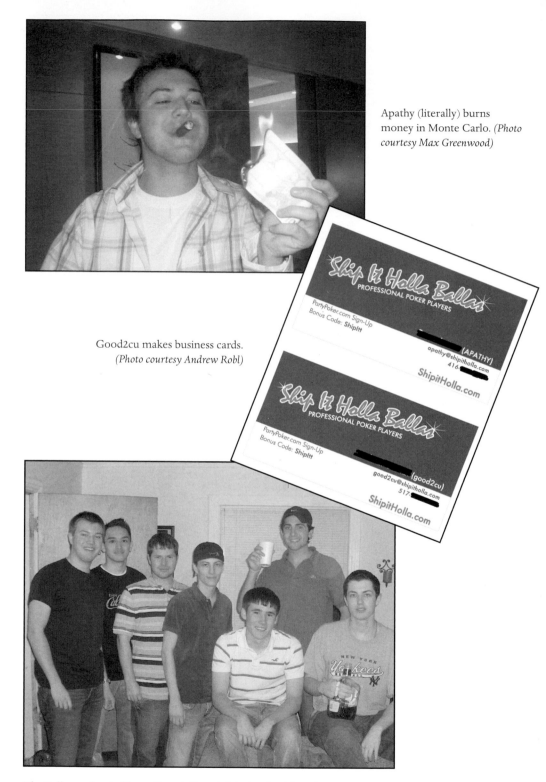

Apathy (literally) burns money in Monte Carlo. *(Photo courtesy Max Greenwood)*

Good2cu makes business cards. *(Photo courtesy Andrew Robl)*

The Ballas gather in Texas (from left to right): Apathy, TheUsher, FieryJustice, Deuce2High, Bonafone, TravestyFund, durrrr. *(Photo courtesy Andrew Robl)*

Good2cu, durrrr, and two new friends in a Dallas nightclub. *(Photo courtesy Peter Jetten)*

DonButtons. *(Photo courtesy Andrew Robl)*

Good2cu in Miami, partying with friends in a stretch limo. *(Photo courtesy Andrew Robl)*

Aruba! (from left to right): TheUsher, Apathy, Raptor, Good2cu. *(Photo courtesy Andrew Robl)*

Raptor, dancing to his own tune. *(Photo courtesy Andrew Robl)*

TheUsher grinds in a hotel room. (Photo courtesy Andrew Robl)

"The Office," Ship It Holla Mansion (from left to right): TheUsher, Raptor, Unarmed, Good2cu. (Photo courtesy Andrew Robl)

Good2cu prepares for his first trip to the World Series of Poker. *(Photo courtesy Andrew Robl)*

A young gambler's tools of the trade. *(Photo courtesy Andrew Robl)*

Good2cu, ready to roll. *(Photo courtesy Andrew Robl)*

The ill-fated BMW M3. *(Photo courtesy Andrew Robl)*

Chantel and Apathy. *(Photo courtesy Peter Jetten)*

Raptor and durrrr made enough money to buy a house together before either turned 21. *(Photo courtesy Andrew Robl)*

A typical Balla home game (from left to right): Empiremaker2, Inyaface, Bonafone. *(Photo courtesy Andrew Robl)*

Exploiting London's less restrictive drinking laws (from left to right): Apathy, TheUsher, Deuce2High, Good2cu. *(Photo courtesy Andrew Robl)*

The Halloween Party in Canada (from left to right): Raptor, Jman, TravestyFund, Good2cu, Deuce2High, Inyaface. *(Photo courtesy Andrew Robl)*

A gift for Apathy from a female fan. *(Photo courtesy Peter Jetten)*

The Candy Fairy, AKA Jman. *(Photo courtesy Andrew Robl)*

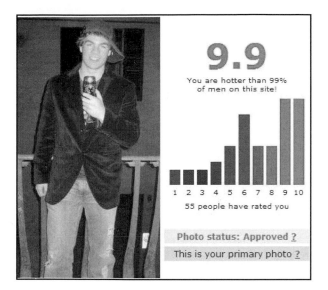

Good2cu gets an ego boost from his self-submitted photo to HotOrNot.com. *(Photo courtesy Andrew Robl)*

Raptor and then-girlfriend Haley.
(Photo courtesy David Benefield)

Good2cu and his brand-new Escalade in East Lansing. *(Photo courtesy Andrew Robl)*

Good2cu and Empiremaker2 meet Lee Jones at the 2007 EPT Polish Open. *(Photo courtesy Andrew Robl)*

Sightseeing in Rome, during a rare break from the online action (from left to right): TheUsher, durrrr, Traheho. *(Photo courtesy Alec Torelli)*

The second Ship It Holla Mansion had its own screening room, rigged to display online poker. *(Photo courtesy Andrew Robl)*

The infinity pool in the Palms' Playboy Suite. *(Photo courtesy Andrew Robl)*

Ballas, circa 2012, outside Manhattan's Per Se restaurant (from left to right): Apathy, durrrr, Raptor. *(Photo courtesy Peter Jetten)*

Newly sponsored Good2cu poses for a publicity photo in Vegas. *(Photo credit Melodie DeWitt)*

27

Overall, I was very impressed by the Ship It Holla Balla Mansion. It is going to be perfect for balling.

—**Good2cu**

LAS VEGAS, NEVADA (June 2006)

For much of its early history, the World Series of Poker hardly lived up to the grandiosity of its name. "World" was an ambitious misnomer, as its participants—almost exclusively old, white men—hailed mainly from Texas and never numbered more than a hundred.

The event wasn't intended to be a proving ground as much as performance art—its host and creator, Benny Binion, hoped that a living exhibition of the world's greatest poker players would pull a little extra foot traffic into the Horseshoe, his downtown Las Vegas casino. For their part, the cardsharps, hustlers, and road gamblers who gathered there embraced the rare opportunity to connect with so many like-minded souls, giving birth to an annual tradition.

Little by little, the World Series' Main Event evolved from circus sideshow into main attraction. Younger players with college educations began to infiltrate the ranks—in 1978, a twenty-eight-year-old former Oklahoma State student named Bobby Baldwin won the championship. Then came "foreigners" like the brash New Yorker Stu Ungar, who won back-to-back titles in the early eighties, and actual immigrants like Chinese-born Johnny Chan, who managed the same feat in 1987 and 1988.

Part of the WSOP Main Event's charm was that it was open to everyone. As long as you had $10,000 to pay for the buy-in, you could sit down and play. The creation of satellite tournaments opened the field to a wider clientele, and by the end of the eighties, the tournament routinely drew two hundred players. Bigger fields meant bigger money—1991 winner Brad Daugherty became the first player to earn $1 million. The Main Event grew steadily until 2003, when The Moneymaker Effect turned the enterprise into an entirely different animal.

The 2006 World Series crams forty-five tournaments into six hectic weeks. Several thousand people are expected to enter the Main Event, and there is speculation that the winner could take home $10 million or more. Las Vegas is swarming with journalists, not just from the poker-centric rags, but also ESPN, CNN, the *Chicago Tribune,* and *The New York Times*. If the Ship It Holla Ballas are going to take the poker world by storm, this is clearly the place to start.

As promised, Inyaface secures a short-term rental: a 3,000-square-foot house in a quiet, family-friendly neighborhood near the Southern Highlands. It comes with a pool, hot tub, billiards table, and absolutely no interference from parental or authority figures.

Welcome to the Ship It Holla Balla Mansion.

Despite losing a gamble in the Utah desert—Apathy and Inyaface blow past the LAST GAS FOR 100 MILES sign with less than half a tank, necessitating a middle-of-the-night rescue from a truck driver who looks like the killer in a cheesy horror movie—the two Canadians arrive first and claim the two master bedrooms for themselves. Good2cu caught a 7:30 AM flight in hopes of beating them to the house, but, upon discovering that they had intentionally misrepresented their arrival time, has to content himself with the Asian-themed guest room. The last three members of the household—Unarmed, TheUsher, and Jman—claim the remaining rooms as they trickle into town.

It's Sunday—a sacred day for online poker players, as most of the major Internet sites hold their biggest tournaments of the week that day—so the first order of business is setting up shop. They transform the otherwise useless dining-room table (like the group's ever going to sit down to a meal) into a communal workstation, a tangled mess of power cords and flat-screen monitors, and get to grinding.

Raptor joins them after lunch. The way he carves out a space for himself at the table, clearing the area around his laptop and doling out the twelve-pack of ice-cold Cokes he picked up on the way over, makes it clear: he's the unofficial seventh member of the household. While he still has a room at DocHolatchya's place, Raptor sees a chance to have the kind of fraternal experience he missed out on when he ditched school. He's also happy to avoid the Doc and Chantel Show: one minute they're talking about having a baby, the next they're screaming divorce.

Everyone settles into an online trance until late afternoon, when they get a call from Irieguy inviting them to dinner at an Outback Steakhouse.

Irieguy can't exactly call himself a father figure to these kids—he's more like a cool older brother who lets you borrow his ID and teaches you how to talk to strippers. Whatever sense of paternalism he might feel has been overwhelmed by awe at when he considers how much they've accomplished in such a short period of time. Most of them are already playing at higher stakes than he does, and he's been playing for more than a decade.

Irieguy may not be able to teach these kids much about strategy, but he's happy to dispense wisdom from his other realms of expertise. Like how the drug MDMA can permanently affect cognitive function (hint: not for the better). Or whether or not Raptor and Good2cu should use fake IDs to enter World Series events, an idea they're both seriously considering. (Hell no: The IRS, gripped by its own version of The Moneymaker Effect—the opportunity to tax the many millions that will be doled out to the winners—has been pressuring the tournament's organizers to check and double-check IDs; getting caught could result in a lifetime ban from the world's most prestigious poker tournament.)

Irieguy also has a few opinions about dining etiquette. He'll teach Good2cu, for example, that women never pay. And when the Ballas finish their meal at the Outback, he shows them how to resolve the inevitable clusterfuck over who owes what with a simple game called Credit Card Roulette.

Everyone hands a credit card to the server, who shuffles the cards and returns them to their respective owners one at a time. Whoever's card gets drawn last pays the entire bill. The game immediately becomes a Ship It Holla Balla ritual. Tonight TheUsher gets stuck with the $400 tab.

After dinner Irieguy heads home, while the young Ballas pile into cars and drive to the Rio All Suites Hotel and Casino, two red and purple glass towers a half-mile west of the Strip. TheUsher, who's lost another contest, has to ride in Apathy's trunk the entire way. They pull up to the valet, exiting in unlikely numbers from every conceivable orifice like a circus troupe from a clown car, and enter poker's new holy ground.

In the months following Moneymaker's victory, Benny Binion's heirs took advantage of the spotlight cast on their father's casino to sell the Horseshoe to Harrah's Entertainment, a gaming corporation that owns dozens of hotels and casinos around the world. Harrah's wasn't particularly interested in the decrepit gaming hall—they sold the building a few days later, holding on to the asset that actually motivated the deal: the World Series of Poker.

Last year, Harrah's moved the tournament to the more upscale Rio, staging it in its Amazon Room, a banquet hall that makes up for a lack of character with sheer size. It's as big as Grand Central Station and, right now, equally hectic. The air is filled with what sounds like a massive swarm of crickets, the familiar hum of several thousand anxious poker players continuously riffling their chips. Every one of the two-hundred-plus tables in the room is full, and every aisle leading to those tables is packed with fans. From above, Mount Rushmore–sized photos of the Main Event's past winners silently observe the spectacle, betraying no hint of what would surely be amazement at what Benny Binion's little marketing ploy has turned into.

Good2cu notices one of the men in the photos, 2001 world champion Chris "Jesus" Ferguson, sitting at a table, alongside two other players he's grown up watching on TV, Mike Matusow and Daniel Negreanu. It's chilly inside the misleadingly named Amazon Room, but that isn't what's raising goose bumps on his arms. He wants to run over to the table and ask for autographs. Shit, he wants to *play* against these guys.

Raptor knows exactly what Good2cu's thinking. "We'll get our chance," he tells his friend. "Just not this year."

Someone on Two Plus Two was like, "Where are the chicks? You guys are losers. You're not hanging out with any girls."

—Inyaface

LAS VEGAS, NEVADA (June 2006)

With the exception of Inyaface, none of the Ballas are enrolled in college anymore. They would never complain about the loss of their academic lives, but there are certain rites of passage built into the collegiate experience they can't help but yearn for. One of them is Spring Break.

This is their Spring Break.

If you've ever rented a vacation house with a large group of friends, then you're no doubt familiar with the ritual that is the first trip to the grocery store. Loading up on food for the week is more than an act of self-sufficiency; it's the symbolic start to an adventure, a celebration of freedom ("Let's buy ten boxes of Fruity Pebbles and eat them for dinner!") and a warm-up exercise in group dynamics ("Who, besides you, is going to eat *that*?")

They drive directly from the Rio to a twenty-four-hour Food 4 Less. This time it's Good2cu's turn to ride in the trunk, and he emerges with a full head of steam. His rowdiness is contagious. They blow through the store like a hurricane, twelve hands transferring whatever strikes their fancy from the shelves to their shopping carts.

It's after midnight, so the store's manager can't help but notice six extremely loud kids running down the aisles, spewing profanities, using their carts as bumper cars. He confronts them, wondering aloud if they actually intend to buy any of this stuff. Two of the carts contain nothing but liquor and beer. Another has been reserved exclusively for fireworks.

"Don't worry," Good2cu assures him. "We're rich."

The manager moves to another part of the store, but Inyaface is willing to concede that he might have a point. "Do we really need all this shit?" He points to the cart filled with smoke bombs and bottle rockets. "Why don't we make a 'Stupid Pile' for the stuff that's not essential."

After some debate, the Ballas admit they might have gotten carried away in the healthy-eating department and move a single carton of strawberries, the lone fruit or vegetable to make it into their carts, into the Stupid Pile.

There's no line at the checkout counter, but it still takes the cashier almost twenty minutes to ring them up. "A hundred bucks says it's over fifteen hundred," says Good2cu.

"I'll take the under," Jman replies.

"Book it!"

The receipt is four feet long. Good2cu wins by a comfortable margin.

"How do you want to pay?" asks the cashier.

"Shot not!" yells TheUsher, raising a finger to his nose.

The others quickly follow suit, but Unarmed is the slowest. He hands the cashier his credit card. They cram the groceries into their trunks, all except for the fireworks, and race home down Flamingo Road, shooting bottle rockets and lobbing smoke bombs from one car to the other, laughing the entire way.

For a long time they were two very separate worlds, and the people in the different worlds didn't like each other very much. The Internet players thought all the tournament players sucked at poker and were just lucky to be famous, and the live players thought Internet players were arrogant and young and out of control. Both sides were probably right.

—Good2cu

LAS VEGAS, NEVADA (July 2006)

The house doesn't exactly turn out to be a pussy magnet.

Apathy and Inyaface lure a couple of girls from Canada back to the lair, and some friends of friends from Michigan stop by to visit Good2cu for a couple of nights on their way across the country. Beyond that, nearly all of the interactions the Ballas have with the opposite sex take place in strip clubs. The wild parties they imagined have turned out to be a bunch of dudes getting drunk and high and breaking things. The dream was the Playboy Mansion. The reality is a frat house.

Alpha Ship It Pi.

They throw beer cans at walls and have shoot-outs with bottle rockets inside the house. The place reeks of sweat, pizza, and workout supplements. One night, Good2cu gets drunk and throws a pool ball through a window. The ball travels across the property line through a window next door. When the angry neighbors arrive at their door, threatening to call the police, Good2cu sheepishly blames the incident on an imaginary "drunk friend" who's hiding upstairs. He defuses the situation by offering to pay for *all* their windows to be replaced. With cash.

Membership in the fraternity is fluid. At any given moment it's hard to say for sure who's living in the house and who's just passing through. Raptor spends so much time here he might as well be paying rent, and the "couple of days" Bonafone told them he'd be crashing on one of the couches turns into weeks. Two of Inyaface's buddies from L.A., intrigued by Good2cu's posts on the Ship It Holla Balla Web site, have rolled out sleeping bags on the floor.

Up close, the most astonishing thing about the Ballas isn't their fondness for sophomoric hijinks, but the way these kids seem to be minting money on a daily basis. They gather around the dining-room table each afternoon, sitting in front of computers and chugging sodas. While they're sharing the same physical space, they rarely cross paths at the online tables. As confident as they are in their own abilities, colluding—even if it were possible—doesn't interest them, but they do interact in a way that might be just as effective: pooling knowledge, sharing strategies, offering emotional support, and applying enormous peer pressure to play their A games. These communal sessions help the Ballas improve, individually, by leaps and bounds, and Inyaface's buddies are astonished by the amount of money they're winning.

Inyaface's friends aren't the only ones who have been reading Good-2cu's posts. Complete strangers are finding their way to the Web site, leaving comments that cleave more or less evenly between shout-outs and flames. The plan Good2cu set in motion is starting to deliver results—the Ballas are becoming Internet famous.

Apathy is playing a cash game at the Rio when a Swedish kid introduces himself. It's H@llingol, a well-known high-stakes player who for a time was crushing the action at PokerStars until he ran into a steamroller named durrrr.

"Wait a minute," H@llingol says after Apathy identifies himself. "You're not one of the Ship It Holla Ballas, are you?"

Apathy nods hesitantly, not quite sure how his admission will be received.

"I think that site is great!"

Apathy later runs into Gank—the stoner from The Crew—who also confesses to being a fan.

But there are just as many haters. A polarizing debate takes shape, especially on Two Plus Two, as to whether these kids are living the dream or acting like total idiots. The image that the Ballas have embraced makes them perfect poster children for an emerging subculture that could only have been birthed by the Internet—college dropouts who have struck it rich playing online poker and enjoy spending their newfound wealth conspicuously. The Two Plus Two old-timers tend to see them as trainwrecks in the making, novices who have taken advantage of a few tricks and run lucky for a time, but whose luck will inevitably run out. To their supporters, the Ballas are adventurous souls charting a path into the unknown and having a damn good time along the way.

The mainstream poker world doesn't see them at all, or at least it hadn't until now. Very few live pros have done well playing on the Internet. They've written off their lack of success to online poker being a different game, the way an NBA star might explain how he got shown up by an unknown in a street game at Harlem's Rucker Park. And they might have a point. LeBron James wouldn't be the same player without referees to protect him; Doyle Brunson's not Doyle Brunson if he can't stare you in the eyes and read your soul.

But the "unknown" at Rucker Park might very well be a legend on the street, a player who possesses skills polished by thousands of hours spent on the asphalt. There's an argument to be made that what online players like the Ballas are doing—racking up millions of hands a year online, or what an excited statistician might call a *ginormous* sample size—is a better test of poker skill than that offered by the live game. The more hands you play, the less impact chance will have to wreak havoc on your bottom line.

Chance is the only reason a lot of the well-known live pros are even famous at all. Most of them only garnered mainstream attention after winning a major tournament. But tournaments represent a very small sample size. In such a condensed environment there's no escaping the vagaries of luck, no matter how flawlessly and patiently you play. All it takes is one unfortunate card to end your day. The winner of most poker tournaments is rarely the best player in the field, but rather the best player who didn't get unlucky at the wrong time.

Which is why it doesn't make any sense, at least to the Ship It Holla Ballas, that some luckbox who wins a major live tournament should get so much media attention, while the players who grind out a profit online, day after day, get none.

They used to idolize the pros, cheering for guys like Sammy Farha, Daniel Negreanu, and Phil Hellmuth whenever they saw them on TV. But now that they're in Las Vegas, observing them in their element, the hero worship is starting to fade. Whether it's envy or fact, they feel like most of the pros are overrated blowhards.

As for what the pros think of the Ballas: *Who?*

So far, online poker's only noticeable contribution to the live tournament world has come from amateurs—salarymen pursuing the dream that has the entire country and half the world enthralled. Allowing Chris Moneymaker to take $2.5 million out of the poker economy didn't sit well with all of the pros, but it has paid enormous dividends both in terms of prize money and sponsorship opportunities, thanks to all the dead money that keeps flowing in.

The live pros, when they've bothered to acknowledge them at all, have mocked online players. But at this year's World Series, they are being introduced to an entirely new breed of online player, as the first wave of kids—the eighteen-year-olds who discovered poker watching Moneymaker's victory on TV and who have been playing on the Internet every day since—have finally turned 21.

At first, their presence is confusing to the veterans. These tournaments carry four- and five-digit entry fees. *Where the hell are these kids getting the money?* Watching them play only deepens the mystery. Tournament newbies generally trend toward caution and respect. Not these kids—they come out firing, playing with hyperaggression, almost as if they're in a hurry to lose all their chips. And, oh boy, are they cocky.

The Ballas who are old enough to play in World Series events feel like they're going to win every tournament they enter, but halfway through the Series, they don't have anything to show for their efforts. Finally, in the eighteenth event, a pot-limit Hold'em tournament with a first prize of more than $300,000, a breakthrough: Not only have Apathy and Jman survived "the bubble" (they're both guaranteed to win prize money) but with fifty-four players left, Apathy is the chip leader.

Jman, who sits only four spots behind him on the leader board, begins the tournament's second day at the featured table, where he butts heads with one of the best known pros in the world, Men "the Master" Nguyen. A clash of cultures—online versus live, young versus old—is inevitable. A former boat person from Vietnam, Nguyen compensates for his lack of height with big-heeled shoes and an oversized personality. He doesn't have any idea who Jman is. Why should he? He's Men the Master, winner of six WSOP bracelets as well as millions of dollars. Jman is a twenty-one-year-old kid who looks like the boy in *American Pie* who assaults a warm pastry on the kitchen table.

But the kid has something Nguyen doesn't: a cheering section. After fortifying themselves at the house with several rounds of Crown and Cokes, the rest of the Ballas have crowded the bleachers that surround the table. They scream "Ship it!" every time Jman wins a hand—even the tiny pot he takes by default when everyone folds to him before the flop, the poker equivalent of cheering wildly for a baseball player who draws an intentional walk. Their behavior is starting to drive Nguyen a little crazy, which becomes apparent when he sarcastically mimics their war cry.

Good2cu smiles—being obnoxious is certainly one way to get attention. He leads his friends in a raucous cheer when Nguyen gets eliminated from the tournament. The room nears pandemonium when a seating redraw lands Jman and Apathy at the same table. The older players don't look happy. A security guard threatens to toss the Ballas out of the casino if they don't quiet down.

Ultimately it's bad luck that mutes their enthusiasm. Jman gets knocked out in thirty-first place. Apathy manages to hold on for another hour before a bad beat decimates his chip stack. Moments later, the reigning World Series of Poker champion Joe Hachem eliminates him in twenty-fourth place.

None of the Ballas will be getting famous today, but Apathy does leave the Rio with a little more than $5,000 in prize money and an unanticipated consolation prize. He has spent much of the day flirting with a player at his table, an attractive brunette who has done a little modeling for Ralph Lauren. When she informs him that she's breaking up with her live-in boyfriend and needs a place to stay, Apathy tells her she's welcome to crash at the Balla Mansion until she finds a place of her own.

He's surprised but not at all displeased when she accepts. He brings her home to meet the guys. Leave it to Apathy to not only bring a beautiful woman back to the house (finally!), but a beautiful woman who's actually psyched to hang out with them.

Only Raptor fails to greet the household's newest addition with enthusiasm. Hard to blame him, given that he actually witnessed the woman's breakup with her "live-in boyfriend," who more accurately could be described as her husband, his friend and landlord, Doc-Holatchya.

"Hi, Chantel," Raptor says through gritted teeth.

30

My mom to this day doesn't want me to be in Vegas for the Fourth of July because I always have bad stuff happen to me.

—Inyaface

LAS VEGAS, NEVADA (July 2006)

According to BMW's marketing department, the M3 can accelerate from zero to sixty in under six seconds. Good2cu is currently putting that assertion to the test on a half-finished stretch of road at the southern end of the Las Vegas Strip. They're on their way home from the gym—Inyaface riding shotgun, Unarmed in the backseat—enjoying a testosterone- and adrenaline-fueled buzz. None of them can say for sure how fast it took to get the car up to sixty miles per hour, but it was damn quick.

Encouraged by his passengers' awed expressions, Good2cu applies the tiniest bit of extra pressure to the gas, and now they're going eighty. The desert landscape shoots by, its hypnotic uniformity interrupted by the occasional construction vehicle. A billion-dollar investment in this undeveloped portion of the Strip has just been announced, but the work is barely under way. What has been completed is the road: long, straight, flat, and almost completely empty.

So there really isn't any question, when they fly past a police car headed in the opposite direction, as to whether or not they've been spotted.

"Shit," says Good2cu.

"Shit," Inyaface agrees.

Poker is a game of critical decisions. Weigh the factors, plot a course, and commit. Sometimes the decisions get complicated, but most boil down to a simple binary: raise or fold.

Sometimes life is a lot like poker. For Good2cu, folding here means pulling over for the cop. Coming up with a reasonable excuse as to why he's driving so fast in a car that doesn't technically belong to him. Definitely getting a ticket. Possibly losing his license.

Good2cu decides to raise. A little more pressure on the gas, and the car does what it was designed to do.

90 . . . 100 . . . 110 . . .

"What are you doing?" screams Inyaface.

"Getting away!"

"I mean about the traffic light!"

$ $ $

The idea had come to Good2cu while riding shotgun in Raptor's race-ready Subaru: it's time for an automotive upgrade. Past time, really. He's still driving a ten-year-old Saturn that looks like it couldn't even make it to the junkyard. Meanwhile, he's won more than $70,000 in the past month, and there's no reason to think the roll he's on is going to end anytime soon. The purchase makes sense for a young balla—if buying a new laptop and flashy watch are the first two items on the shopping list, a respectable ride is number three.

Good2cu figures he can budget $50,000—around 25 percent of his net worth—for a new set of wheels, although a nittier recess of his poker mind knows that buying new is for suckers. Cars lose a significant portion of their value the moment you drive them off the lot. So he spends a couple of days scanning the classifieds until he settles on the perfect intersection between style and common sense: a slightly used BMW M3.

Any asshole can drive a BMW. But the M3 isn't any old BMW. The factory-issued paneling has been traded out for a more aerodynamic design, the wheel wells expanded to make room for racing tires. But the most important difference is under the hood, a high-performance engine that can produce 333 horsepower.

Good2cu spots an ad for a year-old M3 whose price is right. His good feelings about the car grow stronger when he meets its owner, a guy we'll call Mike Sparks, who he recognizes from the poker tables—a week earlier Sparks made the final table of a World Series event.

Not only is this BMW a balla car, it also has a pedigree.

While Good2cu is kicking the tires and gazing under the hood, pretending he has some clue as to how to judge the condition of a car, Sparks casually asks him what he does for a living.

"I'm a poker player," Good2cu replies.

"A poker player? No way! Me too. Want to play for the car?"

"Are you serious?"

"We'll play heads-up. You win, I'll give you the car. I win, I keep the car, plus another $50,000 from you."

Good2cu has to laugh. *I love this fucking town.* He wants to say yes so badly. But he also knows that Sparks must be a pretty good player, and Midwestern common sense overrides any urge Good2cu might have to gamble with this guy.

"Nah, I'm happy just to pay you for it."

"All right. You got the cash on you?"

"I'm going to have to move some money around. Can I give you five grand now and the rest tomorrow?"

Sparks tosses him the keys.

For the next twenty-four hours, Good2cu drives the car like he's trying to avoid spilling his morning cup of coffee. A near stranger has entrusted him with a sports car in exchange for five grand and a handshake. *This is how professional poker players do business,* Good2cu thinks. *How cool is that?*

The next day he gives Sparks the rest of the cash.

"Don't we need to transfer the title?" Good2cu asks.

"The DMV is closed for the Fourth of July weekend," replies Sparks. "We can do it first thing next week. Until then, treat her right!"

"Of course," says Good2cu, emitting his trademark donkey laugh. "What do you think I am, an idiot?"

$ $ $

Good2cu has been paying too much attention to his rearview mirror—*Did we really just ditch that cop?*—to register the traffic light Inyaface is pointing to. It's not red, which is good, but it's not green either. It's nonoperational, the power being saved for a future time when this section of road is complete. Without working lights providing guidance, the upcoming intersection is supposed to be a four-way stop.

But the BMW wasn't designed to go from 110 to 0 in under two seconds, and the Ford Explorer that's barreling through the intersection straight for them certainly won't be able to do it either.

Raise or fold. Hit the gas or slam on the brakes. Good2cu's survival instinct steers him toward the brakes. But slowing the M3 only seems to bring the Explorer that much closer. Taking his foot off the brake, he stomps on the gas and swerves like a stunt driver would. Only he's no stunt driver.

The Explorer slams into the passenger side, propelling them into a third car that's idling on the far side of the intersection. The BMW comes to rest in a crumpled heap.

Good2cu tries to orient himself. He's dimly aware of someone outside the car pointing a finger at him and yelling, "You fucked up my car! You fucked up my car!"

Inyaface looks shaken but unhurt. Good2cu pivots to look at Unarmed. He has blood all over his face.

"Oh my god. . . . I killed Unarmed!"

"Calm down," says Inyaface. "He's going to be fine."

Unarmed mumbles something that indicates this might be true.

Good2cu takes a second look at Inyaface. "Dude, you're bleeding too."

Inyaface looks down at his feet. His shoe is soaked with blood. When the door caved in, it sliced into the back of his leg. Suddenly he doesn't feel so good.

An ambulance takes Inyaface and Unarmed to the hospital to get stitched up. Despite appearances, both will be fine.

The car is a different story. It's clearly totaled. It's also still registered—and presumably insured—in Mike Sparks's name. Good2cu calls him and brings him up to speed.

"You were drag racing, weren't you?" Sparks laughs. "Whatever. Just tell the cops you were borrowing my car. It's still in my name, so my insurance will take care of it. Then when they send me a check to pay for the car, I'll just ship it to you. Deal?"

"Totally. Thanks for being so cool about this."

"No problem. That's what friends are for."

Man, thinks Good2cu, *everyone is so cool here. I love this fucking town.*

31

We currently have a hot ex-Ralph Lauren model who just moved in with us and is a real sweetheart, futilely trying to clean the house as we speak. If we weren't all such assholes, we'd be helping right now.

—Good2cu

LAS VEGAS, NEVADA (July 2006)

The maids used to clean the house every other day, but it's been nearly a week since their last visit. Common sense says they've quit and are never coming back. In their absence entropy has been allowed to take over. The living room reeks of rotting steak and molding orange juice. Half-eaten containers of Chinese takeout sit on the kitchen table for a week until Good2cu shifts them to the floor to make room for a poker game. Ants have taken up permanent residency in the kitchen, feasting on fried rice and potato chips.

Outside it only gets worse. The pool area is littered with shards of glass, remnants of the bottles TheUsher has been smashing against the wall every time he gets knocked out of a tournament. The hot tub is coated with a foul orange skim—last week, Unarmed dumped a Costco-sized carton of Goldfish crackers into it because, you know, fish need water.

The crowd that's gathered around the dining-room table is oblivious to the wreckage. The Ballas, joined by their new houseguest Chantel, are focused on durrrr. He's playing ten high-stakes no-limit cash games at the same time, each requiring a $10,000 investment. He clicks rapidly among them, making nearly instantaneous decisions determining the outcome of four- and five-figure pots. Durrrr might be immune to the tension, but no one else is. The mood in the room is electric.

Like Good2cu and Raptor, durrrr is too young to play in any of the WSOP events. So instead of competing on poker's biggest stage, he's pushing online poker to its limits.

For all their bluster, the Ballas have made most of their money in relative safety. They've played Sit N Gos by an almost mechanical set of rules, enjoying a steady rate of return. Having made the switch from Sit N Gos to no-limit cash games long ago, durrrr is flying without a net, risking a huge portion of his net worth every time he plays. He's grown accustomed to winning and losing more in a single session than most of his friends have in their online accounts. His friends are suitably awed. They feel like they're watching a race car driver stress testing a vehicle at its extremes—one minute headed for disaster; the next redefining what everyone thought was possible. Durrrr has only been playing seriously for a little more than two years, but people are already starting to compare him to Stu Ungar, the poker wunderkind who won his first two world championships before his thirtieth birthday.

Jman is one of the first to follow durrrr's lead. Giving online cash games his full attention, he's begun playing for higher and higher stakes. At the moment he's considering taking a shot at one of the biggest games available. The final nudge comes from Good2cu and Apathy, who agree to invest in his test flight in exchange for a piece of his winnings.

They sit behind him, sweating every hand, cheering and wincing. The cheers outnumber the winces: Jman finishes the session up $70,000, and promptly transfers his partners their shares.

Good2cu and Apathy celebrate the unexpected windfall by taking Chantel out to dinner, remembering to follow Irieguy's advice that the woman never pays. In return, she serves as an ideal wingwoman: beautiful, outgoing, and flirtatious. After dinner she guides them into Tryst, a popular nightclub. When she peels off for a visit to the bathroom, Good2cu gives Apathy a knowing look.

"You know neither one of us can hook up with her, right?"

"Because?"

"Because of TheUsher." While all the guys are developing crushes on Chantel, TheUsher has fallen the hardest. Earlier that day, he took her to the mall for a $1,500 lingerie-and-swimsuit shopping spree. "If he sees one of us macking on her, it would create way too much drama."

"You're probably right."

They roll back to the house at sunrise, and are surprised to find Jman still hunched over his computer. He looks like a guy whose dog just got run over by a bus.

"What's going on?" asks Apathy.

"Running bad," Jman says.

"You're still—"

"Yeah. Hold on. This clown just check-raised me all in on the turn."

Jman doesn't have a very good hand—a king and a queen, neither of which has paired with the board. He's exhausted and should have gone to bed hours ago. But his instincts, honed by the many thousands of hands he's played online and later discussed with his friends, tell him that his opponent is bluffing. With a simple click of his mouse, he calls a bet that could otherwise pay for a new car.

It's an amazing call. Not only was his opponent bluffing, but he was bluffing with a king and a jack, a hand that Jman has, in the parlance of poker, *dominated*—with one card to come, Jman's odds of winning the hand are roughly 93 percent.

"You are a poker god!" yells Good2cu.

Good2cu, Apathy, and Chantel are jumping up and down, hugging and high-fiving, yelling loud enough to wake up the neighbors. Jman never takes his eyes off the screen, so he's the first to see the unlikely jack fall on the river.

Of all the bad beats Jman has suffered during this session, this one is the worst. He closes his laptop, leans back in his chair, and releases a sound like a small animal dying. In the course of one brutal night, he's gone from being a $70,000 winner to losing every cent in his Full Tilt account, 80 percent of his entire bankroll.

"You all right?" Apathy asks.

"I'm a little sad, but I'll be fine. Just a minor setback."

A sense of discomfort settles across the room, until Good2cu addresses it head-on. "It doesn't seem right that you made money for us, then we just took off like that. I sorta feel like we hit-and-ran you."

"What are you saying?" asks Jman. "That you guys are on the hook for part of the loss?"

It's an odd moment for the group. On the one hand they're friends, and what are friends if not the people who support one another in a situation like this? Some friends might even return some of their winnings to Jman, helping to ease his pain.

But they're also professional poker players, or at least aspire to be. While there may not be much in the way of a gambler's code of ethics, a deal is a deal. And their deal ended when Good2cu and Apathy took their shares.

"You know that's not how it works," Jman says. "Our deal was done. I appreciate the concern. But I'll be all right."

The loss stings, but it's an impressive victory for professionalism. Everyone slinks off to their respective beds.

Two nights later, Apathy and Chantel will be sharing one.

I asked them if their power was out, to which they responded, "No, we've had power all day." Which I found very odd, seeing as *our* power was out, but I didn't think anything more of it since I'm a Ship It Holla Balla, and I don't give a fuck.

—**Good2cu**

LAS VEGAS, NEVADA (July 2006)

Good2cu wakes up covered in sweat.

It's got to be a hundred degrees in his room. He's confused—central air-conditioning usually means a comfortable seventy-two—but not enough to question it too deeply. He has larger concerns. He's awake, so he should be playing poker.

The house is quiet, but not strangely so. The Rolex says noon, which means everyone else has already left for the Rio or is still sleeping. Good2cu stumbles downstairs and tries to start up his laptop, but the screen stays black, even after he double-checks that it's plugged in. He moves on to the TV, the GameCube, the refrigerator. None of them work. Coupled with the lack of air-conditioning, it's pretty clear, even to his foggy brain, that the power is out.

A quick dip in the dirty swimming pool proves mildly restorative, but it's already so hot Good2cu starts sweating again as soon as he climbs out. He walks next door to check with the neighbors, who have been treating him like an old friend ever since he replaced all of their windows. Their power is working just fine.

He wishes Inyaface were here to deal with this, but he's already left for the Rio. As the house slowly stirs to life, the various houseguests give Good2cu a hard time about how (literally) uncool it is, shaming him into calling the electric company. A surprisingly helpful human being promises to send a repair truck to the house right away.

Everyone moves into the pool area to wait it out. Some kid no one's ever seen before pokes his head over the wall. "Is your power out?"

"Yeah," says Good2cu. "We called the power company. Supposedly a guy is on its way."

The kid blinks a few times and disappears behind the wall.

It takes the repairman two hours to arrive, but the issue is identified and resolved in under a minute.

"Something tripped your circuit breaker," the repairman explains, eyeing the myriad laptops, computer monitors, and gaming devices in the house. "You might want to unplug a few things. If it happens again, just flip the switch."

The air-conditioning rumbles to life. So do the laptops. Bonafone passes around a bong. Time to play poker.

They're not even an hour into their session when the power conks out again.

"What did the guy say to do?" Good2cu asks.

"Something about the circuit breaker," mumbles Bonafone.

"Right. Where was that again?"

"The basement?"

"Does this house even have a basement?"

"Fuck this. We need air-conditioning, or we'll die. Let's go to a casino."

They hit the Strip. The houseguests want to play blackjack, and because Good2cu is a Balla, he agrees to stake them. They lose a few hundred dollars, decide blackjack is rigged, and move to a roulette table, where Good2cu bets $200 on red four spins in a row. The wheel stops on black each time.

"Maybe we should've stuck to blackjack," offers one of his friends.

"Yo, Dan!" Good2cu yells at sixty-year-old Dan Harrington, poker's world champion in 1995 who is cashing out chips at the casino cage. Harrington smiles weakly and heads in the opposite direction. Clearly he hasn't heard of the Ship It Holla Ballas yet.

Good2cu's phone buzzes. "You need to come back to the house," Jman tells him. "Now."

"I know. The power's out."

"Yeah, there's that. And the house sort of got robbed."

$ $ $

Without the household electronics to provide cover, the detritus the Ballas have produced over the last few weeks has been promoted to center stage. A policeman stands in the living room, taking notes, eyeing the spent bottle rockets and empty beer cans. "Whoever did it really trashed the place," he says.

"Terrible," Good2cu replies. "Just terrible."

"So what exactly got stolen?"

Everybody starts talking at once. Fourteen laptops. A couple of desktop computers and flat-screen monitors. A few digital cameras and iPods. Bonafone's video camera—considered priceless, as it contained the footage of Good2cu chucking the pool ball through the neighbor's window. Around $10,000 in cash and casino chips.

The cop puts down his pen. These kids are clearly shitting him. "You know insurance fraud is a serious crime."

"It can't be insurance fraud," Raptor assures him, "when you don't have insurance."

In the background, typically mild-mannered Inyaface is screaming into his phone. "We don't have time for this bullshit, Bindar! You've got to freeze these accounts right now!" He covers the phone's mouthpiece and turns to his friends. "Fucking Party Poker. They want everyone's screen names and passwords before they'll put a hold on our accounts."

Inyaface's stress is warranted. Whatever's been taken from the house is chicken feed compared to all the money they've got in their online poker accounts. If the burglars use the stolen computers to log into these accounts, this royal mess is going to become a holy catastrophe. He removes his hand from the phone and resumes screaming. "If you hang up this phone, I will fucking slap you!"

"Well," says the cop, "It seems like you have your hands full. We'll let you know if we make any progress."

Inyaface finishes the call and wipes the sweat off his brow. "What's up with the air-conditioning? It's got to be a hundred and fifty degrees in here."

"Yeah, about that," Good2cu says. "You don't happen to know where the circuit breaker is, do you?"

"Probably on the outside of the house. Why?"

And that's when they remember the kid who poked his head over the fence earlier in the day. The burglars weren't some criminal masterminds. They simply shut off their power and waited for the heat to drive them out of the house. Maybe Dan Harrington and the rest of the poker world don't have any idea who the Ballas are, but they've obviously succeeded in attracting the attention of a few of Vegas's small-time thieves.

Good2cu suddenly feels awful.

This isn't the summer he planned. He's not taking the poker world by storm. He's not sleeping with beautiful women. Mike Sparks has yet to reimburse him for the totaled BMW, which, until the matter gets resolved, has left a gaping hole in his bankroll where $50,000 should be. Apathy and TheUsher are barely speaking to each other because of Chantel. Jman is still struggling to recover from his massive loss. The only thing Good2cu can depend on is online poker, but now the main tool of his trade, his $3,000 state-of-the-art laptop, is gone. While all the houseguests get drunk on warm beer in the backyard, Good2cu crawls into bed and cries.

A few minutes later, Raptor bursts into the room and starts shaking him.

"Get up. Get dressed. We're going to the Rio."

"Not in the mood to play," Good2cu mumbles.

"Not to play. To sweat TheUsher. He's like five spots away from making a final table!"

33

Super Bowl champions have Disneyland. Poker champions have the Spearmint Rhino. Clearly, we have it better.

—Good2cu

LAS VEGAS, NEVADA (July 2006)

It's just after 9:00 P.M. at the Rio, the seventh hour of the second day of the thirty-second event at this year's World Series of Poker. The game is pot-limit hold'em. Fourteen players remain, competing for nine seats at tomorrow's final table. First prize is more than a half-million dollars. Every move is carefully considered and reconsidered. The pace of play is deliberate, the atmosphere thick with tension.

At least until a pack of extremely loud and clearly intoxicated kids storms into the room. They form a wall along the rail behind one of the youngest players left in the tournament, a twenty-three-year-old, white baseball cap stylishly askew, sitting behind a pile of chips. TheUsher smiles at his friends, then announces he's raising. His friends go apeshit. They cheer even louder when he wins the hand.

"Ship it!"

A few of the players laugh. But not everyone is amused. Chau Giang, one of the most respected high-stakes pros in the world, complains to the tournament director, who warns the Ballas to keep it down. They obey, more or less. Even after TheUsher gets Giang to fold a hand with a well-timed reraise. Even after Giang, in what feels to the Ballas like instant karma, gets eliminated from the tournament.

But the closer TheUsher gets to making the final table the harder it becomes for his friends to contain themselves. On the last hand of the night, TheUsher bets all of his chips against Nam Le, a poker pro from California who, six months ago, won a major televised event on the World Poker Tour. Le calls with pocket queens, but TheUsher has pocket kings. The kings hold up, eliminating Le from the tournament. Not only has TheUsher made tomorrow's final table, he'll be starting the day as the chip leader.

The wall behind him erupts. All the pent-up frustration of the day, of the entire trip, gets discharged in a rowdy celebration. TheUsher's friends pour over the rail to congratulate him.

Good2cu starts crying again, but this time they're tears of joy. "I'm so happy for you!" he says, hugging his friend.

"Thanks, man!"

"Oh, by the way. The house got robbed, and all our shit got stolen."

TheUsher doesn't get much sleep that night, especially after learning that the thieves took his desktop computer and the keys to his car. But when he returns to the Rio the next day his spirits are lifted by the forty-plus fans supporting him from the bleachers. They jump and yell and cheer in a way that would make any soccer hooligan proud. The enthusiasm is infectious: soon even the reporters covering the event are yelling, "Ship it!" after every big pot. It's also effective, or at least not ineffective—at the dinner break, only two players remain, TheUsher and yet another longtime professional player, Jason Lester, who finished fourth in the Main Event the year Chris Moneymaker won.

Ten minutes after the break, TheUsher tries to run a big bluff past the pro, but he's misjudged the strength of his opponent's hand and Lester takes all of his chips. Reporters from various poker magazines and online sites rush to interview Lester, while TheUsher's cheering section looks on in gloomy silence.

One of the reporters, waiting for an opportunity to speak with Lester, turns to TheUsher. "You just won $284,000. What are you going to do next?"

TheUsher breaks into a huge smile. "We're going to the Rhino!"

$ $ $

The Spearmint Rhino sends a party bus to pick them up at the Balla Mansion. When they arrive at the strip club, they're whisked into a private VIP room, complete with its own bar.

Mike Sparks, who has been hanging out with the Ballas so much he's become a sort of honorary member of the crew, makes the first toast of the night. "Meeting you guys has been one of the most amazing experiences of my life. There's a lot I could say, but I think I can sum it up in two words: 'Ship it!' "

What follows is a blur of lap dances, champagne, and top-shelf drinks. Good2cu peppers his friends with philosophical questions while naked women grind into his lap. Raptor and Unarmed do the world's worst robot dance. Durrrr argues with Mike Sparks over whether they should be drinking Monet or Dom until, having downed too much of each, he sprints to the bathroom and pukes. Bonafone complains to anyone who will listen that he has somehow managed to lose the $4,000 in cash he earned from investing in a piece of TheUsher's action.

"You didn't lose it," Good2cu yells at him. "You spent it all on drinks and lap dances!"

Apathy and Chantel canoodle in a dark corner of the room. TheUsher notices, but he's not going to let it bother him, not tonight. He can't decide which is cooler: that he just won a quarter-million dollars, or that he's getting a lap dance in the VIP room while sitting next to Phil Ivey, arguably the best poker player on the planet.

The sun has already risen by the time the Ballas stumble outside and reboard the party bus. For months to come, all of them will swear it was one of the greatest nights of their lives, even if none of them can remember all the details. They don't know exactly how much it cost them, but they have a rough idea—tallying credit card receipts and surveying the absence of cash in their wallets, they figure $40,000, roughly split between drinks and dances.

Fuck it. They can always make more money tomorrow.

34

I imagine that if I had walked down the road and told the neighbors that the owners of this house weren't even twenty-one years old (yet owned the house), they'd have looked at me as if I had a few screws loose.

—Chris Vaughn, "Lifestyles of the $ick and Famous," in *Bluff*

FORT WORTH, TEXAS/EAST LANSING, MICHIGAN (August 2006)

Four days after TheUsher's second-place finish, the World Series Main Event gets under way. Its $10,000 entry fee is no longer unique—there are now dozens of tournaments with similar buy-ins and a few that are even bigger. But the winner still gets to call himself the world champion of poker. Victory here means instant fame. Television appearances. Invitations to celebrity tournaments. Sponsorship deals. And thanks to a record-shattering field of 8,773—most of them winning seats via online satellites—this year's winner will also take home an all-time best $12 million.

But it won't be a Balla. Good2cu, Raptor, durrrr, Deuce2High, and Bonafone are all still too young to play. Inyaface gets eliminated on the first day, Apathy on the second. Jman also falls short of making the money. TheUsher, still running well, survives the longest, making it to Day Four and earning $30,000 for finishing in 391st place.

The World Series didn't provide the splashy debut they'd hoped for, but the Ballas are clearly gaining exposure. Jman gets some face time on ESPN when the network airs footage of his eighteenth-place finish in a tournament he played last winter. Apathy wins a major on-line tournament, then creates an inadvertent controversy on Two Plus Two when he casually mentions having trashed his hotel room in Monte Carlo in the spring. The supporters and haters form the usual battle lines, giving props to his carefree hedonism or slamming him for irresponsible excess.

Somehow the stink never reaches Raptor. In the world of Two Plus Two, he remains a beloved celebrity. The kid who ran $450 into $20,000. The creator of the Quad Monitor Set-Up. The issuer of Raptor Challenges. His posts routinely generate tons of positive feedback from a growing number of fanboys whose devotion is borderline stalkerish.

So it's actually news in the poker world when Raptor, still just twenty, and durrrr, nineteen, buy a half-million-dollar house in Fort Worth. After they post pictures of the place on Two Plus Two, the poker magazine *Bluff* dispatches a reporter to check it out. He writes about the two seventy-three-inch plasma TVs, mounted side by side in the living room. The six Xbox 360s scattered throughout the house. The full-time personal assistant who makes sure the dishes get washed and the bills get paid. The young poker players' habit of tipping visiting laborers and deliverymen with crisp $100 bills and $200 bottles of Johnny Walker Blue.

The reporter jumps at the opportunity to watch them ply their trade. Raptor plays ten tables at once, a mix of Sit N Gos and cash games, spread across two computer monitors. He seems to be suffering throughout, shouting expletives, glowering at the screen in disbelief, but after two hours he leans back in his Herman Miller Aeron chair and casually informs the reporter that he's won $40,000.

Then it's durrrr's turn: multitabling at stakes ten times bigger than the games Raptor just played, he wins nearly $200,000 in just forty-five minutes.

The article gets titled "Lifestyles of the $ick and Famous," which Raptor thinks is pretty funny because he really hasn't been feeling all that $ick lately. Whether it's his new role as a homeowner in an up-scale neighborhood or the weight of a $4,400 monthly mortgage payment, the kid who just six months before advised Good2cu to "jump around the world" and party with strippers is becoming the guy who will scold you for resting your feet on the coffee table. Raptor's turn-ing into a curmudgeon in his young age, eschewing frat parties and crowded bars in favor of cooking at home, shooting pool with durrrr on their new regulation-size table, or watching episodes of *The Wire* in bed with Haley. As far as he's concerned, nothing beats hanging out with your girlfriend in a $10,000 Tempur-Pedic California king.

While Raptor trends older, Good2cu rededicates himself to colle-giate living, minus the inconvenience of classes. He moves into a sprawling off-campus apartment complex near Michigan State, room-ing with a friend of his who's still enrolled at the university. There's a swimming pool and plenty of young women. But this is a way station, not a destination. He's tasted the life he wants to lead, that of a poker celebrity, and remains committed to attaining that goal.

Good2cu hires a designer to create Ship It Holla Balla business cards, although he ends up giving most of them to drunk college kids at parties. Most days he adds new content to the Web site. His writing style is heavily influenced by Tucker Max, the lawyer turned author who's taken up near-permanent residency on the *New York Times* Best Seller List with chronicles of his drunken, debaucherous, and occa-sionally misogynistic behavior. Good2cu hopes to come across as the same sort of charming scoundrel. Take, for example, his account of a keg party at Apathy's house in Ontario, where two sorority sisters—who he calls "Sam" and "Leslie"—get into a fight over Apathy, interrupting Good2cu's chance to score:

> My head was facing the door and I saw her barge in just as her sister was swallowing my penis. This upset her. She screamed, "If I don't get to hook up with Apathy, I expect my sisters not to hook up with his friends." This was a pretty awkward moment so I quickly put my clothes on and did what I always do when awkward moments take place: drink more beer.

The post generates a reaction, just not the one Good2cu intended—evidently grown-ups have discovered the Internet as well. His dad suggests he show some class. Mom sarcastically asks if he was wearing a condom. When Good2cu meets Apathy's parents during a trip to Toronto, they don't seem particularly pleased to meet their son's new friend.

Good2cu doesn't take the condemnation too seriously. He thinks they're missing the big picture. He's just doing what has always felt most natural to him: inhabiting a persona. What are video games, if not an easy and safe way to take on a new identity, someone cooler and more powerful than you are? It's what he does every time he plays poker, hiding behind his avatar and using "Good2cu" to project whatever image at the table he thinks will result in the most success.

Last year, he read *The Game*, author Neil Strauss's autobiographical investigation into the world of self-proclaimed "Master Pick-up Artists," and its lessons have stuck with him. The book's characters would be the first to admit that they used to be geeks, stumbling awkwardly every time they approached a woman. So they studied seduction as if it were a mathematical equation that could be solved using a handful of simple steps. They adopted aliases like "Mystery" and "Styles," figuring that using your real name during a seduction would be like filling out a job application with your World of Warcraft handle. They're two completely different worlds. The goal is not to be yourself, but to inhabit an alter ego free from the emotional baggage that years of geekdom have left behind. At the end of his story, Strauss argues that however you might judge their methods, his characters were able to achieve a kind of self-actualization—when you try on a new personality for a while, you may feel more empowered to change the things you don't like about your old one, effecting a positive transformation that might actually stick.

Like many others—*The Game* hovered around the top of the *New York Times* Best Seller List for a couple of months—Good2cu responded strongly to the book and its message. He is self-aware enough to know that he's creating a persona. "I am not some drunken white gangsta with a serious case of ADD who wanders the world in search of pussy," he writes on the Ship It Holla Balla Web site. "Although I must admit I do think I'm a gangsta."

But the character he's chosen to play has a more serious liability than parental disapproval—unless he's very successful at what he does, he'll come off looking like a horse's ass. While he figures he won close to $70,000 online during his six weeks in Vegas, if you add up the bar tabs, strip clubs, a couple of unsuccessful forays into live cash games (including a $10,000 loss to the legendary entertainer Wayne Newton), and the *still* unreimbursed cost of a totaled BMW M3 (Mike Sparks has stopped returning his calls), he's actually returned to Michigan $30,000 in the red.

Hoping to make up the deficit in a hurry, he tries to expand his multitabling comfort zone, playing as many as eighteen Sit N Gos at a time, and takes occasional shots at bigger no-limit cash games.

And for a while, it works. He fails to accomplish his stated goal of earning six figures in a month, but he does manage to make back the $30,000, allowing him to continue living a lifestyle he's still struggling to define.

35

The biggest disappointment was that nobody random holla'd at the Ship It Holla Ballas today. I guess Europe just doesn't know us yet.

—Apathy

BARCELONA, SPAIN (September 2006)

'm so rich! I made $100,000 last year! Check out my Rolex! I'm a Ship It Holla Balla!"

Even by the (low) standards of this turista bar—a sponge for young backpackers thanks to its proximity to the youth hostel next door—Good2cu is off-the-charts drunk. His earsplitting declarations of greatness can be heard from one end of the crowded room to the other.

Along with Apathy, TheUsher, and Deuce2High, he flew to Barcelona to play in a European Poker Tour event with a $6,500 entry fee. None of them cashed in the tournament, and none of them really care. They're staying at a luxury hotel in the center of the city, eating crazy good food at expensive restaurants whose names they can't remember, and carousing through the streets like sailors on leave. What's not to love?

The love affair hasn't always been mutual. The hostess at the restaurant where they ate earlier in the night quickly appraised them for exactly what they were before leading them to a table hidden away in the farthest corner of the back patio. Four bottles of wine later, they'd proven her right.

Tired of getting the stink eye from the classier joints, they set off in search of a place better suited to their temperament. A helpful cab driver brought them to this bar, where Good2cu is drunkenly ticking off a list of his financial assets in an attempt to impress the señoritas.

Apathy, who's been playing pool with some girls from Australia, doesn't want to be a cockblocker, but he's starting to fear for his friend's safety. "You might want to keep it down," he says to Good2cu after he's pulled him aside. "You're going to get robbed if you don't shut up."

"But I'm a Balla, baby," Good2cu says, his eyes drifting in and out of focus. "A shot calla. Ain't no worries here."

So that didn't work.

The next best way to help him, his friends decide, is to rob him before someone else does. They take Good2cu's wallet, passport, and Rolex, then steer him outside to get some fresh air. They're congratulating themselves on their quick thinking when they see Good2cu wander into the street, with a girl on each arm, disappearing into the night.

"Seriously?" says TheUsher. "A threesome?"

"Somehow I don't think that's going to happen," says Apathy.

The remaining Ballas bounce from the bar to a club and don't get back to the hotel until sunrise. As they approach Good2cu's room, they take bets on whether or not he'll have company. The consensus is *highly improbable*. But the door to his room is slightly ajar and the noise emanating from inside tells a different story. They hear the unmistakable sound of sex. Loud sex. Vigorous sex. *Porn star* sex.

Which is precisely what it is. Good2cu is naked on the bed, but he's alone and snoring loudly. The sex noises are coming from the in-room porn that's playing at full volume on the television. The mystery of how he got home last night, sans wallet, gets solved when they notice Deuce2High's laptop is missing—apparently Good2cu used it as collateral to placate a cab driver angry at being stiffed.

They're able to recover the computer in time to make their plane to London, where they check into another luxury hotel and play another $6,500 buy-in EPT event that none of them cashes in. They're able to laugh off these failed investments because they know they can simply log in to an online card room and make it all back.

This is how Ship It Holla Ballas roll.

36

Religious leaders of all denominations and faiths are seeing gambling problems erode family values. If Congress had not acted, gamblers would soon be able to place bets not just from home computers, but from their cell phones while they drive home from work or their BlackBerries as they wait in line at the movies.

—Representative Jim Leach, (R-IA)

WASHINGTON, D.C. (September 2006)

It's nearly fall in the nation's capitol, and Election Day is approaching. The Republicans, despite controlling the White House and both branches of Congress, are worried.

With good reason: President George W. Bush's approval ratings have dropped below 40 percent thanks to, in no particular order, a perceived failure to step up during Hurricane Katrina, rising dismay and hopelessness over America's involvement in Iraq, and an ongoing scandal surrounding the president's relationship to a corporate lobbyist named Jack Abramoff. As the president is safely ensconced in his second term, it's Congress that's in line to take the expected beating when voters cast their ballots.

In an effort to mobilize the socially conservative wing of the Republican base, House Speaker Dennis Hastert spends the summer pushing forward a red-meat package of ten bills dubbed the "American

Values Agenda." Increased protections for the Pledge of Allegiance, the American flag, and unborn fetuses. Stricter prohibitions against cloning and gay marriage.

Oh, yeah, and a ban on Internet gambling.

The online gambling bill is similar to one that passed the Senate in 2000. For those who enjoy playing the what-if game, the 2000 bill could have terminated the poker boom before it even got started, had it not been scuttled in the House, thanks in large part to the diligent lobbying efforts of Jack Abramoff. Enacting the ban now would help Republicans create distance from the scandal surrounding the lobbyist while appeasing church leaders and anti-gambling groups.

The version that reaches the House floor, merging separate proposals from Representatives Bob Goodlatte of Virginia and Jim Leach of Iowa, would expand the Wire Act—a federal law enacted during the Kennedy administration to prevent gamblers from betting on horse races via telegraph—to include Internet gambling. It doesn't go after the players themselves, but the financial institutions that handle the payments to and from the online casinos.

Goodlatte-Leach passes the House by a healthy 317–93 margin, but it's not expected to survive the Senate. There's not even enough support for the bill to *get* a vote, at least not before Election Day. Goodlatte-Leach appears destined to suffer a quiet demise.

Enter Senator Bill Frist, the Majority Leader who unwittingly added to the Republican woes, a year earlier, when he tried to insert the Senate into the debate over Terri Schiavo, a Florida woman in a vegetative state whose husband sought to remove her from life support. On the day before Congress adjourns for the upcoming elections, Frist holds a vote on a bill called The Port Security Improvement

Act. It's a no-brainer, given the nation's ongoing War on Terror. Who doesn't want safer ports? The bill passes unanimously.

But most of the senators fail to notice or otherwise ignore a new provision that was quietly tacked on in the wee hours prior to the vote: Title VIII, better known as the Unlawful Internet Gambling Enforcement Act (UIGEA). Goodlatte-Leach has passed the Senate.

Two weeks later, President Bush signs the bill into law. It won't do much to sway the elections—the Democratic Party will win a majority in both the House and Senate—but the UIGEA will wreak immediate havoc on the Internet poker industry. Party Poker, home to a whopping 40 percent of the world's online action, announces that they'll no longer be serving American players. The site's corporate parent, the publicly traded British company PartyGaming, watches its stock tank, losing $4 billion in value overnight. Other companies scramble to divest themselves of their American operations, in a couple of cases for a nominal one dollar, in an effort to avoid tangling with the law.

It's not quite a death knell for online poker: in the short run, many American players simply move their business to PokerStars and Full Tilt Poker, privately held companies that are willing to risk tomorrow's legal complications for today's increase in market share.

As for the long-term implications, no one knows what to expect. Good2cu bemoans the uncertain future on the Ship It Holla Web site:

> It now looks like [online poker] may all be over. I have no idea if I'll be able to successfully return to the real world. I fear I may be like one of those ex-college athletes who is doomed to talk about his "glory days" for the rest of his life . . . but if this is the end, it has been one hell of a ride.

37

Now, it's a strange phenomenon of this digital age that you can partially follow someone's course in life simply by reading the person's changing MSN screen name.

—Nick Gair, "Ship It!!!" in *Bluff*

NIAGARA FALLS, CANADA (October 2006)

Like so many other twenty-somethings, Nick Gair is trying to figure out what the hell to do with his life. He's in a band—Max Galactic and the Cloud of Evil—and harbors dreams of becoming the next John Prine, but admits his fear on his MySpace blog that he'll never write a song even half as good as "Donald and Lydia." He has ambitions of becoming a journalist, but on the rare occasions one of the stories he's written on spec actually elicits a response from an editor, it's been "thanks, but no thanks."

Were it not for online poker, he might be forced to try his hand at gainful employment. He's playing a Sit N Go on PokerStars one day when he notices that Inyaface, a tournament regular and an acquaintance from college, has changed his avatar. His new icon is more of a corporate logo, hot pink text over a purple background, promoting a Web site called ShipItHollaBalla.com. Gair doesn't know it, but he's looking at a prize-winning design: Good2cu recently ran a contest on the Ship It Holla Web site, awarding $25 to whomever could create

the best-looking logo, an effort to generate buzz—at least familiarity—
during the many hours spent grinding at the virtual tables.

And right now, it's doing exactly what it was intended to do. Gair
spends the rest of the day on the Ship It Holla site, reading Good2cu's
accounts of the past summer's adventures. When he's finished, Gair
still isn't sure whether the Ballas are poker prodigies or cocky shit-
heads, but one thing is clear—the stories are entertaining as hell. Re-
introducing himself, this time as an interested journalist, he reaches
out to Inyaface.

Good news: the entire crew is getting together for a World Poker
Tour event in Niagara Falls, an easy drive from Gair's apartment in
Toronto. He can follow their progress in the tournament, perhaps
getting lucky enough to see one of the Ballas make the final table.

Bad news: by the time Gair arrives in Niagara Falls, on the second
day of the three-day tournament, all of the Ballas have already been
eliminated.

But that's not the worst part.

He's also missed the chance to see durrrr swim through the fountain just outside the casino's entrance—fulfilling the terms of a $1,000
prop bet—and sprint naked through a Denny's for $500 more.

He's too late to witness their $4,000 adventure in a local strip club
and, later, the wild rumpus at the Ballas's hotel after one of their two
new stripper friends, who passed out in Good2cu's bed, locks herself
out of the room, half-dressed and half-awake, and has to call her husband to come pick her up.

Gair has missed all three noise complaints issued by the hotel as
well as Raptor's attempt to assuage the manager with a fully committed imitation of comedian Dave Chappelle impersonating singer Rick
James—a performance that was, to put it mildly, politically incorrect,

and, as far as the manager was concerned, ample reason for kicking them out of the hotel.

And he didn't get to see durrrr, in the midst of all the chaos, book another ho-hum $140,000 win.

It seems Gair has missed the entire story. With nowhere to stay and no reason to linger, the Ballas are about to skip town and make the eighty-mile road trip to London, Ontario, where one of Apathy's friends is throwing a Halloween party.

Apathy notices the aspiring journalist's disappointment. "You want to come along?"

Gair eagerly accepts.

He follows them to a local Walmart, where he watches them spend $2,000 on Halloween costumes. Durrrr alone drops $500 on a handful of silver necklaces and a business suit he'll never wear again just so he can tell people he's Tom Cruise in *Risky Business*. Jman, the crew's resident funny guy, buys a tutu, tiara, wand, wings, and a large sack of distributable sweets. "I'm the Candy Fairy," he announces.

Outside the store, the Ballas realize that there's no way all of the purchases are going to fit in their cars, so they pay a cab driver $270 to ferry their costumes to the party.

Gair will spend three weeks wrestling with insomnia, agonizing over the article's structure, finally cranking out a draft in a drug- and alcohol-induced frenzy. His first attempt to sell the piece causes him nearly as much pain as the writing. *Canadian Poker Player* magazine rejects it, leading Gair to consider "taking a bath with my toaster." Out of desperation he submits the article to *Bluff*, an American publication with a much larger circulation. To Gair's great surprise, the editors love it, although they won't be able to publish it for another six months.

In a time of twenty-four-hour news cycles and Twitter, six months is an eternity. By the time the article runs, much will have changed for the Ballas. Not so much will change for Gair—the article turns out to be the first and last piece of paid journalism he'll ever write. He'll still devote his creative energy to his band, but Max Galactic and the Cloud of Evil will break up a couple of years later when one of its members heads off to law school. Gair will soon find himself studying to become a financial analyst.

He may never write a song or story that moves its audience in quite the same way that "Donald and Lydia" does, but his article for *Bluff* succeeds in capturing the spirit of the Ship It Holla Ballas, circa 2006:

Now, most kids go off to college and do some things they'd rather their parents didn't know about. The Ballas, around the same age, are up to the same things. However, free from both parental and financial constraints, the Ballas live in a world almost entirely free of rules or boundaries. And, just as there are a range of personalities in the group, the members of the crew engage in various levels of excess.

However, if at any point in the evening someone begins to discuss poker, the atmosphere suddenly changes. Upon the mention of any hand, real or hypothetical, things turn to business. Amidst all the commotion of the frat party, a Balla will consider a proposed situation and offer his sincere opinion of what the correct play is. Although they joke about almost anything else, they take cards very seriously.

The "Ship it Holla Ballas" constantly walk the line between being too-rich and too-young, leading a vacuous lifestyle devoted to foolish spending, and being an inseparable band of comrades, genuine scholars of the science of gambling.

Prior to the Internet, the last technology that had any real effect on the way people sat down and talked together was the table.

—Technologist Clay Shirky

EAST LANSING, MICHIGAN (December 2006)

The Single-Table Tournament Forum isn't the only destination on Two Plus Two. There is a forum for nearly every variation of poker, from the relatively ancient game of Stud to a new creation called Badugi, and every kind of bankroll, from micro limits to high stakes. There are groups dedicated to politics, travel, and golf. One forum is devoted entirely to discussions about poker legislation; another focuses on the psychology of the game. There's even a forum *about* the forums, where members can ask questions concerning the inner workings of the Web site.

But the two most popular areas are Beats, Brags, and Variance (BBV)—a place for players to boast about wins and whine about losses—and News, Views, and Gossip (NVG), where they can discuss current events and trade rumors. NVG is also where players go to post jokes, make lists of favorites, create polls, give shout-outs, issue conspiracy theories, vent rage, and laugh at the misfortune of others.

As salacious as some of the NVG threads are, there are limits as to what can actually be said. The rules stated in Two Plus Two's FAQ are fairly straightforward—participants aren't allowed to post commercial solicitations or any material that is copyrighted, trademarked, or deemed offensive. Moderators are given the power to edit or delete any post that violates these rules and, in more egregious cases, ban the poster. Back home in Michigan, Good2cu gets a firsthand taste of the "banhammer" when he posts a derogatory comment about poker pro Kathy Liebert and gets suspended from the site for a week.

In 2004, responding to an environment that many perceive as being overly regulated, a group of young poker players start a rival Web site. Neverwin Poker promises uncensored conversations about poker players, by poker players, with little editorial control. Profanity and pornography are not only allowed but encouraged. The site aspires to become the TMZ or Perez Hilton of the poker world, printing the stories that Two Plus Two would never touch, like a well-known poker pro's secret past as an actor in a fetish porno.

Despite alienating almost everyone over the age of twenty-five, Neverwin Poker generates enough traffic to sell a few banner ads. But one of NWP's founders, the eponymous Neverwin, has begun to grasp the same idea that Good2cu has been batting around: being Internet famous might be a currency in and of itself.

In the fall of 2006, NWP reporter DanDruff "breaks" the story of a budding romantic relationship between Neverwin and Chantel, who is single after parting ways with both DocHolatchya and Apathy. Dan-Druff's story follows these star-crossed lovers from their chance meeting aboard a poker cruise in March to the moment they both decide to end their current relationships so they can be with each other. The piece is presented as an effort to "set the story straight," a counterpoint to the supposed rumor and innuendo floating around Two Plus Two.

The only problem is that very little of it is actually true. Neverwin and Chantel are sleeping with each other, but everything else in the story is largely embellished.

"We would go home and read all the threads about it and get amusement," Neverwin later admits. "It was always more entertaining to read about yourself or about somebody that you knew really well."

For the next few weeks, Neverwin and Chantel see their fame (infamy?) increase exponentially, at least within the poker community. But their proverbial fifteen minutes gets cut short by a series of even juicier scandals.

The first surrounds the dramatic arrival on the scene of Brandi Hawbaker, a very attractive twenty-four-year-old self-proclaimed "free spirit," who turns Two Plus Two's NVG forum into her personal diary, providing an intimate and ongoing account of a titillating dispute with the fifty-six-year-old poker pro "Captain" Tom Franklin.

According to Brandi, she allowed Captain Tom to mentor her through the poker world, giving her lessons, helping her decide which tournaments to play, and, apparently, managing her bankroll. She naively believed him when he spoke of maintaining propriety—*Wouldn't want to give people the wrong idea about an older man and a younger beauty, now would we?*—until, according to Brandi, their relationship took a sordid turn in a hotel room in Indiana. It was there, Brandi claims, that Captain Tom climbed naked into bed with her and rubbed his penis against her back, an activity he called "huggling." When she refused to play along, Captain Tom responded by tightening his hold on the money she had entrusted him with.

The post kicks off an avalanche of comments. Most are sympathetic to Brandi, until a player named Newhizzle chimes in. It seems that he used to have a similar relationship with Brandi—poker guidance, with blurry sexual boundaries—until she logged into one of his online accounts and lost $30,000 of his money in a high-stakes cash game. According to Newhizzle, the ensuing argument led Brandi to try to kill herself in a hotel bathroom, slicing her wrist with a broken wine bottle and using the blood to write a message on the wall:

I will fly one day.

Brandi responds with venom, using the forum to deny the story and criticize Newhizzle for his shortcomings as both a poker player and a sexual partner. The back-and-forth drags on for weeks, shifting the group consensus: Brandi is mentally unstable, a creator of "drama-bombs," a walking trainwreck. The opinion becomes even more entrenched after she gets into a public altercation with Dutch Boyd at the Bellagio—she calls him a "schizophrenic asshole"; he responds by calling her "an evil bitch." Needless to say, Brandi becomes an instant celebrity on Two Plus Two; from here on out her every move will be chronicled and annotated with detailed descriptions and commentary.

Brandi has to share the spotlight, however, when Two Plus Two's other founder, David Sklansky, uses the site to unreel a series of controversial opinions and personal revelations. Even by comparison to his mercurial partner, Sklansky has always come off as eccentric. He's clearly brilliant, but his intelligence is attached to a social tone deafness that suggests some form of autism. In the past he's used Two Plus Two to speculate about whether chimpanzees could ever be "trained" to be as intelligent as humans (through a process that sounds an awful lot like eugenics) and whether a woman should ever be president (no way, he argues, given the effects of premenstrual syndrome).

This month he issues a $50,000 challenge to Christian fundamentalists—a group he dismisses as "relatively stupid (or uninterested in learning)"—that he can beat any one of them on the math portion of the SAT. The post gets picked up by several other Web sites, drawing the attention of Ken Jennings, a devout Mormon famous for winning the TV game show *Jeopardy!* a record seventy-four times in a row. When Jennings publicly accepts Sklansky's challenge, the poker guru quickly backpedals, revising the wager to exclude members of the Church of Latter-Day Saints.

But the real fun begins when fifty-five-year-old Sklansky reveals that he once had an intimate relationship with a sixteen-year-old runaway. Five years ago, after meeting on an Internet dating site, he and "Saura" lived together for eight months until he discovered that she wasn't really twenty years old, as she'd claimed.

The message boards get flooded with comments, especially after Saura agrees to do a Q&A, fielding a barrage of questions from how much cash she accepted from Sklansky to the size of his penis. Sklansky—who argues that he'd never have engaged in the relationship had he known her real age—handles the hurly burly with what appears to be a detached sense of amusement. He doesn't come across as embarrassed or ashamed, and, as some speculate, he may even be profiting from the controversy. In the online business world, traffic equals money, and the nearly forty pages of questions Saura receives suggest that the site is doing better than ever.

Good2cu loves reading about the drama and being part of such a fascinating community of freewheeling degenerates. Another long, drab winter has descended upon Michigan, but thanks to his Internet connection, he lives in a world that is bigger, stranger, and more wonderful than anything he can see from the windows of his apartment.

39

Regular folks who used to come home from their job as a waiter, construction worker, or retail manager and log on to Party Poker for some relaxation are no longer doing that. Not only have they stopped, they basically think that it is against the law to play online and they are no longer even interested. Now, there are still plenty of fish obviously. America never held the exclusive rights to bad poker play. But removing a few million recreational American players from the pool of fish is likely to have an effect on the ebb and flow of money online.

—Irieguy

EAST LANSING, MICHIGAN/COLORADO SPRINGS, COLORADO (Winter 2006)

So far the UIGEA has turned out to be more smoke than fire. Americans can still play poker online, and many do. But a chill has settled over the once-scorching poker economy. Per the law, banks and credit card companies will no longer transfer money in or out of online poker accounts. It's a small speed bump: Intermediaries like Neteller, a payment processing company located on the Isle of Man where it enjoys protection from prosecution, rush in to fill the breach. But the hostile climate intimidates many new and recreational players, vastly shrinking the pool of easy money, making online poker that much tougher to beat.

Good2cu misses the games on Party Poker. He hasn't enjoyed the same kind of success on Full Tilt and PokerStars, where his opponents don't seem to make as many mistakes as they used to. The days of mindlessly grinding out a steady return seem to be slipping away. Good2cu isn't losing money, but he isn't winning very much either.

That said, he still has almost $200,000 in the bank, a small fortune for a kid sharing the rent on an apartment in a Midwestern college town.

"Imagine being twenty and able to buy all the movies and DVDs you want for like two hours of work," he blogs. "Obviously, you would too."

The holidays are an opportunity to indulge his consumerist impulses while showing everyone how far he's come since his days as a self-described "punkass broke college student." He splurges on Christmas gifts for his family: a $750 Best Buy gift card for his dad, an LCD TV with a built-in DVD player for his mom, and a brand-new laptop for his sister.

Good2cu has grown very comfortable playing this new role. He loves the awed expressions on the faces of the tellers at the bank when he withdraws thousands of dollars in cash. He's overflowing with confidence, or at least bravado. During the long weekend after Thanksgiving, he uploads a picture of himself to a Web site called "Hot or Not," where visitors rate attractiveness on a scale of 1 to 10. Good2cu gets a 9.9, which he brags about on his Web site to all the "gold diggers and hottie-chasers of the world":

APPLY TO BE MY GIRLFRIEND

I've been playing the field for over two years now, and am now ready to stay in my apartment all day long having long sexual marathons.

In case you haven't heard of me I'll sum up the important details (i.e. why you are dying to be my girlfriend).

—I am a 9.9 on Hot or Not

—I make more than your boyfriend

—I also make more than your dad

—I enjoy traveling the world and spending large sums of money

—I am the epitome of an alpha male

—I am famous on the Internet

—Am often accused of being humble

Basically, I'm every woman's dream.

He's joking—mostly. Good2cu isn't someone who takes himself very seriously. But there's a small part of himself that's willing to entertain the notion that at least some of it might be true.

As long as he can keep making money, of course. It would help if Mike Sparks paid him the $50,000 he owes him for the wrecked BMW, but Mike stopped answering his calls months ago. So Good2cu does what he thinks a Balla should do. Using Chantel as a go-between, he sends word to Sparks that he's ready to take legal action if the debt's not settled immediately.

Sparks calls back right away. The conversation is brief and to the point. He tells Good2cu that he's never going to see the money, and if he ever calls again or hires a lawyer, Sparks will have him killed.

Good2cu isn't sure how seriously to take the death threat, but it's enough to convince him to drop the matter, chalking it up to a lesson learned, albeit a painful and expensive one. So much for any romantic notions he had about professional gamblers honoring their word.

He spends the first half of the holidays with his dad in Okemos, the second half with his mom, who is vacationing in Colorado with her new husband. Bonafone lives in Colorado Springs. Good2cu hasn't seen him since the World Series of Poker, but they've maintained their friendship through the forum and the occasional chat online. Good2cu gives him a call.

Bonafone celebrates Good2cu's arrival with a party. They mix generous servings of "Ecto-Coolers," a fluorescent green concoction made with vodka, Red Bull, and Hpnotiq, named for its resemblance to a Hi-C/*Ghostbusters* tie-in from childhood. "You seriously need no game to get laid on this stuff," Good2cu boasts, then sets out to prove it.

His playbook is straight out of *The Game*. He "negs" a girl, telling her that he heard she was a bad kisser, predictably inspiring her to prove him wrong. From there he moves on to "peacocking," showing off his Rolex, dropping hints about his net worth. Smooth or not, the moves work—he winds up skinny-dipping in the hot tub with two girls, before pulling one of them into the snow for a play-wrestling match that carries over into a bedroom.

In the morning, a hungover but freshly sexed Good2cu calls a limo service to pick him up. One of Bonafone's high school friends sees him off.

"I hope I'm as cool as I seem on the Internet," Good2cu tells him.

The expression on the kid's face makes it clear that he is.

$ $ $

Good2cu returns to Michigan ready to take his game to the next level. Fuck Sit N Gos—he's ready to dominate the cash games just like Raptor and durrrr. The journey begins with a $100,000 downswing, including a $65,000 loss in a single day.

"This is not even close to a significant loss at this level," he blogs. "But the psychological damage is much greater than the monetary blow. How am I supposed to grind out a few thousand dollars a day when it is going to take me a month to win back what I lost in one day? Logically, I know it's the only way, but my emotions want to have all the money back, now. This results in me playing an emotional game, which of course results in further losses."

Reeling from the setback, he can't muster the energy to maintain his public persona. When his poker sessions end, he retreats to the couch to watch *The Sopranos*. "Tony Soprano is a motherfucking bad-ass balla," he writes. "And he is depressed too. How depressing."

The news gets worse. On January 15, Stephen Lawrence and John Lefebvre, the two Canadians who founded Neteller, are arrested while traveling through the United States and charged with violating the UIGEA. Neither man is still actively associated with Neteller, but that doesn't stop the FBI from freezing the company's assets, even after the current management announces that they're pulling out of the American market.

Good2cu is unable to access the $30,000 he has in his Neteller account, and he's not sure if he's ever going to see it again. The future of online poker—and, by extension, the lifestyle it's helped him attain—is starting to look bleak. "Logically, I know all of this doesn't matter," he writes. "I am not even of legal drinking age. [But] I am deathly afraid of failing. Poker is my life. I could not go back to living like a normal person. How could I be content making $100,000 a year when I've made that in a month? I could never feel alive at a real job."

He decides to blow off some steam, going to a party with his friend DieselBoy. It feels good not to think about poker for a night. They meet a girl who accompanies them back to Good2cu's apartment. She seems amenable to sleeping with either of them. When she ducks into the bathroom to freshen up, DieselBoy suggests they flip a coin.

"Heads!" calls Good2cu.

The coin lands tails. Good2cu spends the night on the couch, listening to bestial grunts emanating from his bedroom, taking stock of his life.

I am running sooooooo bad.

High-stakes poker is like a hard drug. When you sit down serotonin levels spike, your hands sweat and when everything goes just right you are in a state of pure bliss. But just like hard drugs, poker is a double-edged sword. The highs are always followed by a long, slow, soul-hollowing crash.

—**Good2cu**

FORT WORTH, TEXAS (February 2007)

Living under the same roof as durrrr has clearly had a profound effect on Raptor. He's just having trouble deciding if this is a good or bad thing.

In the plus column, he gets to watch durrrr play poker. There's little doubt in Raptor's mind that his friend has a gift—like the chess master Bobby Fischer, durrrr can see the game in a way that nobody else can. He routinely makes plays that are unorthodox, brilliant, and highly profitable. Sweating durrrr while he explains the thought process behind each move is like getting a graduate education in shipping it.

Even better, he can use durrrr as a resource. Raptor is deep into a high-stakes session when an opponent makes a big bet on the river. "Shit!" he yells, staring at a decent but far from unbeatable hand. "I don't know whether to call this idiot or fold."

Durrrr glances over Raptor's shoulder, taking about three milliseconds to process all of the variables involved. "Dude, what the fuck?" he says. "*Shove.*"

The idea of reraising with all of his chips hadn't even occurred to Raptor, but its brilliance is immediately apparent: force the other guy to make the tough decision.

Quantifying durrrr's impact on his game is as easy as glancing at one of the detailed spreadsheets Raptor uses to track his play. Since they became housemates, Raptor has been making money by the metric ton while playing higher stakes than ever before. His bankroll is quietly nearing the million-dollar mark.

Most twenty-year-olds would be bursting with joy, but Raptor's not like most kids his age. He understands that the good times can't possibly last forever because nothing ever does. At times he seems more interested in protecting his bankroll than adding to it. He often puts more effort into scouring the online tables for juicy games than he does playing in them, and he'll rarely risk any significant amount of money unless he believes he has a considerable edge over his competition.

He doesn't understand how durrrr stays unfazed by the rollercoaster ups and downs, calmly winning and losing six-figure sums on a daily basis. Raptor worries that he lacks the constitution to do the same.

One afternoon he watches durrrr spread all of the money he's got in one of his poker accounts across four tables, playing heads-up against the same opponent. Sure, it's what Raptor did a couple of years earlier, during his second pass at college, but that was $450; durrrr has put $45,000 in play. Raptor can't bear to watch. *This is not right*, screams the little voice inside his head. He escapes into the next room to watch a movie.

When he returns, durrrr has run the money all the way up to $200,000. Raptor's happy for his friend, but the doubts linger. The game is making him rich, but it's also eroding his connection to anything other than poker. He's having trouble relating to the things kids his age consider normal: stressing about schoolwork, griping about shitty jobs, and setting goals, often centering around money, that in all likelihood they will never attain.

He's rarely presented with the opportunity to have a "normal" conversation. The minute people find out that Raptor is a professional poker player, that's all they want to talk about. Attempts to steer the conversation in another direction come off as dismissive; answer the questions, and there will always be more, each loaded with transparent envy.

You don't want to be me, he wants to tell them. *Do you really want to spend most of your waking hours staring at a computer screen, lying to professional liars? Absorbing losses that can be thought of in units like "sports cars" or "annual incomes"? Having expected value always hanging over your head, reminding you that every non-poker activity—a TV show, a romantic evening with your girlfriend, a walk around the block—is costing you hundreds, even thousands, of dollars that you could be earning at the poker table?*

Nobody wants to hear the bitching and whining. They only want to hear about the time Raptor played against some famous pro, the size of the biggest pot he's ever won, and his thoughts about how long it will take them to make as much money as him if they quit school and join the professional circuit.

If you can't beat them, avoid them. Raptor begins steering clear of bars and clubs, tightening his circle of friends and acquaintances. He spends most of his free time with Haley, but even she occasionally takes issue with his abrupt shifts in mood and unconventional life-style. Still a student at TCU, she does her best to help him stay grounded and self-aware. Which is why he can't talk to her about poker—there's no way Haley could ever get her head around the idea of treating huge sums of money with such indifference. So there are times, many more than he'd like, when he's forced to plaster a smile on his face to get through a romantic dinner when, on the inside, he's agonizing over a losing session that could have been the down payment on some family's dream home.

Money has no meaning, he tells himself. *It's just a tool of the trade, like a carpenter's hammer or level.*

While this line of thinking gives him short-term comfort, it also leaves him vulnerable to the existential despair that's taken root in him.

If money has no meaning, then what's the point of pursuing it?

He finds himself struggling to stay motivated. He tries to give himself a jump-start by posting a new Raptor Challenge on Two Plus Two; he's going to make enough money to buy a $1.4-million vacation home in Costa Rica. *Then I'll be happy,* he promises himself, putting in even more hours in front of the computer screen. *This daily suffering is just a means to an end.*

It's a clever trick, but it comes with another unintended side effect. The card game he loves is starting to feel an awful lot like a j-o-b.

41

When I win the Main Event, I'm going to buy a thirty-second Super Bowl commercial. Filmed like a home movie, the commercial will start with me waking up in my black pj's next to a scantily clad supermodel. I'll yawn, stumble out of bed, and make my way to my kitchen, where I will grab an empty bowl and pour some cereal into it. I will open my refrigerator, grab a bottle of Cristal, and proceed to dump it on the cereal. I will then take a bite, smile, and the text "balla" will appear onscreen as it fades to black.

—Good2cu

WARSAW, POLAND (March 2007)

Empiremaker2 is only nineteen, but in Good2cu's opinion, the kid is already a bigger degenerate than he is. This is meant as high praise. Tonight the two of them are in an unspoken competition to see who can drink more from the open bar PokerStars has set up at the Hyatt Regency in Warsaw, Poland.

Like Internet start-ups from a decade before, online poker companies aren't afraid to spend outrageous amounts of money on extravagant parties, especially when they're trying to lure players to a tournament in Eastern Europe. Good2cu didn't need much arm-twisting—he's hoping a little international travel will help pull him out of his malaise. So far it's working. He and Empiremaker2 are becoming more hilarious and charming with every drink.

In their own minds, anyway. Irish poker pro Andy Black calls them "Beavis and Butthead" every time he walks by. When Good2cu jokingly complains to a server that the champagne isn't Dom Pérignon, an English player scoffs at him. "Nineteen-year-old kids drinking Dom? Show some class."

"Are you joking?" replies Good2cu. "We're Americans."

For the last few months, Good2cu has felt like a superhero, only in reverse. By day, he lives like a balla. He's got more money than all his friends in East Lansing combined, so he can flaunt the best clothes, the best liquor, and the best weed. He picks up the tab at bars and restaurants. He buys a vintage Montblanc Sir Henry Tate fountain pen on eBay just because he can. He finally ditches his Saturn for a black Cadillac Escalade, the ride favored by rappers and basketball stars.

When Neverwin Poker publishes an alleged post from Brandi describing, in graphic sexual terms, how horny she's feeling for an online poker player named Micon (accompanied by a few topless photos), Good2cu sends her a private message, which he posts publicly on ShipItHollaBalla.com:

Brandi,

I see you have still not filled out the date application on my Web site. I would like to remind you that not only am I much much better looking than Micon, but I am also much richer. I will be in Vegas sometime in the next few weeks to meet up with my accountants and was wondering if you would like to go to dinner.

Brandi doesn't reply. Good2cu isn't surprised. Inside he knows his persona is predicated on a dream that is rapidly slipping away. He's struggling to maintain his status as a hundred-thousandaire. Ambitious forays into high-stakes games are killing whatever small profit he's able to eke out playing Sit N Gos. To buy the Escalade, he needs his mom to cosign the loan.

His growing frustration about his lack of success gets amplified every time he hears how well his friends are doing. Raptor, Apathy, and Jman are regularly crushing the high-stakes cash games online. Durrrr recently won a million dollars online. In a single night.

Good2cu's hoping his travels with Empiremaker2 will be the tonic that restores his mojo. They're supposed to be playing in tomorrow's Polish Open, a $5,000 European Poker Tour event that will pay the winner nearly a half-million dollars, but when they try to register for the tournament, they learn that it's sold out. All they can do now is pound drinks and complain about the injustice of it all. As loud as they are, it doesn't take long for word to reach Lee Jones.

Jones, a fifty-one-year-old with a masters in Electrical Engineering who was just named the EPT's new tournament director, is something of a celebrity in the poker world. Two years ago, while working as PokerStars' card room manager, he wrote *Winning Low Limit Hold'em*, one of the first strategy guides to specifically address online poker. The popular book includes a new system for beating Sit N Gos, developed with the help of a math professor, that outperforms the now outdated Independent Chip Model and helps hasten the end of the days when proprietary knowledge can give those in the know such an extreme edge.

Jones walks Good2cu and Empiremaker2 to the registration desk and helps them sign up for the tournament. Empiremaker2 uses the moment to address one of online poker's most popular urban legends.

"Hey, Lee," he says. "You used to work at PokerStars, right? Can you get them to shut off the doomswitch for me? Ever since I pulled $50,000 out of my account, it's been one bad beat after another. I've lost like $200,000 in the past couple months."

According to conspiracy theorists, the "doomswitch" is a secret computer algorithm that punishes players for making big withdrawals from their poker accounts. Trigger the doomswitch, and you're going to suffer an improbable run of bad "luck" for some indeterminate period of time.

Jones laughs. "There's no such thing as a doomswitch," he says. "But I can tell you this—the only people who should be losing $200,000 are people who are already set up for life."

Good2cu feels a twinge of regret. *I had $200,000 not that long ago. Why didn't I put any of it away? I could have bought a place like Raptor did. Instead I'm going to end up broke with nothing to show for it.* "Good point, Lee," he says, washing down the insecurities with another swig of champagne. "But it's just so much more fun to spend all our money now."

Producing a weak smile, Jones wishes them good luck and moves on to a quieter section of the room.

Empiremaker2 slaps Good2cu on the back of the head. "Fuck this place!" he yells. "Let's go find a strip club."

42

Heads-up for rollz!

—**A popular online poker challenge**

ROME, ITALY (April 2007)

After spending his birthday partying in Poland with Good2cu and Empiremaker2, twenty-year-old Traheho flies to Italy to meet up with durrrr and TheUsher. He finds them holed up in a luxury hotel in Rome playing a near-endless loop of high-stakes cash games online, often sharing a single account to minimize the individual risk.

Pooling bankrolls is one of the many responses to online poker's new reality: the games have gotten significantly harder to beat. Six months after the UIGEA's passage, the full extent of its effect is starting to become clear. The recreational players that once fueled the poker economy with their habitual $100 deposits on Friday nights have all but vanished. With fewer fish to eat, the sharks are now forced to go after each other. By sharing risk, durrrr and TheUsher are increasing their chances of not only success but survival.

They prefer to play in shorthanded games—fewer players at the table mean you get to play a lot more hands, which in theory should mitigate luck and emphasize skill. Heads-up poker takes this argument to the extreme: against a single opponent, you've got to play almost every hand or else get steamrolled into oblivion. It's a completely different experience than a nine- or even six-player game, far less methodical and mathematical, way more instinctive and psychological.

Heads-up games have always enjoyed a storied perch in the poker world. In 1951, nearly twenty years before the creation of the WSOP, Benny Binion hosted a series of matches between one of the greatest poker players to ever play the game, Johnny Moss, and the legendary gambler Nick "The Greek" Dandalos. The publicity stunt dragged on for five months, only ending after Moss had tapped Dandalos for a reputed two or three million dollars—or around $20 million by today's standards.

When NBC decided to bring poker to network television for the first time in 2005, it revived the format. The National Heads-Up Poker Championship, a $20,000 buy-in, single-elimination invitational tournament, mixed the world's most popular poker players with a handful of celebrities and Internet qualifiers. It's the highest-rated poker show on television. Entrance into the tournament's sixty-four-player field has become one of the most sought-after invitations in the poker world.

Durrrr has yet to score an invitation, but that's got more to do with his age—he's still not old enough to gamble legally in the United States—than his ability. Online, he's regularly been playing heads-up against anyone who dares sit across from him. While in Rome with TheUsher and Traheho, durrrr has spent most of his time battling a guy called PerkyShmerky.

Perky's not a terrible player. Against average competition, he wins as much as he loses. But he tends to bet in a way that tips off the strength of his hand, a flaw that observant players like durrrr and

TheUsher are happy to exploit. Even better, Perky's a trust fund kid from Manhattan with what appears to be an inexhaustible bankroll. He regularly plays with $50,000 in front of him, and if he loses that, he simply reloads with $50,000 more.

Traheho isn't a trust funder. Growing up in Orange County, he wasn't poor, but he wasn't rich either. Both of his parents worked full time. He attended public schools. When he was sixteen, he won $12 playing poker at a friend's house, a small taste of success that made him hungry for more. He went home and did the math, trying to figure out how many times he'd have to replicate the feat to be able to afford his dream car, a BMW M3.

Way too many, he decided. But he kept playing anyway, slowly moving up through the ranks. His skills and bankroll have developed to the point where he now feels comfortable teaming up with durrrr and TheUsher and taking on a player like Perky, whose wealth allows him to employ an unpredictable style and laugh off losses that would cause severe mental trauma for nearly everyone else.

Traheho quickly becomes one of Perky's favorite opponents. Some online players might as well be robots the way they play, hiding behind their computer monitors, silently clicking their mice, but both Traheho and Perky enjoy talking trash, using the chat box to poke fun at each other whenever they get a chance. They even exchange phone numbers, so they can better torment each other.

One night, in the midst of one of their heads-up matches, Perky catches a lucky card to rob Traheho of a six-figure pot.

Ten seconds later, Traheho's phone rings.

"Hey, you prick, how do you feel about a jack on the river for a hundred-and-twenty K?" Perky cackles into the phone. "Got you, bitch!"

Click.

Traheho has to laugh. He knows there's no real malice behind Perky's words. But the exchange plants a seed in Traheho's mind, and he looks forward to the day when he can deliver an appropriate response.

Traheho is back home in Orange County when that day arrives. Perky challenges him to a series of three $50,000 heads-up battles, and Traheho wins all three. His take, after giving his partners their share, is $90,000.

He celebrates by heading straight to the nearest BMW dealership. A salesman informs him that the M3 he's had his eye on is out of stock. They do, however, have the next model up—an M6—that happens to cost around $90,000. Traheho pays cash and adorns his new car with a vanity license plate that will always remind him exactly who he has to thank for his good fortune.

TYPERKY.

43

Everybody will eventually run worse than they thought was possible. The difference between a winner and a loser is that the latter thinks they do not deserve it.

—Irieguy

EAST LANSING, MICHIGAN (May 2007)

Traheho posts a picture of his new car—license plate front and center—on the Two Plus Two site. Good2cu smiles when he sees it, but he can't help but feel jealous. It feels like all his friends are becoming poker superstars, while he remains mired in a slump he can't seem to shake.

Maybe the games are harder. Maybe he doesn't have what it takes. Maybe he's suffering what statisticians call a "regression to the mean," the idea that extreme results tend to become less extreme over time. Maybe he got lucky to win the $200,000 and, in reality, he's more of a break-even player.

It's a phenomenon Irieguy observed several years earlier. "I am beginning to realize that most people don't have the psychological fortitude or spiritual perspective to manage the vicissitudes of this game," he wrote in a post on Two Plus Two. "I also believe that of the very small number of professional poker players who have been successful for more than a few years, most of them are actually quite lucky. I believe that there are many pros who will fail once they begin to experience average luck."

For Good2cu, there's only one consolation: *At least I haven't gone busto.* These days the News, Views, and Gossip Forum is full of stories about spectacular flameouts. Forced by the rapidly shrinking player pool to go after one another, players who steadily built up large bankrolls over the course of several years are suddenly "blowing up," losing it all in just a fraction of the time.

In *Fooled by Randomness*, a book written for Wall Street investors but popular among poker players for its observations about the role of luck in our lives, Nassim Nicholas Taleb provides a definition of the phrase that works equally well in either world: *"Blow up* in the lingo has a precise meaning; it does not just mean to lose money; it means to lose more money than one ever expected, to the point of being thrown out of the business (the equivalent of a doctor losing his license to practice or a lawyer being disbarred)."

The idea that he could do the same terrifies Good2cu. "What worries me is that dozens of other kids were also in my position and they blew up," he confesses in his blog. "They went on crazy monkey tilt and blew their roll and went back to school a psychological mess."

There's Grimstarr, a young Two Plus Twoer who was almost a millionaire earlier this year. Now nearly broke, he's become infamous for challenging players to heads-up matches, quitting while he's ahead should he win the first hand, hurling insults at his opponents when he doesn't.

Go play in traffic.

I'll murder you.

Die in a grease fire.

Neverwin, of Neverwin Poker fame, has not only gone busto, but is in debt to a long and increasingly impatient line of players. One of them is Newhizzle, Brandi's former sparring partner, who is in the process of frittering away in high-stakes cash games the $1.5 million he won in a WPT tournament less than a year ago. Compounding his misfortunes at the poker table: bad loans to players like Neverwin, the $30,000 Brandi squandered while using one of his accounts, and an $80,000 loss playing shuffleboard at this year's PokerStars Caribbean Adventure—half of which found its way into the pockets of Apathy, durrrr, and Raptor.

Good2cu doesn't want to join them as a character in some cautionary tale. He's momentarily cheered when Nick Gair's article about the Ballas appears in *Bluff*—the crew comes off looking like rock stars—but a close read dulls his enthusiasm. He only gets mentioned a few times, mostly in the beginning where the author notes his "passion for hijinks" and "disdain for the rules of grammar." Oh, and near the end, when the author mentions that Good2cu is "on a bit of a downswing."

The article underscores Good2cu's feeling that he's the only Ship It Holla Balla whose career isn't on the rise. Apathy seems to have a knack for cashing in at major online tournaments, while Inyaface continues to grind out a steady profit in whatever types of games he chooses to play. Durrrr and Raptor have made a relatively easy transition to high-stakes cash games, pushing their bankrolls into seven figures. And Fiery-Justice just won more than a million dollars in a World Poker Tour event at the Mirage that will be televised next March.

But Jman's ascent might be the most spectacular. A year ago he was still making a rocky transition from Sit N Gos to cash games. Now he's playing every bit as high as durrrr and Raptor. Thanks to his growing reputation and some friends in the right places, Jman gets invited to appear on *High Stakes Poker*, one of the most popular poker shows on

TV. His appearance is brief—he's bumped after a single day for the more ratings-friendly celebrity poker pro Daniel Negreanu—but he spends enough time matching wits with famous pros like Sammy Farha and Phil Hellmuth to form an opinion about their play.

"America still thinks that my table (besides me) is full of the best poker players in the world," he tells his friends on Two Plus Two, "when I would've salivated over playing any of them heads-up."

Good2cu wants to believe that he's every bit as good at poker as his friends, that they've just gotten a little luckier than him, that his time will come. But the facts say otherwise. He hasn't been a consistent winner for almost a year. With that in mind he walks into Michigan State's admissions office and tells them that, after taking a year off to find himself, he's ready to reenroll.

Come September, he'll reenter civilian life as a student.

44

IM 21!!!!!! I CAN PLAY THE LIVE POKAHS NOW!!!! WHOOOOOHOOOOOOO!!!

—**Raptor**

LAS VEGAS, NEVADA (May–June 2007)

Two weeks before the start of the 2007 World Series of Poker, Raptor turns twenty-one. In the eyes of the law, he'll finally be able to drink, gamble, and go to strip clubs. Pardon him for not getting too excited, as these aren't exactly novel experiences. Some friends help him celebrate at a Las Vegas club. He's home and in bed by midnight.

But there's one aspect of being twenty-one he does appreciate: he's finally going to get to play in the World Series of Poker. Hoping to recapture some of the good times that took place last summer, he signs on to live with the rest of the crew in whatever rental property Inyaface can secure for them. The directive given to Responsible Guy this time around: *go bigger*.

Inyaface delivers what can more accurately be described as a compound than a mansion, the kind of property that demands entry through an imposing front gate. The main house is surrounded by four guest cottages, a pool, a tennis court, and a fifty-foot-wide putting green.

Good2cu flies in from Michigan, Raptor and TravestyFund from Texas, Jman from Wisconsin. Apathy and Inyaface, joined by their friend BigT, make another epic road trip from Canada in the Pontiac Pursuit, this year's highlight a random stumble across a Vanilla Ice concert in Des Moines. TheUsher arrives from Rome. Durrrr, who's still too young to play in any of the WSOP tournaments, promises to join them in a few days—rumor has it he and Traheho have been playing $100,000 heads-up matches against PerkyShmerky in New York City.

To divvy up the bedrooms, the Ballas plug a laptop into the projector in the home theater and fill the sixteen-by-nine screen on the wall with a randomly chosen low-stakes Sit N Go. Everyone picks an unknown player to root for, injecting the contest with the same uncertainty as a cockroach race. Apathy's player busts first, relegating him to the shabbiest guest house, a shedlike structure at the back of the compound previously occupied by a bunch of feral cats. Raptor has flowers delivered to Apathy's quarters to cheer him up.

The night before the Series begins, the crew meets Irieguy at the Spearmint Rhino. Raptor jokingly promises one of the lap dancers that he'll make seven final tables and win four gold bracelets this summer. Irieguy laughs. Winning a single bracelet is hard enough. But he wouldn't bet against any of these guys. Not only are they improving at Internet speed, they've been on a roll. Three months ago, TravestyFund won an event at the L.A. Poker Classic that paid him $160,000. A month later, TheUsher won $140,000 after taking down a tournament at the Wynn.

Made worse by high expectations, Raptor's first World Series event is a huge bummer. He sails into the dinner break with a healthy pile of chips, then takes two horrific beats in a row to get eliminated. His results don't get any better in the weeks that follow. Fortunately there's a consolation prize: cash games.

"I'm here for the cash games" is one of the more frequent refrains you'll hear during the Series, and it's not just idle talk. For six weeks every summer, the Las Vegas poker economy goes bananas. Recreational players come to town to watch or to enter an event or two, then retreat to the cash games eager to re-create the excitement. The tables are packed, the action loose, the games juicy.

Frustrated by his tournament results, Raptor begins to devote more of his attention to these games. Now that he's twenty-one and able to report his earnings to the I.R.S. he no longer has to tiptoe his way around the card rooms. He can play anywhere he wants. For his first foray into the live high-stakes games, he chooses Bobby's Room, the special section of the Bellagio's card room that's home to some of the biggest games in the world.

The room is named after Bobby Baldwin, poker's original whiz kid. In the early 1970s Baldwin dropped out of Oklahoma State and moved to Las Vegas, hoping to defy the odds and make a living as a professional gambler. After some incredible ups and downs—he once turned $75 into $180,000 over the course of a weekend, then lost it all—he ditched craps and sports betting to focus on poker. He was only twenty-eight when he won the 1978 WSOP Main Event, making him the youngest ever to do so by a good decade and a half.

Baldwin went on to earn three more gold bracelets in World Series events, but the biggest win of his career came during a cash game against the rising business mogul Steve Wynn. Impressed by the acumen of the guy who just cleaned him out, Wynn asked Baldwin if he'd be interested in doing some consulting for his casino, the Golden Nugget. Two years later, Wynn made Baldwin the Nugget's president.

While Wynn was building his second resort, the Mirage, he sought Baldwin's input on everything from financing to design, and when the doors opened on what was then the most expensive casino in history, Baldwin was the man in charge. When Wynn decided to build an even more extravagant casino modeled after a luxury resort on the shores of Italy's Lake Como, he didn't have to look very far to find the perfect guy to run the Bellagio.

At the time, most Las Vegas casinos were replacing their poker rooms with slot machines, an effort driven by an influx of MBAs looking to squeeze bigger profits out of every square foot on the casino floor. But Baldwin saw the wisdom of going against the grain at the Bellagio, creating an amenity-filled card room that quickly became the most popular in town. He also added a sanctuary, cordoned off from the tourists by etched glass windows, where his friends could play high-stakes poker in relative privacy.

Bobby's Room could be considered poker's Yankee Stadium, home to the most talented (and richest) players in the world, only without the fans. Few can handle the steep price of admission. Raptor's a little nervous when he steps into the room, like he felt three years ago when he first mustered the nerve to sit down at a table at the Poker Box with $100 in front of him. Only this time it's $100,000.

The one open seat at the table is being reserved for Bobby Baldwin himself, but the floorman tells Raptor he can use it until the boss arrives. Pot-limit Omaha really isn't Raptor's best game, but that's what they're playing and he's not in any position to request a change. To calm the butterflies in his stomach, he stares at the "i" in "Bellagio" written on the table's felt and focuses on his breath.

Inhale. . . . Exhale. . . . Inhale. . . . Exhale. . . .

He'd be far more anxious if, in true Raptor fashion, he hadn't carefully researched the competition. Like the rest of the players in the room, Raptor hopes to take advantage of the presence of a single person at the table, a bald man in his late forties with a slight French accent. Guy Laliberté, the billionaire owner of Cirque du Soleil, fell in love with high-stakes poker a little more than a year ago and has been paying through the nose for "lessons" ever since. (He will reportedly lose $16 million playing online poker in 2008.)

But when Raptor starts chatting with Laliberté, he discovers that he's more interested in learning about the man's storybook life—a Canadian hippie who began his improbable career as a street performer—than separating him from his money. Laliberté radiates passion, a commodity Raptor suspects is an essential ingredient to a successful life. It feels inspiring to talk to a man who became so prosperous doing what he loved most.

Bobby Baldwin shows up an hour later to claim his seat. The other players at the table aren't particularly happy to see Raptor leave—he wins a $200,000 pot within minutes of sitting down, and manages to hold on to most of it for the rest of the session. But as he shakes hands with Laliberté, Raptor suspects that only a small percentage of his newfound wealth is monetary.

45

I do have to say, though a great poker player, durrrr is one of the biggest prop betting fish I know.

—Jman

LAS VEGAS, NEVADA (July 2007)

Durrrr arrives at the compound carrying a backpack stuffed with bricks of bundled hundred-dollar bills. He counts out $350,000 and matter-of-factly hands it to TheUsher—his share of the action they agreed to split while they were in Italy, an arrangement TheUsher had forgotten all about.

The sheer mass of the money makes it a moment to remember, even in the midst of a summer where $10,000 bricks are just another prop in the Ship It Holla Balla mise en scène, as ubiquitous as the piles of dirty laundry. Now that most of the Ballas can legally play in tournaments and live games, cash rivals the money in their online accounts as the currency of choice and the principal method of exchange between them. When they're not playing poker, they're often devising schemes that will hasten the flow of this cash from one to the other.

Raptor and Apathy spend many afternoons playing Rapathy Golf—each player throws a golf ball into the farthest reaches of the compound, then uses a putter to return the ball to the green, avoiding whatever obstacles lie between the ball's original position and the hole. Pretty silly stuff, unless you're playing for hundreds of dollars a hole.

Even larger sums trade hands on the tennis court, which is frequently in use, even though none of the Ballas brought rackets with them. After hearing through the Two Plus Two grapevine about all the high-dollar action taking place there, PerkyShmerky arrives in a chauffeur-driven Rolls-Royce Phantom to challenge a Two Plus Twoer named Chuddo to a series of $5,000 matches.

But when it comes to gambling serious money, durrrr has no rival. Over the last few months, several anecdotal accounts on the message boards have him donking off hundreds of thousands of dollars while multitabling high-stakes cash games. According to HighstakesDB—a Web site launched earlier in the year to track the results of Internet poker's biggest players—durrrr has lost half a million dollars since January. When a player with his abilities can lose so much money so quickly, it creates a ripple of concern among his friends: *If durrrr can go broke . . .*

So the backpack full of cash is a welcome sight.

"I'd heard you'd gone busto," says Apathy. "Glad to see that was a bunch of BS."

"Unfortunately, the rumors of my demise are partially accurate. I'm down about two mil over the past four months." Durrrr sighs, before perking up. "But, hey, I started with three."

While its comforting to see durrrr and his backpack full of cash, it's *hilarious* to see durrrr and his backpack full of cash when all the lights in the house suddenly go out, instantly producing a collective panic: *Oh shit, are we about to get jacked* again? Durrrr cinches the backpack's straps tightly to his chest and paces nervously, expecting robbers to burst through the door at any moment, until the power comes back on a few minutes later.

Durrrr's dramatically fluctuating bankroll has done little to curb his appetite for big prop bets. He's eating dinner at P. F. Chang's with Raptor when the conversation turns to chess. Durrrr claims he could beat a Grandmaster if his opponent began the game down a rook.

"Bullshit," Raptor coughs into his napkin.

"I'm serious. I'll bet you fifty K."

"Book it," Raptor says, then pulls out his phone and calls Curtains, a fellow Two Plus Twoer who's in town for the WSOP.

"Hey, it's Raptor. You're a chess Grandmaster, right?"

"Incorrect," replies Curtains. "I'm an International Master."

"What's that, like, a step below?"

"Two steps, actually."

"Well, could you beat durrrr in a match if you started down a rook?"

"Maybe. What's he rated?"

Raptor looks across the table at durrrr and his smug grin. "He doesn't have a rating."

"Then I'd place my odds of winning at around a hundred percent."

The chess match becomes a must-see event. Two Plus Twoers arrive at the compound in droves to sweat the action, betting thousands on the outcome. For those who can't make it in person, Raptor provides running commentary on the message boards.

Durrrr plays defensively, so it takes Curtains a bit longer than he expected to sweep the best two-out-of-three series. Durrrr removes a few bricks from his backpack and tosses them to Raptor, who pays Curtains $8,000 for his troubles and pockets the rest.

Durrrr shrugs off the loss. *There's a reason money doesn't come with handles on it.*

The hubbub on the message boards has barely subsided when Chuddo gives durrrr fifty-to-one odds that he can't sink three long putts in a row on the green in the backyard. A few minutes and three incredibly lucky putts later, durrrr's won his $50,000 back.

It was easily [one of the] top five sickest nights of my life and I'd bet everyone would say the same.

—Traheho

LAS VEGAS, NEVADA (July 2007)

If you're unfamiliar with the concept of an "infinity pool," it's a swimming pool that uses architectural design and structural engineering to trick the eye into believing that one of its edges extends forever, when in fact it drops abruptly, sometimes off the side of a cliff.

The infinity pool in the Hugh Hefner Sky Villa, at the top of the Palms Hotel's Fantasy Tower, thrills guests both ways. You're not sure whether to feel exhilarated by the gods-eye view of the Las Vegas Strip and the seemingly endless horizon beyond or terrified by the 40-story drop into the abyss.

The pool is just one of the many amenities you get when renting the most expensive accommodations in what is arguably the city's most rocking hotel, a joint venture between the jet-setting, hard-partying, NBA-team-owning Maloof brothers and their corporate partner Playboy Enterprises. The informal name of this 9,000-square-foot villa is the Playboy Suite—during off-hours it doubles as the set of the Playmate-centric reality TV show *Girls Next Door*. Taking up two floors at the very top of the hotel, it boasts pop-up plasma TVs in every room, beds that rotate to exploit the view, tables for poker and Ping-Pong, a Jacuzzi, a sauna, a wet bar, and a fully equipped gym. It even comes with a butler. Tonight his duties will include lighting joints, procuring pharmaceuticals, and shepherding drunk, hot girls from the casino up to the suite.

Good2cu is one of a group of friends who have rented the suite to celebrate the twentieth birthday of WestMenloAA, a kid from California in the midst of a year that will see him win more than $1 million and receive *CardPlayer* magazine's inaugural Online Player of the Year award. They stock the bar with $2,000 worth of top-shelf liquor and invite as many hot chicks as they know, including a couple of Good2cu's friends who are visiting from East Lansing.

Good2cu has plenty to celebrate. Living in the Ship It Holla compound has completely altered his poker fortunes. His confidence started building the moment he got there. Immersed in a space buzzing with advice, ideas, and support, he gains much needed perspective on his downswing, separating what was bad play from bad luck, restoring his belief that he might actually have some talent for the game.

But the more serendipitous discovery comes during a discussion with one of the compound's many couch crashers, a friend of Inyaface from Toronto who shows Good2cu how to set up a Virtual Private Network.

VPNs are typically used by businesses to give their employees in the field secure access to the same resources they'd have at the office, allowing them to log on to the corporate network from anywhere in the world and use their computers as if they were sitting at their desks. They can also be used, as Inyaface's friend demonstrates, to dupe an online poker site into believing that you're playing from a foreign country. A few minutes later, he and Good2cu have negoti-ated a deal to open a Canadian bank account together, allowing Good2cu to return to Party Poker, the site where he experienced most of his early success.

He's happy to discover that the exodus of Americans from the site hasn't done anything to slow down the action. Party Poker remains a sea full of fish. Their poor play, coupled with the reassurance that comes from returning to a place where so many good things have hap-pened in the past, helps Good2cu go on a tear. In July alone he earns more than $100,000.

Good2cu's not the only one who's having a great summer. TheUsher and TravestyFund both win more than $100,000 in World Series events. Raptor's tournament experience doesn't live up to the promise he made to the dancer at the Rhino—he manages only one cash, barely making back his entry fee—but he backs two players who win gold bracelets and pockets a healthy percentage of their scores. And durrrr has bounced back from the downswing he suf-fered at the beginning of the year in a big way—according to PokerDB, he's been crushing the cash games online all summer, making more than $750,000.

Good2cu is the first to arrive at the Playboy Suite. He wants to show it off to his two lady friends before the party begins. They can't linger long. They've reserved a table for twelve at Shintaro, the Bel-lagio's high-end Japanese restaurant, to celebrate WestMenloAA's birthday. But they're there long enough for the luxury hotel room to work its magic: Good2cu is in the middle of a threesome when the butler accidentally walks in on them.

At Shintaro the rowdy crew devours brontosaurus-sized portions of Kobe beef and lays waste to the local lobster supply, washing it all down with bottles of Dom Pérignon and Cristal. At the end of the feast, they're presented with a $12,000 bill. Each of them hands a credit card to the server, who seems as thrilled by the suggestion of Credit Card Roulette as they are. Good2cu dodges a bullet when his card is the second-to-last drawn; it's the birthday boy, magnanimously tossing in four credit cards to cover some of his less fortunate friends, who gets stuck with the tab for his own celebration.

They take a limo from the Bellagio to the Palms, where they ride the private glass elevator up to the Playboy Suite. Guests arrive in small boisterous groups. Almost everyone is under twenty-one. Some play beer pong for thousands of dollars a game, while spectators gamble even more. Room service arrives with one of everything. Drinks are served by a beautiful bartender. Joints get sparked and passed around the balcony. One of the guests, who's just won a major poker tournament, brings a baggie of cocaine that everyone agrees, is very, very good; the ever-dutiful butler finds a mirror to help them rack the lines. No one is entirely certain how the sixty Vicodins materialize, but, you know, gift horses.

A phone call alerts them that the hookers are coming up the wrong elevator, so ambassadors are dispatched to receive them. This leads to an amusing encounter in the elevator lobby with the famous rap star who's staying in one of the adjoining villas—he's sending his female companion home just as the two hired to entertain WestMenloAA are arriving.

The bartender, who has been drinking as much as everybody else, starts making out with one of the guests, who guides her into the Jacuzzi. He orally pleasures her on the edge of the hot tub, setting some sort of record for the number of *entendres* that can be milked out of "wet bar." On the other side of the glass doors, half of the party jostles for a better view.

The next morning, Good2cu wraps a towel around his waist and walks from room to room, surveying the damage. People are passed out in every corner of the suite, several sporting fresh hickeys and bruises they won't remember acquiring. One guest wakes up in the hallway with a dim memory of betting—and losing—$100,000 on a single hand of blackjack. Food and drink are spilled everywhere. Artwork has been removed from the walls, apparently mistaken for party favors. A used condom floats in the pool.

The hotel bill, with damages, will exceed $20,000, but no one will complain. The night will be reconstructed and reexamined on the message boards, *Rashomon*-style, for weeks to come.

Good2cu drops the towel and slips into the infinity pool, resting the back of his head against its edge. Even by the light of day, the Las Vegas Strip seems to twinkle like a cluster of stars and the horizon looks every bit as infinite and full of possibility as it did the night before. He can't think of a place he'd rather be. It's perfect—as long as you don't get too close to the edge.

47

I die a lot in my dreams.

—**Raptor**

FORT WORTH, TEXAS (August 2007)

After six weeks in the Balla compound, Raptor is ready to return to the relative normalcy of Fort Worth. It only takes a few days of normalcy for the gloom to creep back in.

He can't make sense of it. He's got more than a million dollars safely earning interest in money market funds. A sweet car. A girlfriend who not only tolerates his lifestyle but genuinely cares about him. A house that's nicer than the one he grew up in. And he's only twenty-one. He knows he should be doing cartwheels down the street.

So why do I feel like crap all of the time?

He dreams about dying. He gets shot in the chest and run over by cars. One recurring nightmare has him happily zooming along in a Corvette . . . until—BAM!—he gets hit by a truck. The car crumples in on him, slowly squeezing him to death, before he wakes up in a sweat.

Maybe it's his diet. During his time in Vegas this summer, the four basic food groups were pastries, waffle fries, cheeseburgers, and sour gummy bears. He begins to keep a precise log of everything he ingests. He reads about nutrition and, for a week or two, flirts with veganism.

Maybe it's the lethargy that comes from sitting at his computer all day long. He starts working out five or six times a week, practicing High Intensity Training to burn his muscles to the point of failure. He tries to stay offline as much as possible, carving out time to go shopping with his girlfriend or see a film.

One night he's driving home from the movie theater with a couple of friends when traffic slows to a crawl. Three lanes are being funneled into one. They creep into a disorienting haze of blinking colored lights where emergency vehicles are gathered under an overpass. Floodlights illuminate a circle of traffic cones in the center of the road. A group of medics mill about inside the perimeter, blithely shooting the breeze like they might at a cocktail party.

As his car inches past, Raptor gets a better look. It's a girl, about his age, skinny as a basketball pole. She's got black hair. Pockmarks on her face. A tattoo of a black star on her wrist. One of her legs is twisted at an almost impossible angle.

How long has she been lying there like that? Nobody's helping her, so she has to be dead, right? Why hasn't anyone bothered to move her? Shouldn't they cover her up?

The next morning, Raptor's not sure whether the girl was real or part of another morbid dream. He scans the local paper. It doesn't take long to find the story. She was twenty-one, a cashier at Central Market, a gourmet grocery store where he's shopped dozens of times. According to witnesses, she got into an argument with her boyfriend, jumped out of his car when he stopped for a light, and leapt from the overpass onto the highway below.

Raptor tries to shake the image of her body, all mangled and twisted in the middle of the road. How unfazed the medics seemed to be in the presence of a life cut so short. *Just another jumper,* he imagines them saying.

He can't see himself ever getting depressed enough to jump off a bridge, but at the same time he knows he isn't getting any happier. He gets a momentary thrill every time he achieves one of the many goals he's set for himself, but that joy never lingers long. And when he tries to articulate his feelings, either to himself or others, he feels guilty about having such a woe-is-me attitude.

I'm only twenty-one, and I've already earned more money than most people in the world will see in a lifetime. What do I really have to complain about? God, I'm such a whiny emo bitch.

Hoping to shove the darkness to the back of his mind, he orders a few more books on nutrition, vows to put in an extra day at the gym, and gets back to grinding online.

If I ever want to return to college, it's really going to present some problems for me.

—Good2cu

EAST LANSING, MICHIGAN (Fall 2007)

Shortly after Good2cu returns to Michigan State, an Australian newspaper—the *Sydney Morning Herald*—runs an article about the explosive growth of online poker. The piece is effusive in its admiration for him and his friends:

In the world of online poker, they're known as ballas (pronounced ballers). They party hard, spend big and live large. Their website boasts of $40,000 nights on the town complete with strippers, limos and Kristal [sic] champagne. And while most of us would baulk at wagering $50, let alone $500, on a hand, ballas bet big to win big.

The author, who has obviously relied on ShipItHollaBalla.com as a primary source, portrays Good2cu as the very exemplar of the high-rolling excitement that's luring so many people to the game. According to the article, Good2cu made $145,000 last year while riding in limousines and partying with strippers. "Not bad," writes the journalist, "for a 22 year old who lists 'travelling the world,' 'fine dining,' and 'waking up after 3 pm' among his hobbies."

Good2cu chuckles. He isn't twenty-two. He won't turn twenty-one for another couple of days. And the strippers and limos feel like part of a blurry past. His current reality is a shitty off-campus house that he shares with three guys he's been friends with since high school. They're united by their love of partying, so there's plenty of debauchery, but this is still East Lansing. A big night out means paying five dollars for a plastic cup at a keg party and, if you're lucky, hooking up with a sorority girl.

Still, he's pretty sure coming back to school was the right decision. The only mistake he made was signing up for a full course load, a situation he quickly rectifies by dropping everything but Econ and Interpersonal Communications, leaving him plenty of time to play poker.

The one thing the article does get right is his income. Well, sort of. Since his return from Vegas, he's actually been doing quite a bit better than that. In his first month back at school, he adds another $100,000 to his bankroll, averaging $700 an hour in the process.

Flush enough to throw himself a twenty-first birthday party the campus won't soon forget, he hires a DJ and buys a dozen cases of Dom Pérignon. The event will never be mistaken for what took place at the Playboy Suite, but by East Lansing standards, it's Mardi Gras and Burning Man rolled into one.

The party is hardly indicative of his (second) collegiate experience. Most nights Good2cu holes up in his room, headphones on, grinding away. How can he afford *not* to, given all the uncertainty surrounding online poker's future? He feels like he's got to keep making as much money as he can for as long as he can.

That's the rational argument, anyway. The emotional component is this: he loves playing poker and can't imagine doing anything else. He misses the total immersion in the poker world he experienced during the summer. Discussing hands and trading strategies. Tapping into the collective energy of a group of guys who are starting to prove that they have a genuine talent for the game. The nonstop party atmosphere maintained by his current roommates is starting to feel less like fun and more like a distraction from the work that he's supposed to be doing, that he *wants* to be doing.

He puts in so many hours at the table in October that he only manages to add two new posts to the Web site. The first announces that TravestyFund just made the final table of a tournament in Aruba. The second congratulates him for winning the $800,000 first-place prize. TravestyFund's hot streak will earn him a place on *CardPlayer* magazine's list of the top one hundred players of the year, where he will join TheUsher and FieryJustice.

His friends' success scares Good2cu a little, like they've all hopped aboard a train that's rapidly speeding away while he's left standing at the station. But in his shitty off-campus house he's still the resident tycoon. He pretty much pays for all of the non-rent expenses because, why not? The guys he lives with are usually broke, so he's happy to help them out, buying groceries, alcohol, and the occasional bag of weed. When one of his housemates, on sabbatical from both school and the workforce, can no longer come up with his share of the rent, everyone just assumes Good2cu will pick up the slack. The presumption bothers him.

What the hell am I doing here?

It's meant to be a rhetorical question, so he's surprised when he gets an actual response. From some deep recess in his brain, he can hear the advice Irieguy gave him a year and a half ago, now reverberating louder than ever: "Vegas is where you want to be if you are a card-player."

Good2cu doesn't bother officially dropping his last two classes, believing his complete absence should get the point across, and by the time he informs his housemates of his decision to leave, he's already settled in his new condo in Las Vegas.

My life has recently been single-mindedly focused on my career as I spend eight hours a day, six days a week playing poker. I wish I spent more time away from my computer, but as a job I can hardly think of anything I'd rather do. I don't know how long the games will be beatable, or how long I can sustain this level of play and I'm going to try to make as much money as I can.

—Good2cu

LAS VEGAS, NEVADA (January 2008)

Sky Las Vegas is a brand-new, forty-five-story tower of luxury condos right in the middle of the action on Las Vegas Boulevard, a five-minute drive to the Bellagio and the biggest cash games in the world. Good2cu's two-bedroom rental comes with granite countertops, marble floors, and an unobstructed view of the Strip. He spends $9,000 stocking his bar: liquor, a few cases of Dom, as per usual, but also some fine red wines he's read about—he's not living in a frat house anymore.

Now that he's twenty-one he can finally enter the major tournaments, and there's no shortage of them in Las Vegas. He arrives in town just in time to play in the Doyle Brunson Five Diamond World Poker Classic at the Bellagio. On the second day he finds himself at the same table as one of his poker heroes, Daniel Negreanu.

"So," asks Negreanu, "you an online pro?"

"Me? No, I won a five dollar satellite on PokerStars to get here," lies Good2cu, inwardly chuckling.

In Michigan he felt like a minor celebrity; here he's almost completely anonymous. Aside from TheUsher and Irieguy, who both live about ten minutes away, Good2cu doesn't know anyone in Las Vegas, but hopes to quickly expand his social circle, starting with the dancers at the Spearmint Rhino.

"One of my top priorities here in Vegas is to be on a first-name basis with the top strippers in town," he blogs. "Learning their names should not be hard, since there are only around five or six stripper names. Hopefully they learn mine quick."

But a part of Good2cu embraces the anonymity as an opportunity to reinvent himself once again. In the past several months his "balla" persona has started to feel like a caricature of itself, and it's beginning to bother him.

He gets two or three e-mails every week from complete strangers calling him an arrogant idiot or an attention whore. Someone even compares him to Brandi Hawbaker. Every post he makes on Two Plus Two invites a flurry of abusive ad hominem attacks.

You're a loser.

You suck at poker.

Your forehead is too big.

Your forehead is so big it should be called a "fivehead."

You look like John Edwards . . . with Down syndrome.

Some of these insults are given life in distorted pictures created by Two Plus Twoers with rudimentary Photoshop skills and too much time on their hands. Good2cu laughs but it's still painful. He's self-aware enough to know that he's asking for most of the abuse, thanks to the image he's created for himself. What bothers him the most is the way it's interfering with anyone taking him seriously as a poker player. And his performance at the Doyle Brunson Classic shows how ready he is to be taken seriously: he tallies his first two major tournament scores, cashing twice in the series for almost $40,000 each time.

Good2cu goes into problem-solving mode. He starts a thread on Two Plus Two's Psychology forum titled, "Why do people on the internet (2p2) hate me?" He knows he's painting a target on his back, and plenty of zingers do get hurled his way, but some of the replies are genuinely heartfelt and sympathetic. "Ship It Holla Ballas? Really?" writes one respondent. "You're better than that; I don't even know you, but you've got to be better than that."

The truth is he *is* better than that. The image he created for himself online was designed to attract attention for himself and his friends. He hoped it would be a shortcut to fame; it's turning into a major source of frustration. With that in mind Good2cu decides to retire—or at least rethink—his image. The goal has always been to enjoy a long career as a professional poker player. It's time to emphasize the "professional" part.

The first order of business is replacing ShipItHollaBalla.com and its emphasis on hedonistic excess with a more businesslike Web site. To do the job, he hires WildBill, a Two Plus Twoer he's already been working with for a few months.

WildBill runs RakeAid, a Web site designed to exploit online poker's affiliate system—he signs up players and directs them to certain poker rooms, receiving a commission each month based on the number of hands they play. He returns most of the commission to the players (their motivation for signing up with him) but keeps a sliver for himself (his motivation for running the business). Good2cu has been driving traffic from ShipItHollaBalla.com to RakeAid in exchange for a percentage of the percentage. It's been a successful arrangement so far, as Good2cu has served up a few extremely high-volume players—FieryJustice, for example, often plays enough hands in a month to generate as much as $50,000 in commission.

With WildBill working on a new Web site, Good2cu tackles the next issue: if he's going to be a serious poker player, he's going to have to focus even more of his attention on the game. He can't allow himself to get distracted by the mundanities of everyday life. Buying groceries. Doing laundry. Going to the bank. Filling the car with gas. Paying bills. Booking travel. The mathematically correct play, Good2cu decides, is to hire a personal assistant. He places an ad online, offering $20 an hour plus free poker lessons.

He gets more than a thousand responses.

Sifting through a thousand resumes is exactly the kind of mundane bullshit he doesn't have time to deal with, an irony that isn't lost on Good2cu. He's debating whether to toss them all into the trash when WildBill suggests that he save himself the time and hire Trent, who's been handling RakeAid's customer service needs.

A former athlete at the University of Southern California, Trent is also a pretty good poker player, theoretically capable of grinding out $10,000 a month playing low- and middle-stakes games, were it not for his propensity to give it all back at the high-stakes tables. The cycle has repeated itself enough times for Trent to see the wisdom of maintaining a steady income independent of his online poker accounts. In addition to RakeAid, he also works part time as a personal assistant to the Finnish poker star Patrik Antonius, but he's happy to take on more work.

Good2cu can't help falling in love with the idea. An ex-jock, the kind of guy who probably would have ignored him before he became a poker player, wants to work for him for $20 an hour, *and* he gets to share an assistant with one of poker's most famous young players. Good2cu hires Trent as fast as he can.

Free to concentrate on poker, Good2cu gets to work. And it truly is work. He can see that most of the young poker players he's crossed paths with don't treat the game like a job. They've made a lot of money and enjoyed an extravagant lifestyle by playing a computer game, but that doesn't mean they're professional in their approach. The online world is becoming increasingly cannibalistic, and if Good2cu's going to survive, he's going to have to keep improving his game, which is going to take focus and discipline.

In one of the final posts he'll make on the Ship It Holla Balla Web site, Good2cu reveals his desire to adopt an entirely new set of habits and his goal of becoming one of the best all-around poker players in the world. To aid him in that endeavor, he devises a daily schedule that promotes hard work, good health, and personal growth over hard partying, late nights, and unhealthy living.

—Do 30 minutes of cardio as soon as I wake up

—Make a list of what I want to accomplish on said day

—Lift weights five times a week

—Play poker 50 hours a week

—Do some writing once a week

—Constantly review my poker play

—Avoid drugs and alcohol (Beside an occasional drink/joint)

Here is what I picture my normal day being:

9:00 am: Wake up

9:15–10:00 am: Go to gym downstairs and do some cardio

10:00–10:45: Shower, eat, sauna, steam room, etc.

10:45 am–5:00 pm: Play online/live, read, run errands

5:00–7:00: Dinner with friends

7:00–10:00: Play more poker

10:00–11:00: Weight room

11:00 pm–12:30 am: Review hands, read, write

12:30–9:00: sleep

His schedule bears a striking resemblance to the one implemented by another Midwesterner, although F. Scott Fitzgerald's Jay Gatsby is a fictional character—not to mention an earlier riser.

I'm not really too worried about my play deteriorating, as I spend a lot of time reviewing hands and discussing them with friends. I AM worried about my mental state though, and how poker will affect me later in life. Many of us have been given the opportunity to make epic amounts of money at a very young age, and I am curious to see how many (including myself) are turning out in the next ten to fifteen years.

—**Raptor**

FORT WORTH, TEXAS (Winter 2007–2008)

Like most of his poker buddies, Raptor grew up playing video games. Many of them still do—durrrr seems to have an Xbox in almost every room of the house. Raptor likes to think he's outgrowing the habit, but lately he's found himself getting sucked into a game called Defense of the Ancients.

DotA is a mod of the popular real-time strategy game Warcraft III. Raptor enjoys losing himself in a fantasy world where heroes battle over the Internet, earning gold for each opponent they slay. To, you know, escape from the real world where he battles poker players over the Internet, earning gold for each opponent he slays.

When he's not playing DotA, he's talking to people on AIM or browsing the Two Plus Two threads. In other words, procrastinating.

I must be really sick of poker.

It's true. The game no longer captivates him the way it once did. After playing no-limit Hold'em nearly every day for four years, he frequently finds himself playing by rote.

He dabbles in other forms of poker, like the more nuanced pot-limit Omaha, hoping to reignite his passion. But at the end of the day, he's still staring at cards on a screen.

I feel like I'm just going through the motions like I would at some job I hated. Part of the reason I wanted to make poker a profession was to prevent these feelings, yet here they are.

One night he has an eye-opening conversation with his friend John, who once flushed his entire bankroll down the toilet in a single high-stakes session. After a few miserable attempts at recouping his losses, John decided to move on from online poker and get a real job.

"How's *that* going?" Raptor asks.

"Every day I wake up at the asscrack of dawn," John tells him. "I go into an office and do the shit that someone else tells me to do for eight hours. But you know what's funny? I like it. Sometimes I work late even when I don't have to."

Raptor's got to admit that John seems a lot happier. He was a great poker player, but an angry one—he'd curse loudly, kick walls, and pulverize computer mice. Now he sounds relaxed, like he's actually enjoying life.

Raptor reminds himself that there's a world beyond poker. He could be backpacking in New Zealand or learning to salsa in Argentina. He has enough money in the bank to stay abroad for as long as he wants, immersing himself in a new culture and language.

But like his dream of buying that vacation home in Costa Rica, he never gets past the planning stage.

Real estate seems like something he *should* be interested in, so he scours Fort Worth for a rental property to buy. He reads books, has long conversations with realtors, and researches MLS listings online. He passes on the first four places he sees, until he stumbles across a fourplex, one block from the TCU campus, that promises to bring in positive cash flow for years to come. It feels great to sign the paperwork.

For a moment, anyway. Then the moment's gone. With it goes any motivation to repeat the exercise.

He tries to get serious about golf, taking lessons and playing nearly every day, until, several months in, he abruptly quits. He joins Haley for a few bikram yoga classes; they're enjoyable and make him feel great for hours afterward, but they too fail to become a habit. He fares better with jiujitsu. It's a great workout—he almost blacks out during his first sparring session—and he loves the competition. Everyone at his gym can kick his ass, quickly tapping him out. So he starts training five or six days a week, sometimes twice a day, setting his eyes on a blue belt.

He's practicing takedowns when he falls awkwardly on his side, and for a moment his shoulder, the same one he injured in high school, slips out of place. He hasn't done too much damage—he's able to get back on the mat after a couple of weeks of rest—but the incident gets him thinking about his torn labrum and baseball and what might have been.

What if I'd never injured my shoulder? I'd probably be getting ready for spring training. I'd be a junior in college. I wouldn't be playing poker much, if at all. I'd be a regular guy. And who knows? I might even be happier.

Living a normal life is surprisingly appealing to him, but it's hard to be normal when you're a twenty-one-year-old millionaire. When his friend Kurosh talks smack about his DotA skills, Raptor finds himself challenging the kid to a best-of-eleven series.

For $10,000.

Just like a regular guy would.

51

At the time, no other online players really played those games at
the Bellagio, mostly because online poker players are kind of lazy. It's
easier to stay at home than to have to go to the casino and sit there
and play for hours. But to me, poker rooms were more glamorous. I
liked being in the casino around all of the characters. I wanted to be
a gambler.

—Good2cu

LAS VEGAS, NEVADA (April 2008)

Ever since watching Chris Moneymaker go toe-to-toe with Sammy
Farha, Good2cu has maintained certain fantasies about the life of
a Vegas gambler. A carefree existence devoid of soul-crushing responsi-
bilities. The freedom to play poker whenever and wherever he chooses.
Nights that last until noon. Colorful characters. Suitcases full of money.
A hot girlfriend. *Stripper* hot.

Hiring Trent has proven to be a great first step along the path he
hopes will lead him there; on the best days, it appears to be a master-
stroke of brilliance. Any good personal assistant can shield his employer from life's petty distractions, but how many can help his boss
scout online card rooms for juicy games and high-rolling fish ready to
tilt off tens of thousands of dollars? Trent is also the kind of guy who
doesn't blink when Good2cu asks him if he wants to join a blackjack

team, à la the M.I.T. kids described in Ben Mezrich's *Bringing Down the House*. Their four-man team only lasts two weeks, but they manage to make $50,000 before getting barred from the casinos.

Right now it feels like everything Good2cu touches turns to gold. He's added, on average, more than $100,000 to his online accounts each month since leaving Michigan. But he didn't move to Vegas to sit in front of a computer. He came to the center of the gambling universe to become a professional gambler. To play in the biggest cash games in the world. To stare down guys like Sammy Farha for hundred-thousand-dollar pots. To become a colorful character himself.

Which means spending more time in the Bellagio's card room, particularly Bobby's Room. There, he gets to play with some of the well-known pros he recognizes from television: Doyle Brunson, Barry Greenstein, Daniel Negreanu, even Phil Ivey. But not all of the players are famous—he loves interacting with the Machiavellian cast of characters who haunt the periphery of the big games. Like Tweety, a chubby connoisseur of debauchery who grew up hustling pool in Cleveland and now wears a Rolex Masterpiece and drives a $300,000 car. Or 20K Jay, who might pass for *Scooby-Doo's* Shaggy, if Shaggy wore stylish glasses and hip-hop clothes and talked like a wannabe rap star.

Traheho is every bit as fascinated by this shadow world as Good2cu is. The two of them are discussing the viability of a prop bet Trent is considering—living in one of the rooms at the Bellagio for a month—when 20K Jay snorts dismissively from across the table.

"I could live in the *bathroom* of one of these rooms for a month, yo."

"Yeah, right," Good2cu replies.

"Care to put some money on it?"

A few minutes later, the terms have been settled. They rent a room where, for the next thirty days, Jay will be confined to the lavatory. No visitors, no computer, no drugs to help pass the time. He's allowed an air mattress, a portable DVD player, a cell phone with four hundred minutes of talk time, and up to four visits from room service a day. Break any of the rules, and Jay owes Good2cu and Traheho $20,000. Succeed, and they owe Jay twice as much. The loser also has to foot the tab for the room.

"How do I know y'all will pay me my money?" Jay asks.

Good2cu understands the implication—he hasn't been around long enough to have earned anyone's trust. They agree to put the $60,000 that's at stake into escrow in a safe deposit box at the Bellagio. The box is registered in Jay's name, but Good2cu gets to hold on to the only key.

Good2cu and Trent watch Jay set up camp in the bathroom. He's whistling "We're in the Money," although his enthusiasm noticeably wanes as he inflates the mattress, shrinking the bathroom into a human-sized doggie crate.

"Don't worry," Trent whispers to Good2cu. "He's never going to make it. He's already cracking up."

"How can you tell?"

Trent points to the first DVD Jay's selected: *Sex and the City*, Season One.

"It's gonna get lonely in here, yo," 20K Jay explains, holding up a bottle of lotion and grinning.

News of the bet quickly spreads to the Internet. Trent sets up a live Webcam to monitor Jay's behavior, streaming the footage on ShipIt-HollaBalla.com. Good2cu offers a $500 reward to any viewer who catches Jay violating the rules, attracting thousands of visitors to the site. *Card Player* sends a reporter who films a ten-minute segment about the bet for the magazine's Web site.

A few nights later Good2cu is hanging out at Spearmint Rhino with his buddy tsarrast, who's dating one of the dancers. She introduces Good2cu to one of her coworkers. He asks her for her number. She gives it to him. And just like that, Good2cu has a girlfriend who's stripper hot.

He doesn't want to celebrate prematurely, but, just a few months after leaving Michigan, all his fantasies about life as a professional gambler in Las Vegas seem to be coming true.

This explains why people who look too closely at randomness burn out, their emotions drained by the series of pangs they experience. Regardless of what people claim, a negative pang is not offset by a positive one (some psychologists estimate the negative effect for an average loss to be up to 2.5 the magnitude of a positive one); it will lead to an emotional deficit.

—Nassim Nicholas Taleb, *Fooled by Randomness*

FORT WORTH, TEXAS (April 2008)

Hey, guys," Raptor writes. "Today I would like to talk about something I would imagine most wouldn't in their first CR blog post . . . downswings. Currently, I am pulling myself out of the biggest one of my life, ~375K. I was playing in games where I thought I had a pretty good edge, but the swings are just so epic, that sometimes it's hard to tell."

It's the first day of Raptor's new "job," if you really want to call it work. About once a week he plays a Sit N Go or a cash game, narrating his thoughts along the way, a presentation that gets turned into an instructional video. He's also expected to make occasional entries to a blog.

His new bosses are only a couple years older than he is. Green Plastic and Muddywater met in 2005 at the University of Illinois, where both were developing reputations as successful online players. Tired of answering the same questions over and over about how to win at the game, they created videos of themselves playing real hands, describing the thought process behind each move, and posted them on a Web site. No good deed goes unpunished: they were quickly besieged with requests for more. So they decided to make it worth their while, offering access to their growing catalogue of poker how-tos for a monthly fee.

Three years and ten thousand subscribers later, CardRunners has become the world's largest poker training Web site. They're making a push to get even bigger, having persuaded Lee Jones to ditch his job with the European Poker Tour to come onboard as chief operating officer. They're also bringing in some fresh talent to join their team of instructors, such as the young online poker legend who once took $450 and turned it into $20,000 in just thirty-six hours.

Raptor doesn't need the money. For him, it's more of a lateral career move. Lately, he's been feeling like if he really wants to be a professional poker player, then he needs to fully commit and put himself in the best position to succeed. That means moving to Las Vegas and pursuing a sponsorship deal.

He figures making videos for CardRunners is a great way to increase his marketability in a way that doesn't make him want to puke. While he loves all of the Ship It Holla Ballas as individuals, he's always been a little too self-conscious to promote himself as part of the group, politely declining whenever Good2cu invited him to post on the site. CardRunners, on the other hand, is a highly respected company within the industry, generating more than $3 million in revenue the previous year.

There's more: Green Plastic and Muddywater are currently working out the details of a partnership with Full Tilt Poker that, should everything fall into place, could make Raptor a sponsored pro on the site. This would be an incredible opportunity, as Full Tilt has become one of the biggest online poker sites in the world. Ever since Party Poker's departure from the American market two years ago, Full Tilt has been battling for supremacy with PokerStars. So far it's been a dead heat, with PokerStars corralling most of the online tournament action and Full Tilt hosting the bigger cash games.

Raptor already spends most of his time on Full Tilt, so the idea of getting paid to play there is more than enough incentive to encourage him to make a few videos. All he's got to do is talk while he plays, remembering to keep the swearing to a minimum.

He isn't so sure what to make of the blog. The other pros on the site mostly use the space to discuss interesting hands, linking to videos that will hopefully encourage casual readers to become paying customers. But when Raptor sits down to write his first post, he has trouble focusing on any particular hands. He's too consumed by the agita that has accompanied the biggest downswing of his career.

Over the last two weeks, he's lost nearly $400,000.

He knows, intellectually, that these kinds of swings are a normal part of the "nosebleeds" he's been testing, games where the typical buy-in is $60,000 and pots often climb into six-figure territory. His bankroll is large enough to withstand the volatility. Aside from his own continuing success at the tables, he has made several very successful investments in other players and still has a stable of affiliates generating a steady income for him each month. Spreadsheets help him keep track of all his assets—online poker accounts, bank accounts, cars, real estate—down to the last dollar. While his contemporaries are graduating college and scrambling for crappy entry-level jobs, Raptor has already built a net worth close to $3 million.

So a $400,000 loss shouldn't bother him too much. But he can't help thinking about the money in real-world terms: he's lost a dozen nice cars, a house, a retirement nest egg. Which only gets him more aggravated, because this is the kind of thinking that has the potential to make it even worse.

You have to blow off the losses, call it a bad day at the office, and move on. Your bankroll is just a number on a screen. The cards don't care whether you're running hot or cold; neither should you. Psychological distress is just noise that will distract you from picking up the signals you should be paying attention to if you want to stay on your A game.

But right now the noise is *REALLY FUCKING LOUD.* It's pounding in his skull as he sits down to write his first blog entry for CardRunners, so how can he possibly write about anything else? Before he knows it, he's poured nearly a thousand words onto the page, an unguarded inquiry into his prospects for a sane life given the occupational hazards of his chosen line of work. As he looks over what he's written, he worries for a moment that he might be revealing too much. But this is the Facebook Age—everybody overshares. He hits the PUBLISH button, flinging his rant out into the world.

It feels so cathartic he's ready to do it again the very next day. This time he makes an effort to do what he's supposed to, describing a few hands he played the night before, but soon finds himself shifting gears.

"Just so everyone knows," he warns his readers, "this is NOT going to be a dedicated poker blog. I do lots of other things rather than poker and fully intend to include those things in this blog. I am trying to expand my 'horizons' and try to get out of the habit of just waking up and getting on the computer for fourteen hours a day. I know a lot of people struggle with this as well, so maybe this can help us both."

He starts blogging almost every single day about whatever strikes his fancy: the Texas Rangers game he took his dad to, the second season of *Lost,* the video games he's playing. He provides obsessively meticulous accounts of his various exercise regimens and diets, offering the precise details of his workouts and breaking each meal down into calories, fat, carbohydrates, fiber, and protein.

He frequently ruminates about the role poker plays in his life—negative, he suspects, as these days it seems to be generating far more pain than pleasure. He's not even a month into the job when he comes right out and admits that lately he's had "no desire whatsoever to play poker."

He knows he's not exactly inspiring his readers; he's just being honest. The blog is a place where he can say the things he's too polite to utter in real life. He describes a dinner he's forced to attend with a bunch of people he hardly knows. When he mentions, between bites, that he's thinking about buying a house in Las Vegas, the relative strangers at the table start hammering him with questions.

"So poker's treating you well? What's your strategy? How much money have you made? Do you want to play heads-up sometime?"

And finally: "Dude, can I crash at your place the next time I'm out there?"

Raptor goes mute for the rest of the meal, afraid to give his new "friends" another opening to hit him up for strategic advice, free lessons, or a place to stay. He pulls out his phone and pretends to send text messages, hoping they'll take the hint and leave him alone.

When he's finally able to escape, Raptor returns home to an in-box inundated with Facebook friend requests from people he doesn't know and e-mails asking if he'd be interested in meeting up for drinks or doing some coaching. He resists the urge to rip off snarky replies, instead using his blog to vent his frustrations, relying heavily on capital letters and exclamation points.

A few days later, he buys a $95,000 Mercedes-Benz on the Internet and has it delivered to the house in Vegas he just closed on. He's looking forward to living in a city where he doesn't have to be embarrassed about his expensive habits and to spending more time with his old poker friends. But what he hopes more than anything is that the move will revive his passion for the game. If it doesn't, he honestly doesn't know what he'll do next.

53

You guys might recall a post a few months ago about moving to Las Vegas and implementing new habits. Well, I worked my plan and achieved results that surpassed even my lofty skills (in just a span of a few months), and still found myself uncontent.

—Good2cu

LAS VEGAS, NEVADA (January—April 2008)

While 20K Jay is serving the twentieth evening of his sentence in a bathroom a few hundred feet above his head, Good2cu is dining in a dramatically different part of the Bellagio, the avant-garde restaurant Fix. It's almost a triple date: Trent and WildBill have both brought their significant others; only Good2cu's girlfriend has begged out, claiming illness. They're drinking vintage wine and having a grand old time until Good2cu reveals the real reason he organized this dinner—a breakup. He tells WildBill that he's tired of waiting around for his new Web site to be built, so he's going to hire somebody else to do it.

WildBill's not happy to hear the news. He anxiously tugs at his New Survivalist beard. "But I've already done a ton of work on it."

"Maybe," says Good2cu. "But I haven't seen any of it. Not even a single screenshot."

WildBill shrugs. "I expect I'll be compensated for my time."

"Why? You offered to build the site for free."

"That was when we were going to split the revenues on the back end. Just give me ten grand, and we'll call it good."

"Ten grand?! That's ridiculous. Besides, you owe me at least that much."

"What are you talking about?"

For Good2cu, this is the more pressing reason for the breakup: he thinks WildBill is stealing from him. The irony is that he never would have suspected it if WildBill hadn't encouraged him to hire Trent, who still handles customer service for RakeAid and is privy to the company's financials.

"I've paid you everything I owe you!" WildBill insists.

"That's not the information I have."

WildBill glares angrily at Trent, grabs his female companion roughly by the arm, and storms out of the restaurant.

Trent laughs. "That went well."

Good2cu calls his girlfriend on the way home. "It's me," he says. "Want to come over?"

"That depends. . . . Are those two whores still there?"

She's referring to a couple of Good2cu's female friends from Michigan who have been crashing in his guest bedroom. "They're not whores." He sighs. "Come on, I want to see you."

"There's something we need to talk about," she says.

Good2cu's phone informs him with a beep that he's got another call coming in. "Hold that thought," he says, clicking over to the other line.

"Guess what?" says Trent. "20K Jay just stepped out of the bathroom."

"Are you sure?"

"We got it on the Webcam."

"Ship it!" Good2cu switches back to the other line. "Good news!"

"Me too," his girlfriend says. "I'm pregnant."

$ $ $

She's not really pregnant. She made up the story because she's angry at him for having two female houseguests. The incident makes Good2cu reevaluate their relationship.

What kind of person fakes a pregnancy just because they're pissed at you? One I don't want to be with, he decides. He breaks up with her, vowing never to date another stripper.

The kid who arrived in Vegas with stars in his eyes, hoping to become a professional gambler, is now getting an up-close view of the city's underbelly. It's not a pleasant sight. Take, for example, the characters at the Bellagio who a couple of months ago seemed so colorful. One of them is now threatening to break his legs, while the other has apparently cheated him, and he's having a hard time deciding which is worse.

The dustup with Tweety is probably Good2cu's fault—not only did he violate a sort of unspoken code, but he clearly underestimated the man.

On the surface, Tweety epitomizes the image of a degenerate gambler. He lives alone. He's balding and overweight. He spends freely on women in return for a variety of favors. He isn't afraid to gamble for millions, even when he's drunk. *Especially* when he's drunk. Part of Good2cu wants to mock the guy. Another part of him worries that he's looking at his future.

Like many of the regulars in Bobby's Room, Tweety tries to develop personal relationships with the rich out-of-towners who occasionally sit in the game, hoping to set up private matches away from the casino where the house won't be taking a rake out of every pot and the IRS can't tax the winnings.

A businessman who usually has Tweety organize games for him whenever he's in town takes a shine to Good2cu and asks for his number. Good2cu isn't trying to hustle anyone, but when the businessman calls and requests that he set up a private game for him, what's he supposed to do, say no? He briefly considers inviting Tweety, but ultimately decides against it.

This doesn't sit well with the veteran poker pro, who explodes when he hears the news. Good2cu gets to see a different aspect of Tweety's personality—the part forged during a fractured childhood spent in a rough neighborhood, honed by the struggle to survive on his own from the time he was fifteen without a high school education. The part that thinks these privileged online kids with their upper-middle-class backgrounds are a bunch of arrogant dickheads.

Tweety delivers a message via the Bellagio's grapevine. "He'd better watch out. He's dealing drugs on my corner and when you deal drugs on someone else's corner, there's going to be serious consequences."

Good2cu won't be making that mistake again. He does his best to mend the rift with Tweety and reminds himself that he needs to be more cautious in the future, a lesson that gets reinforced when 20K Jay refuses to acknowledge that he's lost their bet.

According to Jay, he had to step outside the bathroom to sign some legal paperwork. Good2cu doesn't care about the why—in his mind, Jay has clearly violated the terms they agreed upon.

Jay refuses to accompany him to the safe deposit box, so Good2cu goes on his own. He's too late. Jay has already convinced the Bellagio that he's lost the key—easy to do, as the box is in his name—and asked to have it drilled open. There's not much Good2cu can do about it. Jay's holding all the cards, or in this case, the cash.

Good2cu thinks back to the first time he saw Las Vegas from the sky, two years earlier, and remembers how glamorous he imagined life was below. Now he's starting to understand why hard-bitten poker players call the game the world's hardest way to make any easy living. Survival depends on outrunning bad luck, a task made even more difficult when everyone is trying to trip you up along the way.

Good2cu doesn't need any more proof about how hard it is to keep your head above water in the poker world, but gets it anyway. The message boards are burning up with the news that Brandi Hawbaker has committed suicide in an apartment in Los Angeles. As the story of her topsy-turvy life gets dissected by people who didn't even know her, it becomes clear that many of them feel complicit in her tragedy.

And in a way, they're probably right.

Good2cu didn't even know her, but feels like he did, thanks to her many tell-all confessions on Two Plus Two. Her death leaves him with an uneasy feeling that only worsens when he recalls the title of the first post she ever made on the forum:

NEVER TRUST ANYONE.

54

We were both calling the other side bad, but for different reasons. They were calling us bad because we gave off stuff or acted like nerds or whatever, and they were terrible because they were actually terrible.

—**Raptor**

LAS VEGAS, NEVADA (May 2008)

War has become inevitable.

On one side: the poker establishment. The guys who played poker before society thought it was cool. Old-timers who used to "fade the white line," traveling from town to town in search of backroom games. The generations that followed were respectful because they had to be—without the Internet or decent poker strategy books, the only way to learn the game was at the feet of grizzled veterans. It's been said that it takes ten thousand hours to master a skill. Old-school players put in their time in smoky card rooms, figuring out how to read other players while controlling their own emotions and learning how to methodically build a bankroll. It wasn't a glamorous life, but the survivors of this rough apprenticeship felt safe in the insular, castle-like world they had created.

In the opposite corner: the kids who learned to play poker online. Thanks to the Internet, they've mastered the game faster than anyone could have ever imagined, sharing strategies, pooling bankrolls, and playing as many hands in a single year as the veterans could in ten.

Open gates, enter barbarians. The poker establishment still doesn't know exactly what to make of the growing onslaught of young kids. They wear baseball caps turned backward or sideways or, most confusingly, someplace in between. They seem surgically connected to iPods and wear oversized noise-canceling headphones that look like Mickey Mouse ears. They move with twitchy impatience, throwing chips around like they've got nothing to lose because, well, they *don't* have anything to lose. Having learned the game in front of computer screens, they lack social skills, table manners, and impulse control, yelling stupid things like, "Ship it holla!" whenever they win a pot.

The Internet kids offer a counterargument that sounds a little like this: yes, we're young and annoying—deal with it. We're also smart and talented, so go ahead and deal with that too. Many of us went to college, at least for a while, where we were exposed to a concept called "math." You so-called professionals had better be as good at reading people as you think you are to make up for all of the fundamental mistakes you make when calculating odds or valuing hands. If we're not as nitty with our bankrolls as you are, it's because we don't have to be: we're used to winning and losing large sums of money on a daily basis. An hourly basis. The only reason you guys get so much hype is because you were in the right place at the right time just as the poker boom exploded.

Skirmishes between the two sides are being fought around the country every day as wave after wave of Internet kids turn twenty-one and—facing increasingly difficult games online—start flooding the brick-and-mortar card rooms like animals driven from the hills by a lack of food and water.

This war has been mostly a private affair so far, but in March 2008, it goes public, catalyzed, to no one's great surprise, by the singular durrrr.

Durrrr's invitation to play in the NBC National Heads-Up Championship is a sure sign that the poker community at large is starting to understand what the Internet faction has known for a while. Since turning twenty-one last July, durrrr has steadily demonstrated that he's not just one of the best online players in the world—he's one of the best players in the world period. In the last eight months, he's made final tables in four major tournaments and racked up almost a million dollars in prize money.

Proving that they have a sense of history—and a sense of humor—the show's producers pit durrrr against Phil Hellmuth in a first-round matchup at the featured table.

Nearly two decades ago, Hellmuth was the upstart. He was only twenty-four when he won the WSOP Main Event in 1989, making him the youngest world champion ever crowned, but nineteen years and eleven gold bracelets later he has become the poker establishment. In 2005, he won the first National Heads-Up Championship. But as talented as he is, Hellmuth is equally well known for the explosive temper tantrums at the poker table that have earned him an odd nickname for a forty-three-year-old man to bear: "The Poker Brat."

Before their match begins, the show's hostess Leann Tweeden—a former Hooters girl who has reinvented herself as a sports correspondent—pulls them aside for a pregame interview.

"I think that maybe he's ahead of me online," concedes Hellmuth, who's wearing a hat and hockey jersey promoting his sponsor, Ultimate Bet. "It's a little different in the real world, so we'll see what happens."

Tweeden turns to durrrr, who, with his button-down shirt and jeans, looks like he's on his way to class. "Tell us about the challenge you issued Phil online."

A look of confusion passes over durrrr's face. "I didn't issue it," he says. "He issued it."

"Really?" she asks Hellmuth. "What did you issue?"

"I don't know. Every time I play someone heads-up online and they get a little cocky, I say, 'Let's meet somewhere in the real world,' and I give them the option of flying to California to play me in person, because it's a good test for them."

Their match barely lasts longer than the hype preceding it. On the just the third hand Hellmuth, having been dealt pocket aces—the best starting hand in Hold'em—lures durrrr into risking all of his chips with a pair of tens. Hellmuth has about an 80 percent chance of winning, but durrrr gets lucky and catches a third ten on the turn, eliminating Hellmuth from the tournament.

The Poker Brat is anything but gracious in defeat, lambasting durrrr for his perceived poor play.

Durrrr rolls his eyes. "I was going to say, 'Good game, sorry for the suckout,' but when you phrase it that way, it makes me not want to. That's why you lose money online. Pick your stakes heads-up. We can play right now if you want." To show he's serious, durrrr pulls a handful of high-denomination casino chips from his pocket and tosses them onto the table along with a stinging rebuke. "Learn to play heads-up no-limit."

Word of the confrontation spreads quickly on the message boards.

When NBC releases a clip of the encounter, it goes viral on YouTube, and durrrr becomes a hero for an entire generation of Internet poker players. Not only is he an incredible player, but he's articulated what all of them have been thinking: the older players aren't half as good as they think they are, and they'd better start taking us seriously.

Raptor, who has just moved to Las Vegas, watches the event on TV at TheUsher's condo. The timing of his move feels auspicious: being an Internet player has suddenly become a marketable quality instead of a liability to be overcome. His friends are now getting invited to play on the same poker shows they used to watch on television. First Jman got to play on *High Stakes Poker;* now durrrr and Good2cu are slated to appear on NBC's *Poker After Dark*, where they'll play a cash game against seasoned pros in an episode billed as "Nets vs. Vets."

For the first time in a while, Raptor is revved up to play. He calls the Bellagio and asks the floor manager to lock up a seat for him. But by the time he gets there, his place at the table has already been filled, a slight that thoroughly annoys him. He's debating whether to get his new Mercedes registered or blow off the afternoon to go-cart racing when he runs into Good2cu, who invites him to join the juicy pot-limit Omaha game that's starting up in Bobby's Room.

As he steps into the high-limit area, Raptor takes in Good2cu's swagger. The last time they hung out Good2cu was struggling with his confidence and talking about going back to school. Now he's casually trading barbs with the regulars like he's one of them.

They're joined at the table by a rich businessman and a few high-stakes pros. Raptor recognizes one of them: Sammy Farha, the crafty gambler who Chris Moneymaker defeated at the World Series five years ago, when Raptor and Good2cu were still attending to their first pimples. Now they're playing against him for stakes that then would have seemed unfathomable.

Part of poker's great appeal is the idea that anyone can play with the pros—as long as you've got enough cash to afford the hefty buy-in, of course. But just because everyone can, doesn't mean everyone does.

Losing to Moneymaker thrust Farha into the spotlight, perhaps even more than beating him would have. Ever since, he's been getting challenged by a long line of overeager amateurs, and as far as he's concerned Raptor and Good2cu are just the next two on that list. What he doesn't know and what they're not about to tell him is that even though they're only twenty-two and twenty-one respectively, they've been playing the game nearly every day for the past five years, honing their skills, in anticipation of a moment like this.

Three hands into the session, Good2cu finds himself wrestling over a big pot with Farha, who shoves all of his chips into the middle on the flop. It's the kind of play that should intimidate a kid. But Good2cu calmly thinks for a few minutes, decides he's getting the right odds to call, and winds up winning the $30,000 pot.

"So you guys play on the Internet, huh?" Farha asks, motioning to a chip runner to fetch him a new rack.

"A little," Good2cu confesses.

The new rack of chips is placed in front of Farha.

Two hands later, he pushes them all into the middle of the table once again. This time it's Raptor who calls.

"You have a good hand?" Farha asks.

"It's not bad," Raptor replies, turning over his cards.

The pro's jaw goes slack. He stares at the cards, removing the unlit cigarette from his mouth, replacing it, then removing it again. He rubs his eyes, like he can't believe what he's seeing, but the pips on the cards don't change. Farha throws his cards into the muck, leans back in his chair, and yells as if speaking directly to the poker gods above.

"WHAT THE FUCK WITH THESE INTERNET KIDS?!"

55

I no longer wish to set arbitrary monetary goals that will constantly be reaching higher and higher. This is a recipe for disaster. . . . Setting and reaching goals is not the be all and end all of happiness. There is more out there, something bigger, and I intend to find it.

—Raptor

FORT WORTH, TEXAS (July 2008)

By the time the 2008 World Series of Poker rolls around, the Ship It Holla Ballas are finally getting the mainstream attention they've been clamoring for. As individuals, they've made numerous appearances on TV and in *Card Player, Cigar Aficionado,* even *The New York Times.*

But defining the Ballas as a group has become nearly impossible. The loose confederation that once held them together has been eroded by their respective successes. Good2cu finally pulls the plug on ShipItHollaBalla.com, even before he finds someone to complete his new Web site. Apathy and Inyaface try to re-create the old esprit de corps by renting a sprawling 10,000-square-foot house for the summer, but everyone else has a place in Vegas now. The house gets populated by eight reasonably behaved young men from Canada. No one shoots bottle rockets or throws a pool ball through a window.

This is the first year that all of them—except Bonafone, who's still only twenty—are old enough to play in the World Series, and they don't disappoint. TheUsher goes deep in two events. Durrrr makes two final tables. Apathy nearly becomes the first Balla to win a coveted gold bracelet when he finishes second in the $10,000 Pot-Limit Omaha event, earning more than a half-million dollars. Jman successfully clears the hurdle when he wins the $5,000 Pot-Limit Omaha event, earning over $800,000. Ten days later, Inyaface earns a bracelet of his own in a $1,000 No-Limit Hold'em event that pays him nearly $700,000.

Good2cu only manages to cash once in his World Series debut, but he makes the most of it, finishing third in the $5,000 Limit/No-Limit Hold'em event and earning $144,000. His appearance at the star-laden final table allows Trent—who earns a field promotion from "assistant" to "manager"—to negotiate a one-day sponsorship deal with Full Tilt Poker on his employer's behalf. Decked out in garb promoting the card room, Good2cu finishes just behind ZeeJustin, the Internet player whose career path he once emulated, and Eric Lindgren, a poker pro he grew up watching on TV.

Raptor just misses making the final table in two events and outlasts 99 percent of the field in the Main Event, but the prize money represents only a small portion of his summer haul. Thanks to a few more shrewd investments in other players and his own dominant play online, he adds a million dollars to his bankroll over the course of a single month.

Two years ago, any one of these finishes would have triggered a massive celebration and a few cases of alcohol poisoning. This time around they respond to their achievements like professionals. There is no over-the-top party to end the summer. When the Series comes to a close, a few of them go on vacation. The rest simply get back to work, grinding online or at the nearest card room.

Raptor retreats to his house in Fort Worth to spend some time with his girlfriend. This also means a return to the lifestyle that depressed him so much before.

"For some reason, I am just not all that happy with what I am doing," he confesses in his blog soon after getting back to Texas. "I have made a ton of money, have set myself up for life, but can't seem to get any fulfillment out of poker. I am working on some lifestyle changes, and they are coming along nicely."

Most of them involve his body and his mind. He exercises like a madman. He carefully evaluates every morsel of food that enters his mouth. He employs a poker coach to help him with his motivation and psychological well-being. He reads books about Buddhism. He gets more serious about meditation. He plans a couples vacation to Kauai.

A few weeks into his homecoming, Raptor suffers one of the worst sessions of his career, dropping $140,000 in a single night. What surprises him is how little it bothers him.

Maybe I've turned a corner. This is how it goes at this level, so get used to it. Win a mil in a month, lose a hundred grand in a night, move on.

He's able to dispel the loss from his mind as soon as he logs out of his account. He banters cheerfully with Haley. They go to Whole Foods and buy a vegan cookbook, a carton of egg substitute, and some nondairy butter, and spend the rest of the night experimenting in the kitchen. *Vegan brownies aren't half bad,* he decides.

The next day, he plays more than eight thousand hands. Invoking some of the advice given to him by his poker coach, he stays focused on the present, putting yesterday's setback out of his mind. He knows trying to win back all the money he lost is a good way to lose even more. This attitude helps make the $15,000 loss he suffers feel slightly more bearable.

One day later, he loses $70,000 in less than an hour, then another $70,000 trying to win it back. The day after that, he drops another $100,000, bringing his four-day downswing to nearly $400,000.

Raptor keeps his cool. *Just numbers on a screen,* he reminds himself. He's pleased with the way he's handling this slump. He doesn't have to keep playing these stakes if he doesn't want to—thanks to the new deal between CardRunners and Full Tilt, he has been named a "Red Pro," an arrangement that pays him $35 every hour he plays and returns 100 percent of his rake. He figures he could easily make several hundred dollars an hour multitabling smaller games, assuming he could stand the tedium. For now, he turns off his computer and goes to a yoga class with Haley.

The next day, he practices jiujitsu at the gym, falls asleep in a movie theater watching *The Mummy: Tomb of the Dragon Emperor,* and loses $97,000 online. In just five days, he's down almost a half-million dollars, more than half the money he has in his online accounts. He's far from broke—between his money market savings and his houses in Texas and Vegas, he's still worth more than $3 million—but a sense of panic is starting to creep in. He briefly considers cashing out most of what he has left in his online accounts, forcing him to rebuild his bankroll by playing smaller stakes games. But just thinking about how long it would take to win back all that he's lost makes his mouse hand start to cramp. Instead, he decides to take a sabbatical, burying the Full Tilt Poker and PokerStars icons on his computer in a nest of subfolders:

G:/DOCUMENTS AND SETTINGS/RAPTOR/DESKTOP

/DO NOT CLICK

/ARE U SURE

/ARE U REALLY SURE

/HOW SURE ARE U

/DONT DO IT

/YOU KNOW BETTER

/THEY HAVE DOOMSWITCH

/467K DOWNSWING

/ULL ONLY MAKE IT 500

/POKER IS RIGGED

/TAKE A FUCKING BREAK

/YOUR FUNERAL

He vows to take two weeks off from the game, even if durrrr texts him to say that the five biggest fish in the world are sitting at the same table and there's an open seat. He occasionally glances at his computer to see what games are running, but doesn't allow himself to sit in any of them.

During his time off, he does his best impression of a regular guy. He goes out to dinner with his girlfriend and her parents, something he's never done, he realizes, despite having dated her for two and a half years. He takes that vacation in Kauai, surfing, snorkeling, and diet-busting with cheeseburgers and Oreo cookie smoothies. When he gets back to Texas, he tries to teach himself how to speak Japanese.

The more poker recedes from his mind, the more space there is for other thoughts to enter.

Man, I forgot how much I miss playing baseball.

What would have happened if I hadn't hurt my shoulder?

I probably would have played in college.

I bet I would have been happy going to college.

I wonder if going to college would make me happy now?

Maybe I should give it try.

He begins to look into schools that might accept a two-time drop-out. One possibility is St. John's, a small liberal arts college in New Mexico that employs "The Great Books" program, tossing out text-books, lectures, and examinations in favor of a curriculum devoted to reading and discussing the finest works in the Western canon. Raptor loves that the college consistently ranks in the top ten in both student happiness and academic rigor. Who wouldn't want to go to a school like that?

He sits down at his computer and, in a single frenzied session, bangs out eight pages of essays for the application.

These kids were going to be leaders regardless of what fields they chose. I've talked a little bit about this with them, where I'm not sure that Internet poker is a great thing, because I'm not sure you should be taking these guys and have them committing all their time to playing a stupid game when they could be building bridges and educating other kids and leading their communities and fixing people and building rockets.

—Irieguy

LAS VEGAS, NEVADA (November 2008)

In an effort to milk the World Series of Poker for all it's worth, ESPN breaks up its coverage into an entire season of weekly shows that follow the tournament from beginning to end. A perfectly reasonable strategy, save for one thing: by the time the finale rolls around, everyone has already known the identity of the champion for months.

To restore some of the drama, the final table of this year's Main Event has been delayed until the fall. In the intervening months the November Nine, as the players at the final table come to be known, have been waiting anxiously for their fate to be determined. The unluckiest of them will take home $900,000. The champion will earn ten times that amount.

None of the Ballas are still in the tournament, but Raptor still has a personal interest in the outcome, as one of his buddies from Texas, a twenty-three-year-old online player named Craigmarq, is still alive. Craigmarq ends up being the first player to get eliminated from the final table, but another young online player, lsser from Denmark, goes on to win it all. Only twenty-two years old, lsser becomes poker's youngest world champion, breaking the record set by Phil Hellmuth two decades before. Only one year will pass before the feat gets surpassed by jcada99, a twenty-one-year-old who grew up just ninety miles away from Good2cu. At the time of his victory, jcada99 claims that he's been playing serious poker on the Internet for the past six years. Do the math.

Raptor isn't happy to see his buddy Craigmarq get knocked out of the Main Event's final table so quickly, but some consolation arrives when he finds an extra $42,000 in one of his online accounts. It's a refund from the virtual card room Ultimate Bet—part of its effort to restore trust following the second "superuser" scandal to rock the online poker world in the last thirteen months.

For years players have been speculating about the existence of a tool that would allow an unscrupulous player to see his opponents' hidden hole cards. The notion that so-called "superusers" might actually exist has generally been dismissed as a conspiracy theory and vehemently denied by the online card rooms.

To borrow from *Scooby-Doo*, the cheaters might have gotten away with it, were it not for those meddling kids—or to be more specific, some youthful members of Two Plus Two who have been collecting information about suspicious players who seem to possess far more information than they should. In September 2007, this informal investigation draws the attention of Michael Shackleford, an adjunct professor of casino math at the University of Nevada-Las Vegas, who uses statistical analysis to prove what the aggrieved players suspect: an Absolute Poker player called Potripper can see their cards.

Absolute Poker initially denies the accusations. But a brief internal investigation reveals that a disgruntled employee—"a geek trying to prove to senior management that they were wrong" and "took it too far," according to a company source—has indeed ripped off players to the tune of $1.6 million.

A few days later, thanks to more detective work from Two Plus Twoers, Ultimate Bet announces its own investigation into a similar claim. The ensuing controversy is even more devastating to the poker community as the culprit turns out to be a poker legend. For nearly four years, Russ Hamilton, the 1994 world champion, has been using a superuser tool to take money away from "friends" like Mike Matusow, even loaning them money so they could continue losing to him. The story goes national on *60 Minutes*, where correspondent Scott Pelley calls it "the biggest scandal in the history of online gambling."

When the dust settles, Ultimate Bet starts the painful process of refunding more than $22 million to the players who got cheated. One of the biggest beneficiaries is durrrr, whose reimbursement tops a quarter-million dollars. One of durrrr's greatest rivals in the high-stakes poker scene, former model Patrik Antonius, is also slated to receive a hefty refund, but it never makes it to him—his personal assistant, Trent, intercepts the money and gambles it all away.

Trent's larceny forces Good2cu to audit his own books. *Never trust anyone*, he reminds himself. When he discovers that Trent has been skimming from him as well, Good2cu has no choice but to fire him.

Good2cu's move to Vegas has been insanely profitable. In just six months, he's won over a million dollars. But his day-to-day happiness— or what poker players half-jokingly call "life equity"—has dipped to an all-time low. For at least ten hours a day, he's either sitting in front of a computer or at a table in a casino, interacting with people who can calculate the exact odds of making a straight flush but who would have a hard time telling you the name of the president.

"I've forgotten how to talk to 'normals' (this is what we poker degenerates call normal people)," he confesses on Two Plus Two. "I'm unable to hold more than a brief conversation with people not in the gambling field. I feel that I've become a highly skilled specialist, who is somewhat isolated from the real world. I think I'm starting to realize that making money isn't ultimately the highest purpose of life. Money is a means to an end; not an end in itself."

Unlike Raptor, Good2cu is able to quickly shunt aside these troubling existential thoughts. It might not always be pretty, but this is the life he's chosen. He's back in Bobby's Room the very next day, giving $100 handshakes to the floormen and laughing at jokes he's heard a million times. He even manages to negotiate a truce with Tweety, who offers to take a piece of Good2cu's action in an upcoming match against PerkyShmerky, the New York trust fund kid whose losses paid for Traheho's BMW.

According to the rumors swirling around Two Plus Two, Perky's parents have cut him off, forcing Perky to borrow money just to stay in action. Previously, his opponents had to be mindful of Perky's unlimited bankroll, which allowed him to make bold moves at the table less affluent players would be unlikely to attempt. But now they're starting to view him as a badly wounded animal that needs to be put out of its misery, which is why Tweety is so eager to get his money into the mix.

Good2cu flies to New York, where he finds a very different person from the one who arrived at the Ship It Holla compound in a

Rolls-Royce the summer before. Gone is the tanned, good-looking kid who danced around the tennis court. In his place stands an emaciated shell, pale as a corpse. His sickly appearance gets attached to an explanation a few minutes after they sit down to play at the table Perky has set up in his apartment in Trump Towers. The kid is popping pills into his mouth like they're M&Ms.

"Got a headache?" asks Good2cu.

"No, dumbass. Why do you think I'm called PerkyShmerky?"

"Never really thought about it."

" 'Cause I love me some Percocet."

Perky's soon chopping up the pills with his American Express card and snorting the powder to bypass the built-in time-release mechanism. Good2cu does his best to ignore the distraction, but he can't dismiss the feeling he gets when he returns to the table after a bathroom break. The next hand has already been dealt. Something doesn't feel right. But he keeps his mouth shut and plays the hand, a pair of deuces that becomes much stronger when the flop delivers a third one.

He's made a set—a huge hand and usually a winning one as well, but a minute later, Perky turns over an even bigger set. A stunned Good2cu stumbles down to the streets below a $325,000 loser and calls his partner.

"I think I just got cheated," Good2cu tells Tweety, explaining how he thinks Perky rigged the cards during his trip to the bathroom.

"Don't pay him then," responds Tweety.

"But I'm not *sure* I got cheated. It's just a feeling."

"Trust your gut, kid. Do not pay that motherfucker."

Good2cu wrestles with the decision. He doesn't want be a sucker. If he lets one guy cheat him, everyone will see him as an easy mark and he'll never survive in this world full of angle-shooters and con art-ists he's chosen to inhabit. But he feels slimy not paying Perky based solely on a hunch, so he coughs up the cash he owes him and does his best to banish the incident from his mind.

When he gets back to Vegas, Good2cu receives a call from a floor-man at the Bellagio. A certain "celebutante," a B-list actor more famous for marrying well, is sitting at a table in Bobby's Room next to an actual garbage bag full of cash and chips. The Celebutante is generally a pretty good player unless he's wasted. And, man, is he wasted. Good2cu makes the five-minute drive to the Bellagio in three.

He needn't have hurried; the Celebutante isn't going anywhere anytime soon. He claims that he hasn't slept for thirty-six hours, and his frequent trips to the bathroom—powdering his nose with cocaine, Good2cu suspects—promise to keep him awake, if not altogether co-herent, for many more.

The drugs having turned off his inner filter, the Celebutante seems determined to offend. He propositions a cocktail waitress by tossing two $5,000 chips onto her tray. He rambles. How he used to be afraid of having anal sex with his ex-wife. Venereal disease. How one night, blotto drunk, he managed to cast aside that fear.

Right now Good2cu can't stand to be around this guy. But he also can't afford to leave. As long as the Celebutante keeps reaching into his bag of cash, Good2cu will keep sitting at the table. It's what any professional poker player would do.

The game continues for nearly four straight days. When his energy starts to flag, the Celebutante hires a couple of prostitutes to stand be-hind him and cheer. By the end of the session, he isn't even bothering to visit the bathroom to refresh his buzz; he's snorting bumps right at the table.

When the Celebutante finally bows out of the game, a quick count by the other players at the table estimates his loss at close to $2 million. Good2cu's take exceeds $500,000. His celebration is muted by exhaustion and a bit of disdain.

This, he reminds himself in a weary, cynical voice, *is the life I've chosen.*

57

There is nothing either good or bad, but thinking makes it so.

—*Hamlet*, Act II, Scene II

FORT WORTH, TEXAS (January 2009)

Raptor's been reading a lot of books lately, even more than usual. In one of them he stumbles upon an exercise that seems worth giving a try. He's supposed to imagine that he's a hundred years old and allowed the use of a time machine. What advice should his future self give his present self about how best to pursue happiness?

Do yoga, eat healthfully, and stay in good shape, he writes. *Read often, write even more. Ask everyone you meet what their favorite books are. Go to more ballgames and play more golf with your dad. Go back to school, and major in something that you enjoy learning about. Stop worrying so much about having "x" amount of money in the bank, because x will forever be increasing and focusing on such a hopeless pursuit will suck the life out of you.*

Afterward, he notices that "play more poker" doesn't appear anywhere on his list.

The downswing that started last July reached its worst point in November, when the loss swelled to almost $650,000. He's won back most of that money, but still finds himself less and less compelled by poker. Instead of playing one of the biggest online tournaments of the year, he does yoga by the pool, shops at the mall, cooks dinner for some friends, and watches the Cowboys game on TV. He feels like he's reaching a turning point.

"See, we all KNOW what makes us happy," he blogs. "We KNOW what we need to do; it's not some unreachable mystery that only a select few people are aware of. YOU know what makes you happy. The only thing preventing us from doing these things is apathy and laziness."

Raptor gets more serious about jiujitsu, regularly sparring with blue and purple belts. He meditates without moving for one hundred full breaths—when he first started practicing, a few months earlier, he could barely do five. He adds a new column to his spreadsheet that calculates the percentage he has invested in online poker. He vows not to let it reach the teens.

He wishes his relationship with Haley gave him the same peace of mind. Lately they've been arguing. She says he's too emotionally unavailable and, after three years of dating, she wants to feel more connected to him. The idea of marriage gets tossed around. Raptor loves her, but feels more inclined to sell everything he owns and travel the world than start a family. So he's devastated but not exactly surprised when, during what's supposed to be a romantic New Year's Eve cruise, he finds her making out with a random guy.

The ensuing breakup causes him a lot of pain, but he also feels energized. He has been actively seeking big changes in his life, and now they're beginning to manifest themselves. He receives an acceptance letter from St. John's and starts making arrangements to move to New Mexico in the fall. His plan is to sell everything he owns, all of his houses and cars, and take at least the first semester off from playing poker.

Meanwhile, his old high school baseball coach has taken him up on his offer to help out the baseball program on a volunteer basis. In a couple of weeks Raptor's going to be an assistant coach for the junior varsity team, pitching batting practice to fifteen- and sixteen-year-olds boys.

The shoulder hasn't fully healed. He also hasn't thrown a baseball in more than a year, so he asks a friend to meet him at the field to see if he still can. There's a moment of dread as he steps onto the pitcher's mound. He smacks the ball into his glove a few times, hoping that old habit will help calm him. Then he rears back and throws.

The familiar *thwap* he hears as the ball meets the catcher's mitt makes him break into a huge smile. It isn't a perfect strike, but it will do.

Poker makes you a good decision maker. You're able to analyze and weigh options and everything else, but in terms of practical skills for employment, you really don't have any. You get used to making a lot of money without working that hard.

—Good2cu

SAN DIEGO, CALIFORNIA (April 2009)

Good2cu is generally unabashed when it comes to self-improvement. In an effort to get better at talking to women—and despite a shitstorm of ridicule from his friends—he once contemplated hiring a coach who promised to teach him the secrets of pickup artistry. It's not like his whole life is predicated on chasing women—lately, Good2cu finds himself wishing, more than anything else, for a serious girlfriend to share his life with—but he finds that the techniques recommended by the pickup artist actually make him feel more comfortable talking to people in general.

Last year, looking to shore up his lack of grace on the dance floor, he took a ballet class. Every time he glanced at the floor-to-ceiling mirror he saw how silly he looked in tights. His classmates—a bevy of ten-year-old girls—seemed to agree, tittering every time he moved. At the end of the class, one of the girls helpfully pointed out to Good2cu that he had WBRS.

"What's that stand for?"

"White Boy Rhythm Syndrome," she answered, eliciting a chorus of giggles from her friends. Good2cu has been avoiding the dance floor ever since.

His latest effort at self-betterment involves hiring an accountant to take care of his finances for him, a decision motivated by his complicated tax situation. The government doesn't make it easy for professional poker players to pay their taxes. Any money they win gets taxed at a hefty 25-percent rate, but the IRS doesn't give them a refund, should they lose that money the following year. The accountant tells Good2cu that he's going to have to send Uncle Sam a six-figure check, which might be a huge bummer were it not for the greater implication: poker-wise, Good2cu has had a very good year. He now has a $2 million bankroll, at least until he pays his taxes.

As he's settling the last few details with his accountant, his phone starts blowing up with text messages from his new pal Antonio Esfandiari. There's a part of Good2cu that still can't believe they're friends. He was in high school when Esfandiari, at the height of the poker boom, won a World Poker Tour event. Coverage of the tournament seemed to run in an endless loop on the Travel Channel, immediately turning Esfandiari into one of the game's most recognizable players. Five years ago, Good2cu thought Esfandiari was pretty much a poker god; now they're buddies, going to clubs together and hanging out in each other's condos.

The texts invite Good2cu to join him and some friends for a party weekend at the Ivy Hotel in San Diego. *Ship it!* A few hours later, Good2cu is walking through the lobby of the hotel, smiling at pretty women in bikinis on their way to the rooftop pool. Another message directs him to the luxury suite, where Esfandiari and twenty-five of his closest friends have begun to preparty.

As they toss back tequila shots, introductions get made. Good2cu recognizes one of Esfandiari's friends as another one of his childhood heroes: the professional video gamer Fatal1ty. He also meets a publicist named Courtney who, as it turns out, recently broke up with the author Tucker Max. For a moment it's all too surreal for Good2cu, who sneaks off to call one of his best friends from high school.

"You won't believe who I'm hanging out with right now," he says.

The party moves to the rooftop bar, lit by the glow of San Diego's Gaslamp Quarter. Esfandiari's assistant, Amalie, gamely serves as a wingwoman, introducing herself—and Good2cu—to every woman in the bar. She orders shots with names like "Gummi Bears" and "Blowjobs" and encourages everyone around her to get on the dance floor.

Good2cu hesitates. *I can't do this. I'm going to look like an idiot.*

His friends beckon him. "Come on!" Amalie yells over the music.

Screw it. Let the haters hate. My goofy white boy dance moves are all I got.

He cycles through all of them—the shopping cart, the sprinkler, even some improvised disco. When the DJ puts on House of Pain's "Jump Around," Good2cu abandons any sense of choreography and simply does what the song demands. A few hipsters on the sidelines snicker. Good2cu doesn't care. He's too busy hurling himself into the air with all the force he can muster, reaching for the stars as if he might actually be able to grab one.

Epilogue

We're all born and a bit later we all die. So all we have is each other.

—Irieguy

LAS VEGAS, NEVADA (Present Day)

Irieguy and his girlfriend are out to dinner with another couple. They're having a nice enough time, assisted by a couple bottles of good wine. When the bill arrives, Irieguy barely glances at it. It doesn't matter if it's $5 or $500 (which it is); he wants to gamble for it.

"Credit Card Roulette?"

"What's that?" the other guy's wife asks.

Irieguy quickly takes them through the rules. Since women never pay, only Irieguy and the other guy hand their cards to the server. Irieguy's card gets returned first.

Ship it! yells the voice inside his head, although the expression on his face hardly changes. "Tough break," he says.

As the server turns to leave, the other guy's wife snatches Irieguy's Visa from his hand. "No way!" she demands. "Split it!"

The other guy smiles awkwardly and shrugs: *What can I do?*

"Guess we're splitting it," Irieguy tells the server.

It's one of those moments—and there have been a lot of them

lately—that makes him miss hanging out with the knuckleheads who used to call themselves the Ship It Holla Ballas. Sure, he still sees them from time to time, but it's not the same. As hard as it is for him to believe, the kids have all grown up. Nobody's shoehorning eight people into a car; they all have their own high-performance vehicles. No reason to rent a house when almost everyone keeps a condo in the city. No need for wild parties after every win, when wins have become part of the routine.

The Ship It Holla Ballas were already pulling apart when Black Friday finished the job, bringing to an abrupt end the era that created them and the subculture they helped define.

For the players who are surviving on small profits and rakeback, the poker dream suddenly becomes a lot less viable after April 15, 2011. Bonafone takes over his father's insurance business. TravestyFund uses what's left of his winnings to seed a green energy start-up. Chantel goes to nursing school. Deuce2High joins the family business, a furniture moving company. Green Plastic and Muddywater, the founders of CardRunners, start a new business in San Francisco that allows players to gamble on their fantasy sports teams.

PerkyShmerky ends up in rehab in Malibu, where he meets and begins dating actress Lindsay Lohan. Until she dumps him for a girl. Later there are reports of a scandal at a high-stakes Hollywood home game after Perky and an accomplice are accused of marking cards with infrared ink made visible by special contact lenses.

Jman wins enough money online to buy two penthouse apartments at the top of the trendy A Building in New York City's East Village. He combines them into one and has a giant slide installed inside the resulting megacondo. When Black Friday hits, he lists the place for a shade under $4 million—"Does anyone want to buy a slide?" he tweets—and moves to Vancouver, where he continues to play online.

The shutdown only affects the Canadians peripherally. Apathy and Inyaface continue to play online in Toronto when they're not traveling the world, following the live tournament trail. Both cashed four times at the 2011 World Series of Poker.

Some of the American members of the crew have made an easy and successful transition to live poker. TheUsher still lives in Las Vegas, playing cash games and tournaments. FieryJustice has become one of the top tournament players in the world, with nearly $5 million in winnings to date. He's also written two books and produced his own series of instructional videos.

Durrrr continues to reshape the poker landscape on a near-daily basis.

Six months after his showdown with Phil Hellmuth, he gets invited to join the new season of *High Stakes Poker,* where, after getting taunted by the old pros at the table for his measured play, he proceeds to win $919,600. In a single hand. It's the biggest pot ever won on TV. One year later, he smashes his own record by winning a $1.1 million-dollar pot against the legendary Phil Ivey. In late 2009, after earning more than $7 million during a four-month stretch online, durrrr becomes the first "pure Internet" player to become a fully sponsored pro at Full Tilt Poker. In his first week on the job he loses $4 million.

His sponsorship deal disappears at the same that Black Friday shuts down the company, but durrrr barely blinks, easily moving from the biggest cash games online to the biggest live games on the planet, regularly winning (and occasionally losing) million-dollar pots in Macau, where many online players have resettled to take advantage of a new poker boom. Barely twenty-six, he's considered by many to be the most talented no-limit player alive.

Among the friends Good2cu makes during his stay at the Ivy Hotel is an entrepreneur named Danny Fleyshman, at the time the youngest CEO of any publicly traded company. When Fleyshman launches the online card room Victory Poker a few months later, Good2cu finally gets the sponsorship deal he's been working so hard to attain.

Black Friday brings an end to the business arrangement, but by that time Good2cu has already made an extremely successful transition to brick-and-mortar poker. Today, he shuttles between luxury condos in Las Vegas and Macau, playing in the world's biggest cash games. He still draws more than his fair share of criticism from all the haters online, but, while he once documented his ups and downs with far too much honesty, he's now learned to play his cards a little closer to the vest. He hasn't bothered to inform the haters that he's toned down the debauchery, settled down with a serious girlfriend, and, oh, by the way, he's a multimillionaire.

Before Raptor heads off to St. John's College, where he'll spend the next two years studying philosophy and literature, he announces his official "retirement" from poker, creating a stir on the blogs and message boards. A year later, they're buzzing about his comeback after he wins more than a million dollars in a month.

But Raptor doesn't have any interest in returning to his old life, especially after Columbia University accepts him as a transfer student. Today he's living in Manhattan with his new girlfriend and a 110-pound Newfoundland, studying Chinese and political science. But nobody ever quits poker for good. He still goes to the World Series every year. And he's still making final tables.

Whether you believe they're brilliant young minds who braved uncharted waters to make their wildest fantasies come true or arrogant little pricks who got beaned in the head by good fortune and landed with a horseshoe in the ass, the unique circumstances that spawned the Ship It Holla Ballas are gone forever. While the group's fluid membership and inconsistent accounting methods make it impossible to be precise, collectively they have won close to $20 million in live tournaments and at least as much in live cash games and online. By these metrics, they are the most successful poker crew of all time.

And they're all still under thirty.

Acknowledgments

Anyone who's spent time at a poker table knows that it's a game of courage. But it's still hard for us to fathom the guts it took for the characters in this story to open up their lives, warts and all, to a pair of complete strangers, without any guarantees of a flattering portrayal. Talk about your gambles.

But these aren't just any characters, and winning a lot of money isn't the only way they've beaten the odds. It would have been so easy for these kids to grow up to be assholes. Instead, we discovered a remarkable collection of thoughtful, self-possessed, and charismatic young adults who are just as interested in the world outside of casinos. As incredible as it might seem, given the exuberance of their youthful indiscretions, each and every one of the Ship It Holla Ballas we talked to has grown up to be the kind of person that would make any parent proud.

There would be no book—or, for that matter, a Ship It Holla Balla crew—without our brilliant and fearless tour guide, Andrew Robl. He was subjected to many torturous hours of impertinent interrogation, gamely answering questions that would have driven a lesser man to mortification. Our greatest fear about this book is that we haven't done an adequate enough job of conveying just how far he's come in terms of maturity and personal growth. Thanks for taking the leap with us, Andrew.

Special thanks also to David Benefield, who always found time to set aside his own fears of personal embarrassment to respond to our panicked Facebook messages whenever the waters got murky. His honesty, especially in regard to the emotional highs and lows, was invaluable.

Ditto to Craig Hartman, who has been an instrumental ally throughout, and, as we came to discover, one of the most amazingly cool guys we've ever met.

Peter Jetten, Kevin Boudreau, Alec Torelli, and Aaron O'Rourke all deserve to be thanked twice: once for their generosity in sharing intimate details and photos; a second time for their tolerance in regard to their portrayal. We're sorry for any liberties we might have taken on the way to producing what we hope is a coherent narrative.

Max Greenwood, Mario Silvestri, Jonathan Little, Casey Diener, and Aaron Nadell were all extremely forthcoming with their time and helped us to get the ball rolling. Thanks also to Harry Greenhouse, Chantel McNulty, Travis Rice, Ivan Solotaroff, Melodie DeWitt, Bryan Hadley, and Dustin Woolf.

As proprietary as we've come to feel about the Ballas and their incredible story, we can't take credit for having discovered them—Nick Gair, Michael Kaplan, and Chris Vaughn all wrote about them first.

A shout-out also to Jim McManus, for inspiring us to play and write about the game of poker, and to David Sklansky and Mason Malmuth, for giving poker players a virtual home, plenty to read, and plenty more to talk about.

It's going to be impossible to butter our agent, Daniel Greenberg, with any praise that he hasn't already heard or read in countless other literary acknowledgments; suffice to say that all of it is earned. Same goes for everyone at St. Martin's Press, especially our visionary editor, Marc Resnick, who understood where this book needed to go and what it needed to say long before we did, and his tireless editorial assistant, Kate Canfield. And to Michael Cantwell, the attorney who, with relentless good humor, helped us wrangle our story into legal compliance.

Finally, to our wives and sons, for their unwavering patience and support throughout this project and beyond. There's not enough money in the world to pay the debt we owe you, but hopefully our love, delivered in steady doses, will gradually chip away at it.

Holla!

Jonathan Grotenstein
Storms Reback
June 26, 2012

cmd

cmd → copy to (sethc)

sethc (seth 1)

shift 5x

-> net localgroup Administrator
?

~~-> net localg~~

-> net user <Accou

(Enter passwor   ,

(Still unable to log in?)

-> net user <Account N>

                    /active : yes